DREAMS
AND
SYMBOLS

DREAMS AND SYMBOLS

MAN'S UNCONSCIOUS LANGUAGE

Leopold Caligor & Rollo May

Basic Books, Inc., Publishers

NEW YORK / LONDON

Preface

Freud's observation that "the interpretation of dreams is the royal road to a knowledge of the unconscious activities of the mind" [1] has become an axiom of psychoanalysis. By now, most psychoanalysts would agree, further, that dreams contain the essentials of a person's central conflicts and his ways of coping with them.

This volume grew out of Dr. Caligor's fascination with the way in which intrapsychic changes during psychoanalysis were reflected in a patient's dream life. The idea occurred to him that perhaps the best way to examine just how these changes took place was for someone unfamiliar with a patient to study transcripts of all dreams reported by the patient in the course of psychoanalysis. Dr. Caligor invited Dr. May to be that person.

Dr. May accepted. For some time he had believed, as he writes in his introduction, "that we can often get a more accurate and meaningful picture of the significant changes in the patient's life from the symbols and myths he creates and then molds and re-creates in his dream existence than we can from what he says." This would be an opportunity to test his hypothesis.

[1] Sigmund Freud, *The Interpretation of Dreams*, translated by James Strachey (New York: Basic Books, 1955), p. 608.

The first section of the book is written by Dr. May who, after stating his aims, moves through a step-by-step analysis of the symbols in the dreams of Dr. Caligor's patient, Susan. Dr. May did this "blind" working with the dreams as they unfolded; the only clinical material he used was the transcript of Susan's account of her dreams taken from the recording of her psychoanalytic sessions. Dr. May then examined the additional clinical material available in Dr. Caligor's section and proceeded to make a major new formulation in the field of dream theory and the interpretation of symbols.

In the second section, Dr. Caligor presents a verbatim account of the interaction between the patient and himself around each dream recounted in the course of her psychoanalysis. Also provided are background material about this patient, some diagnostic formulation, and where necessary, information to clarify specific elements in the dreams or her associations to them. A series of human-figure drawings done by the patient early in treatment are included (shown following page 150).

The authors hope that the method they have chosen here, the presentation of specific clinical material together with a theory of symbols through which that material may be viewed, will contribute to psychoanalytic theorizing and examination. In contrast to the usual procedure of selecting clinical material to demonstrate one point of technique or theory, all of the dream material is given unselected. The reader is given the opportunity to do his own examination of the clinical data in its entirety and to draw his own independent conclusions. The process material recorded here helps to convey some of the unquantifiable aspects of the psychoanalytic process: the quality of the empathy between the patient and the analyst who are working together and the subtleties of changes that take place as treatment progresses.

The authors hope that this study will provide a step toward bringing personality theory and clinical observation closer together. Their belief is that what is currently needed is theory making in relation to the primary data of the psychoanalytic process so that the basic assumptions formulated can be publicly examined and tested to insure the development of psycho-analytic theory in a direction that is relevant and applicable to contemporary needs.

L. C.
R. M.

Contents

PART
I

Dreams and Symbols

BY

ROLLO MAY

1

Introduction

When Dr. Caligor invited me to participate in this study of his patient's dreams, I was immediately intrigued because it would give me a chance to ask —and perhaps to answer— some questions about dreams which had rustled around in my mind for years. It is indeed an unusual opportunity to have, as in this study, the entire sequence of a patient's dreams from the beginning of therapy to the end. I was excited by the idea that perhaps we could tell simply on the level of the dreams themselves what is going on in the person's life. And here I found myself resurrecting one of my old and long-believed hypotheses; namely, that we can often get a more accurate and meaningful picture of the significant changes in the patient's life from the symbols and myths he creates and then molds and re-creates in his dream existence than we can from what he says.

The questions I began to ask myself as I pondered whether to accept this invitation were the following. What in man's nature makes it possible for such a thing as dreaming to be? For it is a curious phenomenon, when you stop to think about it, that I can tonight whisk myself to China or ancient Byzantium, and experience it with as high a degree of reality in many ways as if I were there in actuality; that in moments I can live through a complex drama that it would take hours to enact on the stage; that not only can I cross boundaries of continents and centuries and languages, but I can make and mold symbols and myths at will, drench my dreams in all the colors and perfumes of Arabia and all the mysteries of the Congo; and most curious of all, I can cross boundaries of my own awareness and tell myself things which I knew but did not dare to let myself know that I knew in my conscious hours; that I can find an almost infinite depth of sensitivity (beggaring my conscious imagination) and an almost endless series of experiences from what we call by the negative name "*un*conscious," and live them through with delight or terror in these few minutes of sleep. Surely, some-

3

thing much more is going on here than merely communication from my "primitive" thinking.

As I pondered the question of what makes dreaming possible, I recalled that Joseph in Pharaoh's prison believed he was able to foretell the future by interpreting dreams, and Agamemnon's army at Chalcis could not sail across the Aegean to storm the walls of Troy because certain seers among the Greeks had certain dreams. And I could not persuade myself that Joseph and those Greeks were more stupid and less "civilized" than I.

Most fascinating of all are those experiences on nights when I go to sleep concerned with a problem, preoccupied, let us say, with a decision that has been puzzling and plaguing me. Often I find, during the night or the next morning, that my dreams have come up not with the answer as such but with new light on the context of the problem; and though the resolution of the problem is not necessarily clear, at least steps toward its solution seem indicated. This process of getting help from dreams on problems does not, of course, work all the time. But it does work enough to indicate that here is a highly significant process in which dreaming reflects my deepest concerns, a process that is within the sphere of my intentionality, though not my conscious control.

Thus it has seemed to me that dreaming comes out of more profound capacities than we generally assume. I believe also that dreaming has some connection with man's distinctive capacity for transcendence, i.e., his capacity to break through the immediate objective limits of existence and bring together into one dramatic union diverse dimensions of experience.

Another question I found myself asking was related to the above: *What is the source of dreaming?* I have believed for a long time that there is something wrong in our Western tendency to think of dreams as merely prelogical language that we "get over" if we become well-adjusted or integrated enough. There are a number of similarly subtly pejorative ways of regarding dreaming that are our unexamined heritage in a culture that overvaluates rationalism and objectivism. We need to remind ourselves that dreams are *trans*logical as well as *pre*logical. They are a form of communication with ourselves

and our world which includes many dimensions at once, and
therefore it is entirely understandable that they should, as Jung
and Fromm (in his early work) have argued, include insight
and reveal not only greater error and evil but also greater
wisdom and ethical sensitivity than the person was aware he
possessed in his conscious life. In fact, there is now some evidence that dreaming involves the *higher* cerebral centers, in that
patients who have had lobotomies do not dream.[1]

Part of this tendency to see dreams as "primitive" comes
from our belief that consciousness develops out of a more
elementary previous state of unconsciousness, and since dreaming comes from the latter, it is taken to be the language of this
more primitive state. I believe this developmental picture is in
error, and that what goes on in the child is quite different. I
propose that the original elemental state of the newborn infant
is not unconsciousness but generalized *awareness*, a capacity
that we human beings share with all animals. Both *consciousness*
and *unconsciousness* develop out of this original awareness, in
a process beginning shortly after birth but observable by most
of us only some months later. This process is the capacity to be
aware of one's self as subject in a world of objects, a differentiation of self and world. It is the capacity which distinguishes

---

[1] "Therefore, it is more than just an aphorism that one attribute of
homo sapiens seems to be his analyzability, ranking on the level with his
ability to be psychoneurotic, to dream, to daydream. To the observation
of the infrequency of dreams and daydreams after lobotomy, should be
added the simplification of the manifest dream content, when dreams do
occur. The dreams have the character of direct wish fulfillment like
those of children; for example, Anna Freud's strawberry dream in the
Interpretation of Dreams [Freud]. Lobotomized patients dream of deli-
cacies, of getting rich, and so on and have occasional pollution dreams.
The manifest dream content also becomes tamed after lobotmy. For example, a former patient of mine, a schizophrenic doctor, complained before the operation about a recurring nightmare in which he was sur-
rounded by wild animals in an arena; after lobotomy the dream lions did
not roar and were not frightening any longer but walked away silently.
. . . The emotional asymbolia caused by lobotomy drains away a
psychic dimension." Jan Frank, "Some Aspects of Lobotomy (Pre-
frontal Leucotomy) under Psychoanalytic Scrutiny," *Psychiatry*, Vol.
13, No. 1 (February, 1950). I owe the reference to Dr. Frank's study
originally to Dr. Robert Holt, *American Psychologist*, April, 1964.

human beings from the rest of nature; out of it emerge language and the capacity to use symbols.

But lo, this birthright of the human being is a curse as well as
a blessing. Out of this distinguishingly human *Anlage* comes the
capacity for repression and the neurotic problems, as Kubie and
others have pointed out, to which the human being is heir.
Consciousness itself, in that it consists of our ability to differen-
tiate between subject and object, also involves simultaneously
our ability to deny awareness, potentialities, and desires. This is
the "split" between consciousness and unconsciousness often
spoken of, but that terminology is based too much on neurotic
rather than normal experience. I define unconsciousness here as
*the potentialities for awareness and experience which the indi-
vidual is unable or unwilling at that time to actualize.* If it were
true that the unconscious is the primitive, it should follow that
it would be richer in peasants than in highly differentiated
people, but this is manifestly not so. The problem of "primitive" dreams has to do with how the dreams are used (as in
primitive tribes) rather than with the fact of dreaming itself.
Speaking of the non-neurotic person, i.e., the person free from
gross repression, I believe we can say in principle that the richer
his consciousness, the richer his dreams, and vice versa. The
upshot of what I am saying is that there are many different
dimensions of awareness, consciousness, and what we call "unconsciousness"; and what is occurring in dreaming is richer,
more portentous and significant than implied if, following the
usual assumption, we relegate it chiefly to primitive experience
and childhood memories.

Other questions immediately followed as I considered Dr.
Caligor's project. How does a person create and re-create
symbols in his dreams? Does he not mold these symbols together into myths, and in turn form and re-form the myths into
dramas, and is not this his *way of perceiving, coping with, and
giving meaning to his world?* There would not *be* a dream
from the unconscious except as the person is confronting some
issue in his conscious life—some conflict, anxiety, bafflement,
fork in the road, puzzle or situation of compelling curiosity.
That is, the incentive for dreaming—what cues off my particu-

lar dream on a particular night—is my need to "make some-thing" of the world I am living in at the moment. The phrase "make something" includes on the one hand making sense of it, looking at it from various perspectives and re-forming it to make some meaning in a perplexing or apparently meaningless situation, and on the other hand remolding my relationship to this world.[2] And since the self is always inseparable from the world to which it is related and with which it is engaged in dialogue, this implies as well remolding the world "closer to the heart's desire." I use this last phrase in a different sense from "wish fulfillment," as I trust will be clear below.

By this time in my ponderings I became aware that I was so much taken up with questions that might be answered by studying a patient's series of dreams that I had, for better or worse, already given my inner consent to participating in this study. Whether I would regret the "decision" or not, I did not stop to ask, for I kept thinking of other theses Dr. Caligor's study might give a chance to answer. Several years ago I formulated the hypothesis, for example, that every dream situa-tion and every dream has within it some decision, latent as the decision may be. I mean this in a normal sense, not necessarily traumatic. Dr. Caligor's study might give me a chance to test this thesis.

The dreams we get in therapy often come out of traumatic situations experienced now by the patient or reexperienced from childhood. But we should not peg dreaming at this intense or traumatic level. "Play" and "wonder" are included in the term "curiosity" as I have used it above, particularly as we see these states in a child, and particularly as we see them ensuing in dreams that give some answer to creative problems which the dreamer is confronting.[3] The thing we find in common in dreams which come out of intense conflictual dream situations

[2] The dream could be said to be a TAT or projective test par excel-lence; the dream does in a total way what these do only in partial ways.

[3] Wonder and the related state awe are not so different from anxiety: indeed, are they not of the same quality, wonder and awe being the benign form of the awareness of the gap between being and nonbeing, of which anxiety is the painful form?

and those which come out of "play and wonder" is that the person is related to his world in the mode of forming and re-forming it, creating and re-creating, molding and remolding it. The *quantitative* degree of activity and passivity is not the issue here, but rather a certain *quality* of relationship: the person is engaged with his world not only on levels that include consciousness and fantasy but on other levels which are often lumped together in many gradations of "pre-" or "sub-" or "un-" consciousness. Children's play and some adult art have this quality of activity and may not be accompanied by anxiety or trauma in any obvious way. Though anxiety and neurotic problems certainly affect dreams, we cannot understand dreaming as such, or the fact that dreaming is possible, on the basis of such a dichotomy between neurosis and health.

What I am arguing is that unconscious life is also *intentional*. It is oriented in some direction: the dream or fantasy is saying, this is the way I see the world, and this is the way I see myself in it. That is quite different from what has generally been assumed in psychoanalysis, that by *interpreting* the dream we give it meaning; for interpreting has tended to be our transforming the dream into our symbols, rather than listening for the dream's symbols; interpreting it in our formulations, rationalizing it in terms of our particular school. Then lo and behold, the meaning of the dream turns out at worst to be the therapist's meaning rather than the patient's, or at best the patient's formulation in terms and categories he has learned from the therapist. What I am proposing is something different: namely, that the unconscious experience *itself* is intentional, moves toward meaning. It is *protentive*, to borrow Husserl's term. This meaning will not, however, be in logical terms. As Freud made entirely clear, the unconscious brooks contradictions, denials, reversals, and every other thing that horrifies our logic.

Unconscious experience does have its own *form*, however. This form has more in common with art than with logical forms. The language which is unique to unconscious experience is the symbol and myth. Here symbol and myth come into their own, not as rationalized explanations but as their own language. As I shall point out in discussing this patient's dreams, I have

some serious questions about therapists' propensity for rationalizing and interpreting symbols and myths in rational terms.
The purpose of dreaming is to enable the person to *experience*,
rather than *explain*, symbols and myths. Explanations are
useful, by and large, only as they open the person up to a fuller
experiencing of the symbol or myth.[4] The symbol and myth
present a totality of meaning which "grasps" us, a meaning
which contains a union of feeling, willing, and thinking. It
seems to me we lose the power of a dream and other unconscious experience when we reduce them to rationalized words,
for they then become "signs" rather than "symbols." When I
am away from home traveling in the Mediterranean, the flags of
other countries such as Turkey or Egypt or Italy are to me
"signs," pieces of cloth standing for certain nations, which I
decode and file in my mind. But when I see the flag of my own
country, something altogether different happens: I am grasped
emotionally and volitionally as well; I experience a symbol, in
contrast to decoding a sign. This is the powerful language of
symbols and myths in dreams.

It makes no sense to say that a symbol is "less real" than the
reality in which it participates, that the trees in Cézanne's painting are "less real" than the maple tree in my front yard because
the latter is an object which I can walk up to and put my arms
around. The trees in Cézanne's painting, unforgettable once
one has seen them, affect us infinitely more than the thousands
of trees we see every day as objects and forget immediately.
Cézanne's trees on canvas have changed for countless people
their very way of looking at trees, enlarging their consciousness
so that Tree has gained an architectural majesty that literally
did not exist in our relation to trees until Cézanne painted
them. In this pragmatic sense, you can say the trees in Cézanne's painting are "more real" than those in one's front yard.

---

[4] I am not referrring here to the other functions of explanation and
interpretation in therapy in general: as a way of helping a borderline
patient to see the rationality and order in what is going on; as a way of
reducing anxiety when it gets so strong it paralyzes the patient; as a
means of increasing the patient's sense of autonomy since, if events have
antecedents and are not mere fortuitous happenings, he can then hopefully do something more about his own life.

Cézanne's trees are the quintessence of tree expressed in art form, and as this quintessence they have the quality of symbol. By the same token we forget the actual persons whom we have seen playing Hamlet—Barrymore, Gielgud, and Burton merge into each other in our memory. But we never forget Hamlet himself, precisely because *he is a myth which expresses the quintessence of our experience in an art form.* Dreams and other aspects of unconscious phenomena reveal that "reality" has many levels, and by bringing these together, as I shall try to illustrate here, dreams deal with quintessential experience.

Some of the practical questions I asked myself were: Will there be unity and consistency in a person's dream life? If we take the dream as an art form, in which field it would be most analogous to drama, will we be able to discern an inner consistency from one dream to the next? One assumes the patient will be building world after world in dramatic form, and four characters are most likely to be in the dramas, the characters who preoccupy him most in therapy: himself, his father and mother, and the therapist. What inner consistency will we be able to discern within this sequence of worlds in the patient's dreams from the beginning of therapy to the end?

When I finally consciously decided to take this opportunity to study the total sequence of Dr. Caligor's patient's dreams, I set out to take the dreams phenomenologically. That is, I planned to stick as closely as possible to the dreams themselves, to take them as self-revealing phenomena, as "givens," as patterns of data within themselves. Thus my intention was to use the patient's associations and what she and the therapist said *about* the dreams only as secondary material, to check and test the understanding I could come to from the dream itself.

When I began to read the case material, however, I was forced to take an even more rigorously phenomenological approach than I had planned. For I found that what is said in case studies like this *about* the dreams—that is, discussions by the patient of content and excerpts from childhood associations—is already on a level several times removed from the dream itself. So we must distinguish a number of steps in dreams. First, the patient, Susan, has a dream. Second, she remembers it, and her memory already partly distorts the dream. Third, she tells it to the therapist, emphasizing certain elements, leaving out certain others, falsifying still others. Fourth, they talk about it. This generally brings in formulations and theory which may—and I fear too often do—take us further away still from what the dream is trying to say. After my analysis of Susan's dreams was written, I read what she said *about* her dreams, generally given as interpretation immediately after she related the dream and introduced by: "I think the dream means such and such." Almost consistently she gave psychoanalytic clichés and banalities, which sounded sensible enough but were actually intellectualizations that not only did not do justice to the dream but often, in my judgment, seriously watered down the central communication of the dream. This is of course understandable when you come to think about it, for the patient's intellectual reaction to the dream will be a defensive one motivated by the desire to escape the anxiety of the dream (which is generally why she had the dream in the first place). Consistently Susan led an amazing "double life," with her dreams carrying and tackling issues on a considerably more serious, original, and significant level than the relatively banal things she said about them. What continually enthralled me about Susan was that after an important dream which she had managed to render innocuous by banal parlor talk, she would catch herself and the therapist up short the next time with a short, punch-line dream such as, "Let's call a spade a spade," or "This is a soap opera we're engaged in."

I saw, thus, that if I were to start with what she and the therapist said about the dreams, I would be at least four levels removed from reality right off, and subject to four points where confusion could multiply. This results—as so often happens in case conferences—in endless guessing games and speculations among therapists, ending up generally with some parochial cliché or intellectualized formulation.

Therefore, I decided to base my study on *only the dreams themselves* and let them, so far as I could, speak to me. I marked the beginning and end of each dream in Dr. Caligor's total transcript and made a conscientious effort not to let myself read anything else. I waited till I had completed my study and analysis on the whole series of dreams before reading the associations of Susan, the dialogues between her and the therapist about the dreams, and the rest of the case material. I have added footnotes (accompanied by asterisks) in a few places where I refer in the body of my material to what I learned from my later reading of the case sessions.

The discussion and interpretations I present of this sequence of dreams thus are based on knowing nothing about the patient other than that she is a woman in her early thirties, has been in therapy before, that she cuts down the number of hours at two junctures in this therapy, has an affair at one point with Morris, the husband of her friend, and falls in love at another time with a psychiatrist called David. These last two facts were put in by Dr. Caligor in special notes in his transcript. I say that I knew nothing about the patient except these facts: I must hasten to add, which I can do since this introduction is being written after concluding the study itself, that I felt that I knew a very great deal about her after her very first dream, and that very shortly—so vividly is a person revealed in his or her dreams—I felt I had a complex and many-sided acquaintance with a very real person.

Those who are looking in the pages which follow for a systematic analysis will be disappointed. I intentionally did not try to make it systematic in any rigid or external sense. I wished only to listen to the patient's dreams, to try to hear what she is saying in her symbols, and to follow that. I sought to find *her* order, the system which fits her. This requires flexibility and a variety of perspectives: she leads the way down the path and I go along, attempting to cast light on the journey and see what it means. What is necessary in such a venture is clinical perception, a grasping as far as it is humanly possible, of a complex human life in its career over two years.

I have only two main hypotheses to begin with. One is that dreams of a given person are related to personality change— they reveal it, predict it, and cast light upon its meaning. The other is that people communicate their most meaningful experience in symbols and myths—whether what we call symbols and myths are in the form of images, fantasies, dramatic enactments (as in dreams), gestures, the dance, or what not. The linear statement—subject, predicate, object—can communicate something *about* me; but if I want to reveal *me*, which as a self, an organism, always has the character of a totality, I select or form my words in some symbolic or mythic form.[5]

This does not at all imply that our inquiry is hit-and-miss or without categories or tests. I have said that symbols and myths have *form*. They constitute, like any work of art, a Gestalt. There is, then, the test of *inner consistency*. This criterion can be applied to the symbol, as we shall do in the case of the simple symbol of "hair" as it comes up in Susan's first dream. Inner consistency does not necessarily mean unity. There will be plenty of *disunity* in this patient's or anyone's dreams: that is one of the things which brings her for therapy. It is in understanding the mechanisms and dynamisms of the disunity that scientific tests and concepts come into their particular importance. But disunity itself presupposes some unity on the basis of which she, and we, experience and hopefully can understand her disunity. In therapy we should be able to perceive the consistency in the neurotic *disunity* of the patient.

There are other specific factors that make our inquiry not simply a hit-and-miss enterprise. One is the *time dimension*. We shall ask our question of consistency over a period of time; the total series of dreams gives us a test, a long-term dimension of over two years, which is very important. Another factor is the continuous presence of the therapist. If the therapy "takes," the dreams will have much to do with the world the patient is creating with her therapist: he will be an enduring focal point, a relatively constant figure on the stage or in the wings or in the audience, as a central figure among those to whom the dreamer is communicating. By following that thread as well, we try to discern the form or pattern of this patient's relationship to her world.

I am proposing that the *structure of the dream itself* carries a

[5] I shall presently define "symbol" more specifically.

great deal of meaning—perhaps the basic meaning of the dream.[6] For example, Susan dreams of a female moving toward or away from a male. A structural interpretation is possible on the sheer dimension of space; i.e., she has the female move in a certain relation to the male. The discussion of whether the female is herself or her mother or her girl friend or even the therapist is on a secondary, content level. The structural interpretation can tell us a great deal regardless of how the dreamer may distort or falsify the content of the dream in telling it. It is the dreamer who makes the female move this way or that, regardless of who the female is. If at the beginning of therapy the dreamer has all the females moving *away* and at the end moving *toward* the male, we have a datum of considerable importance.

One more question arises. What about the latent meaning in dreams? If we take the dream simply as the given phenomena, are we denying what Freud called, and put most of his emphasis on, the latent in contrast to the manifest meaning of the dream? The answer is no. My hypothesis is, again, that assuming the therapy "takes," *the latent meaning in the early dreams will become manifest in the dreams later on.* Latency refers to a dimension of communication the patient is unable or unwilling as yet to actualize. According to our theory, it will come out gradually and step by step in the later dreams in the therapy (assuming still that the therapy "takes"). Since I am writing this introduction after completing my total study, I can say that I was indeed gratified to discover in this patient that that is exactly what happens.

[6] I am not, of course, arguing at all that the free associations of the patient are not useful in actual therapy, with Susan or any patient. Rather, I am asking, for the specific purpose of this study: What can we learn on limiting ourselves to the dreams alone? Also, what I am proposing is different from supervision, in which the supervisory therapist identifies to some extent with the therapist and therefore already participates to some extent directly in the therapeutic relationship. I had no supervisory function whatever in Dr. Caligor's therapy with this patient, and knew nothing about the case until, several years after the therapy as contained in these sessions was completed, I was asked to participate in this study.

2

Symbols
and Their
Changes
in Dreams

What are symbols, which we have said are the language of dreams, and therefore the language of Susan's dreams? The word *symbol* comes from the Greek *sym* plus *bollein*, meaning, literally, to "throw together," to unite. The symbol is a uniting, a bringing together, into a meaningful pattern, of the person's experience on many different levels—unconscious and conscious, historical and present, sensual and intellectual, social and individual. The symbol has been called a bridging mechanism (Kahler); but it is more than that. It is an image which reveals the living totality of the person, and whether he is speaking to himself or to us, it is his only means of communicating these different dimensions of his existence at once.

The best way to illustrate both what the symbol is and how we investigate the ways a person builds, creates, and re-creates symbols is to turn immediately to Susan's first dream.

Dream 1 / *Session 10*
[First dream mentioned in analysis. Dreamed two nights before the initial interview with the therapist, when the decision to start treatment had already been made.]

I was in the process of changing the color of my hair. I was trying to be blonde. It looked quite dreadful. Then I tried to dye it red. When I was nearly through, I looked into the mirror and was horrified. I desperately wanted to revert to my own original hair color but I could not. I awoke frustrated and anxious.

Immediately, we see the symbol "hair," and the symbolic action that is the theme of the dream. This is stated lucidly:

15

"Changing the color of my hair." First dreams are usually quite lucid, particularly when the person is about to begin therapy. The dream is a kind of prologue to a drama, saying in summary what the play will be about. First, she is "trying to be blonde." The affect that goes with this re-forming of symbol is dread: "It looked quite dreadful." She then tries to "dye it red," looks in the mirror (a secondary symbolic action, or motif), and the affect also is horror. She then wants "to revert to the original hair color"—a most interesting yearning in the dream—but cannot. The affects with which she awakes are frustration and anxiety.

I use both terms *theme* and *motif* for the symbolic action that will be the drama of the dream. *Theme* points toward the unity and inner consistency that are part of the dream and will be (so I hypothesize) characteristic of all the dreams of a given individual, reflecting the unity and consistency which are his character and which his neurotic behavior is an effort to preserve. *Motif* indicates the central thread that will run through the dream or dreams, from the point of view of *motive*, which is the etymological source of the word. A theme is thus also a motive, a dynamic movement, a goal in life one wants consciously or unconsciously to move toward, a motive in the forming and re-forming of one's life.

A symbol is never arbitrary. *Signs* can be arbitrarily selected, like highway signs which direct us to the turn. *Symbols*, in radical contrast, *are an organic expression of the meaning of the total living experience of the person at that time in her history*. Strictly speaking, I am so far in our discussion *hypothesizing* that "hair" is a symbol for Susan—a hypothesis for which that dynamic dream gives us much reason. Obviously the word *hair*, from the time we comb it in the morning till we wash it at night, may be used countless times without any symbolic meaning whatever; it represents a chore we take care of while thinking of something else. What makes two random sticks of wood, when crossed and placed above an altar in a Christian church, become a powerful symbol? The quality and dimension of meaning the sticks, in that particular form, now express. Since the meaning is partly historical and unconscious, we can never set out rationally simply to "make" a symbol. It is inaccurate to speak of a symbol *for* something; it does not *stand for* its meaning, but participates *in* that meaning. It is a symbol *of* something. So far as Susan's symbol of "hair" goes, we shall have to wait to see whether it is enduring, whether it expresses the significant and different dimensions of her experience, and therefore deserves to be called a genuine symbol.

I want now to illustrate the many dimensions of experience symbols in dreams may contain, and their significance. I take the simple "hair," so commonplace that those who think symbols must be exotic will be disappointed at the outset. It is what the patient does with this symbol, however, that is of interest. (We shall find that "hair" comes up time and again at critical points in Susan's analysis.)

First, hair is a biological fact as well as an image; the symbol brings together Susan's biological state with her mental image. Thus, the symbol does not stand for reality; it is not abstracted from the reality; it contains the reality (in this case, the biological reality). The symbol involves senses as well as an idea; indeed, it is closer, as we shall see later, to the senses than it is to an intellectualized image, and needs to be "sensed" as one apprehends it.[1]

The symbol "hair" is certainly social and cultural as well as individual. How one wears one's hair, particularly how a woman wears her hair, has expressed attitudes and relationships to the world throughout all times. We have only to call to mind the long, beautiful hair of the Cretans; the shorter, practical hair of the Romans; and the fact that in different cultures femininity, and specifically virginity, is indicated by the woman's hair. To this day, in primitive parts of Central Europe, when a girl has lost her virginity and must be relegated to the role of

---

[1] "Dream thought is essentially organismic in character. The basic unit of dream thought, the symbol, emerges from the senses as well as the intellect. . . ." The dream "is fired under special conditions of realness, contact, and impact and during a time when the whole person is stirred and involved. These conditions give rise to the common experience that dream thought leaves one more with a 'sense' of things than with an 'idea' of them." Herbert Zucker, "Dreams and Dream Thought," unpublished paper.

prostitute, her hair is cut off. Similarly, the women who collaborated with the enemy in the last war had their hair shaved off.

Biologically, hair is an expression of age, a symbol of growing up and of growing old. The baby has very little hair (this comes up later in Susan's dream); the growing child has abundant hair (and it is often used in the dreams as a parental rather than a child's symbol; that is, to make the child pretty, to make it look like a boy or a girl).[2] The adolescent wears hair as a badge, whether the crew cut of the student or the long hair of the beatnik or Beatle. The adult woman uses it as a means of attraction; and the old lose their hair and become like babies again. Hair is an image of aging and dying; and how a person accepts or refuses to accept these facts may be reflected in the way he relates to his hair. In our culture, people often have their anxiety dreams in terms of their hair graying or falling out —expressions of their fear of growing old and dying, which since the Renaissance seem to be particularly dreaded in Western culture.

Susan's hair seems to be a social symbol also in the particularly American sense of the "accent on youth" ; in the attitude that one can make one's self over, take one's self in hand,[3] do something to make one's self attractive or hide one's age, all by changing one's hair. At the time of this particular analysis, a widely used advertising slogan displayed in beauty salons and recited over TV went: "You have only one life to live, so live it as a Clairol blonde." We also see the obvious individual elements in how Susan uses the socially and biologically given symbol. She "tries" to be a blonde (which draws your eye), suggesting an assertive desire to be seen, a cry for attention. Then she dyes her hair red (which strikes your eye), reflecting an aggressive attitude toward others and an aggressive manipulation of herself as a tool in her aggression.

[2] Early in these dreams I found myself hypothesizing that Susan had been the favorite of her mother, had been "prettied" up like a doll as a child. This was later borne out.

[3] I use the phrase "in hand" in its specific meaning of "manipulate," which comes from the Latin *manus*, hand. Susan is telling us in this first dream that she is preoccupied with manipulating herself and others.

I mention these things merely to illustrate the variety and richness of a simple symbol like hair. To what extent hair and the symbolic action of dyeing it mean these specific things or others to Susan remains to be seen. Some symbols have such deep biological and cultural roots, such as symbols related to birth and death, that they may well be universal, as Freud and Jung proposed. Even so, how any one individual relates to a universal symbol depends upon an infinite number of factors in him. How he selects, forms, and re-creates a universal symbol is what we seek to determine in order to understand him. A symbol that is so closely bound up with the social, cultural situation as hair certainly tells us much about Susan's individual attitudes toward herself and the world. We must carefully analyze the content she in later dreams gives the symbol, as this will tell us how she speaks out her conflicts, identity problems, and interpersonal relationships. The task of the therapist is not to prejudge the symbol, but rather to be aware of the almost infinite possibilities in it, and to be aware, too, of his own hypotheses about it. We all form hypotheses, presuppositions, assumptions as soon as a patient mentions a symbolic theme such as changing her hair. It is impossible to listen intelligently and imaginatively without forming presuppositions. The error is in hearing only what is in our own minds to start with, thus forcing on the patient our own interpretation of the symbol in question, or the formulation of our particular school of analysis. My purpose here is the exact opposite: to expand our consciousness about the symbol so that we can be more open and flexible toward it, so that we can hear on expanded dimensions what the patient is trying to tell us. By the same token, the purpose of interpreting a symbol or a dream is not to tell the patient what it means, and certainly not to intellectualize it, but to expand his consciousness so that he may more deeply and fully experience what he is saying, and more fully experience himself in relation to himself and us who partly constitute his world at the moment. The interpretation of the meaning of a symbol or a dream is not an end in itself but a bridge to the patient's experiencing the symbol and the actions that go with it.

Thus, in considering Susan's dreams we shall ask: (1) What are the significant symbols and myths by means of which she is communicating to us? (2) What drama is she playing out with these symbols or myths? [4] How is she, on the stage she sets in the dream, forming and re-forming these symbols? How is she creating and re-creating them? (3) What intentionality, what orientation toward willing, what decisions are shown in the dream? (4) What symptoms does this involve? It is the symptoms which trouble the patient and bring him to therapy; therapy, on the other hand, works somewhat in the reverse. First there is the anxiety, desperation, frustration which the patient experiences and which trouble him at the moment; the therapy moves back through the conflicts in identity and relationship which underlie the symptoms, through the patient's intentionality and willing, which are involved in his acting in the dream. All along, symbols and myths are the basic, underlying forms in which he sees and communicates his life. In actual practice, of course, therapy works on different levels simultaneously, depending on what the patient brings up.

Since we have discussed hair as a symbol, let us ask our second question in reference to this prologue dream of Susan's. What she is playing out in the drama will reflect particularly her *problem of identity in her world*. The dream is an answer of sorts to the three-sided question: What am I? What am I in relation to these persons in my world? What do I want to be? It is important to emphasize that a person experiences his identity not through ideas but through symbols. He gets his identity through concepts when these are reborn in symbols or myths, as the idea of success becomes a myth in Horatio

[4] This "playing out" of the drama is acting, but it should not be confused with what is called "acting out." Acting out is generally an escape from insight, an acting to avoid seeing one's self. What we mean here is the acting that occurs in all dreams, which is normal and meaningful. The analogy is to the dream as a stage on which the dreamer sets various characters and has them act out the meaningful picture of his life which he is trying to communicate. The acting in the dream, as in a drama, is an encountering of experience on all dimensions at once— seeing, feeling, intentionality, and physical action. The ways these different dimensions are brought together represent the symbols and myths.

Alger, or Marxist formulations become a symbol of the proletarian revolutionary. Susan is struggling to find some identity through "being" a blonde or a redhead; and she does it by changing her external appearance. She tries "blondness" on for size: "I *am* a blonde now," or "I *am* a redhead, and how is this?" The "looking in the mirror" is a vivid element in its own right. "Mirror" is an exceedingly rich symbol and could be phenomenologically described at great length, as the way we are seen, the way the self is constituted by how it appears to others, a means of self-evaluation and self-criticism, and so on. At first blush, Susan's dream does not seem interpersonal: she has no other persons in it. But she is not dyeing her hair for herself alone. At first I thought she was dyeing it chiefly for men, but later I began to feel it was more: "Look, Mom! Are you impressed?" In any case, the mirror is an eloquent symbol of the interpersonal world, but a world with no people in it, a world in which others exist only in terms of reflections, only in reference to "How do I look?" I hypothesize that Susan's interpersonal world is empty, barren, and considerably depersonalized.

We ask our third question specifically about this dream: What is the intentionality, the orientation toward willing, the decision or act of willing in the dream? It is my belief that every dream situation has within it some crisis which to begin with was the occasion for the person's having the dream on this particular night. The dream is an answer, however obscured, to the question posed by this crisis. Thus, the hypothesis makes sense that every dream has within it some decision, latent, repressed, or contradictory as it may be. In Susan's dream, the intentionality and the decision are clear: she puts forth a good deal of effort "trying" to be a blonde or a redhead, whatever this may mean for her. She struggles hard "trying to be"; and we assume that she is a person who tries to find her identity by forcing, controlling, manipulating, not only others, but, as indicated in the dream, herself. There is also the element of intentionality in the "desperate wanting" to get back to her original identity, to have her own hair back again. It is interesting and presents a note of pathos that it does not seem to occur to her that she could get back her original hair color simply by letting her hair be. It is of the essence of such an identity conflict that she cannot see that identity comes by being what you are; she has not been able to be what she is, and this is why she is in analysis.

With respect to our question about her symptoms, we see these in what she overtly states—dread, horror, some desperation, frustration, and anxiety. There are also the symptoms of disorientation and self-doubt, which are partly stated and partly acted out in the dream.

The second dream does not come until session 32 and is, also, not a dream she's had during therapy but a recurrent nightmare from childhood. We note but put aside for the moment the question why during therapy she has had no dreams. This suggests, in line with our hypothesis, a rigidity in Susan, a considerable need for her to control the situation.

Dream 2 / Session 32

[Recurrent childhood nightmare.] I would have these nightmares of semi-human characters who walked on two legs and had faces covered with hair like animals. They were called "busses." They lived in family units. I would somehow wander into the area of the city they lived in. I would usually have some kind of warning but not heed it. The most frightening thing about these creatures was that they used words that always had an opposite than the usual meaning. I would awaken terrified.

Here the stage is filled with "semi-human characters," symbolic creatures who are like human beings in that they walk on two legs and have faces, but their faces (the part of the body we normally recognize, by which we identify a person) are "covered with *hair* like animals." This again raises the question of identity, hers or any human beings as she sees them; and it sets the problem more specifically as that of the relation of animal nature, her animal elements, to the fact of being human. The relationship of these creatures is in terms of "family units," although this is vague in the dream—it is stated and not shown.

This tells us what we would assume anyway: the fundamental connection of her identity problems with her family background. I put aside the symbol of "busses," though interesting data could probably be obtained from Susan through free association. The symbol is "spoken" and consists of an inanimate word: to my mind, the more significant message of the dream is communicated chiefly in the figures of the *persons*, and particularly in their *movements*, what they are *doing*. So important is the movement that one has the impression in many dreams that the central and most forceful meaning would be communicated if they were in pantomime.

We turn now to Susan's movement in the dream. It is vague, a "wandering" into the part of the city in which these animal-human creatures live, as though pulled by some attraction of which she is unaware, the rational "warning" disobeyed, betraying some complicity on her part, some ambivalence masked as indecisiveness. This is a clear intentionality in the dream (what we call "decision"), masked and hidden, as is often the case with neurotic patients, as well as with normal people. Her movements reflect a passive-active dilemma—"somehow wandering," not "heeding."

The capacity to speak is the distinctively *human* capacity: when she has her half-animal creatures act, their words have an opposite meaning. She must have grown up with adults who lied to her, who said one thing but felt (the little child picking it up empathically) something opposite. This dramatic picture of the creatures using words which are oppositional—*against*—leads us also to ask: oppositional to what in her? It suggests she has become a person of defiant behavior. What particularly comes to mind is the "opposition" to the female elements in herself, the passive-active theme as a conflict in herself. She may well be telling us that this unresolved oppositional conflict between male and female aspects of herself is basic to her problem of who and what she is.

Finally, the symptoms are consistent with the previous dreams reported, and what we would expect; namely, "fright" and "terror" strong enough to make a recurrent nightmare.

Dream 3 / *Session 34*

I was necking with this boy. I thought my parents were upstairs. My father came in and got angry. He ordered the boy out of the house. Then my father turned to me and was really furious. As a punishment for what I did, he forced me to have intercourse with him. I protested. But he in a fury insisted that I straddle him while he sat on a chair. We had intercourse. I woke up in a cold sweat.

This dream, still not from the period of therapy, is an adolescent dream recalled from age fifteen. It looks at first glance like a powerful Oedipal dream in the Freudian sense, which on one level it is. But if we drew that conclusion to begin with, we would be in grave danger of short-circuiting the dream and missing what Susan is trying to communicate to herself and to us. An intelligent person like Susan, and practically every patient in private therapy these days, knows about the Oedipus pattern; no dream or fantasy of wanting to have intercourse with one's parent has the power to shock anyone or even requires much censorship in our culture, where this is common cocktail talk. So if Susan were not trying to tell us more than that, why would she have remembered this dream from adolescence?

When we take a further look at the dream, we see that the Oedipus content is in a highly *oppositional* dramatic situation, with the power, "force" in the dream, exerted along those lines. The father "ordered" the boy out; then "forced" her; she "protested" ; he "insisted." The word "straddle" is significant—*she* straddles *him*—with respect to the ambivalence we mentioned in the passive-active conflict in the previous dream.[5] "Intercourse"—the term literally means "running between," a communication—can occur only in the context of all this op-

[5] * The term "straddle" becomes important, always typical, for such situations later: her mother *straddles* her in dream 8; she *straddles* her boyfriend, etc. [*Asterisk designates notes made after I had read all the dreams.*]

position: the father to the boy, the father to her and vice versa, and, we may assume, opposition of both her and her father to the mother. This is much more than censorship of sexual content: she is very specific in the dream that sex can occur only in rage, fury. All of which protests the guise of passivity we have already seen in her.

This dream introduces the problem of *latency*, which we mentioned earlier. Previously latent meaning is now emerging: the *oppositional* theme, which emerged with "animal nature," is here, appropriately enough, related specifically to sexuality. There is also latent material casting light on why Susan has such difficulty being feminine: to be a woman is to be *forced* by others. Other obvious questions come to mind. *Whose* fury is it in the dream, her father's or hers? To what extent is her being "violated" her own desire and strategy? Is the recalling of the dream at this stage in analysis related to her anger at the therapist because of the growing intimacy between them? Does it reflect a desire that he force her to greater intimacy—which she will not have to acknowledge or take responsibility for, but can fight against? We ask these questions but do not answer them, waiting for Susan to bring any or all these possible latent meanings into the open later.[6]

As she struggles with considerable anxiety, desperation, and frustration, she presents three themes to us so far, all interrelated around the central question of who she is in her world. First, her identity as a woman, and the social "splash" she makes, coming out in her "mirror" relation to others. Second, the wider problem that people do not have identity as human beings but as animal-human creatures who use language oppositionally; and here her apparent "passivity" comes into view. Third, the oppositional problem in her identity comes directly into the center of the stage in the "forced," rage-filled sexual relationship with her father. Sex is the content and the "playground" (to use Freud's term) in which the conflicts are played out, though it does not decide the form and meaning of the struggles.

[6] * Such latent meaning does later come out.

Dream 4 / *Session 37*

It was a mixed-up dream. During the beginning of the dream I was going somewhere with a girl friend, someone I knew in high school. At one point in the dream there was some kind of physical contact—I think a kiss, though I'm not sure—and in the dream I had a real immediate response, a violent physical reaction. This disturbs me because I have never been attracted to women before. In the dream, someone was going to wash my underwear, probably the girl friend. I took off my pants and they were sopping wet with excitement.

Then there was this fellow I knew in college. I didn't know where we were going or what we were doing. He began to kiss and fondle me on the street and said he would love to have intercourse with me. So we started to take our clothes off in the street—it was dark. We did a weird dance, I following his movements. Then I realized how inappropriate it was to be naked in the street. I tried desperately to get inside, to get away from this public place where I was totally naked. I awoke feeling anxious.

This is the first dream Susan has actually in therapy. The fact that it appears as late as session 37 substantiates our assumption of her need to keep a controlling hand on herself and the therapy, her fear of dependence, her fear of "opening up." (I wonder what has been going on in the therapy during these two and a half months when she had reported no current dream.)

Let us take the dream as a stage that she sets up and peoples —her microcosm—on which she has herself and the other figures move in this direction and that, in and out of relationships, in a drama directed to finding and living out some existence, however unsatisfactory so far, in a meaningful human world. We see the first movement in this dream is toward a girl, a physical contact with a violent sexual reaction. Whether or not Susan has pronounced Lesbian tendencies is to be left in abeyance; but the fact that she moves toward a girl after telling the dream about her father is significant. The element of having the girl wash her underwear is minor, though not to be ignored. It suggests to me that she makes other people (chiefly her mother, probably) take care of her, do her menial chores, as compensation for the fact that she plays a relatively passive role and cannot act with regard to her main problems. I hypothesize that her mother tied her to her as a child, and in return her mother did Susan's chores for her. Again on the main theme: the movement now on the stage is toward a man; it is about as clear a setting of the sexual roles in opposition to each other as could be imagined, and a "trying on" of different roles to see which fits. She continues in the passive, *reactive* role; she has the man doing the *wanting*: he would "love to have sexual intercourse with her," and *so* (the adverb is important) "we take off our clothes . . . I following his movements" in the dance.

The man—"this fellow," she calls him—is presumably the therapist, among others. She has him doing the directing, she following ("I didn't know where we were going or what we were doing"). My feeling from this dream is that she is exercising considerable camouflaged control over the therapy but hides behind her passivity, thus avoiding responsibility for what is happening. The "desperate" reaction to "being totally naked in public" seems to reflect the humiliation of the controlling person at being unclothed, uncovered, fully seen by another person.

Her anxiety, at times taking the severe form of desperation, at times being expressed in frustration and rage, is to my mind a positive element all through here. It shows that she is in genuine conflict, which, though she tries to hide it, tells that a good deal is at stake in this world she creates and struggles in. The anxiety is a sign of the presence of energy and potentiality to change and grow. The therapeutic problem is to help her to keep the anxiety as a motive and propelling force, which seems to be what is now happening, as exemplified in her searching in the next dream.

Dream 5 / *Session 43*

The dream involved Irwin, and I was trying to get something that belonged to me from his apartment. We were civil to each other; there was no overt hostility. It was important to me that he think well of me.

Then another woman entered the picture. She was Irwin's fiancée and I wanted her to like me, too. I wanted her to see me as reasonable. I tried very hard to be sweet to both. I was still going through drawers looking for whatever it was when I woke up; I was looking for some information I had left in the apartment.

Most important, I wanted Irwin's fiancée to have a good opinion of me.

She now shifts the scene of the search to the location of Irwin, her previous husband, looking through drawers for "some information I had left in the apartment." What can she find about herself in that previous world of failure in marriage? The mirror motif is present all through here: four times she mentions that she wants Irwin and his fiancée to "like" her, have a good opinion of her, think of her as "reasonable." How much effort she expends in this protective front of "being sweet"! Here the mirror preoccupation (how do others see me?) seems to be a strategy and technique by which she keeps the world controlled and unruffled about her while she goes about a much more important quest.

Dream 6 / *Session 46*

[Susan had a vague dream about Leah and Morris breaking off, and she was glad.]

The dream before this introduced the "eternal triangle": Susan, her previous husband, and his fiancée. We now see a clear triangle subtheme: herself, another woman with her man, and she, the patient, breaking them apart.

I want here to introduce the triangle as a symbol. We have seen it several times in the past few dreams, referring to the "triangle" of marriages. But the importance of the symbol goes far beyond this vernacular use and involves many significant dimensions. The triangle is one of the earliest symbols in art forms, emerging in the neolithic paintings on Egyptian vases. Apparently (so says Sir Herbert Read), the original art forms were drawings of water reeds and the legs of ibises, which then evolved into the well-known triangle design on the vases used by the Greeks and others on countless varieties of early pottery. From this art form was abstracted the triangle for mathematical use. The triangle constitutes the smallest possible number of straight lines which can make a *form* with *content*. The triangle, then, was important in the technology of the Egyptians and in later science: by triangulation, the Egyptians measured the rise and fall of the waters of the Nile, predicted seasons, and learned something of the movement of the heavenly bodies, since symbols such as the triangle are reflected in the relationship of all bodies in nature. Human beings and animals similarly judge distance by the triangulation that is possible because we have two eyes, in relation to which is located the third point, the object we wish to see.

In medieval culture, the triangle was the dominant symbol, being present in the trinity of theology, in philosophy, and in the triad of nature, man, and God. It is basic to the art of the Gothic cathedral, graphically shown, for example, in Mount-Saint-Michel, where the rock emerging out of the sea serves as a base for the Gothic structure that rises in many triangular pinnacles into one large triangular form, thus uniting nature in the form of rocks and sea with the man-made cathedral pointing up in its graceful apex to God.

The triangle is present in human existence more profoundly than one would think from its use by Hollywood. The triangle is the smallest unit of *procreation*—man, woman, and baby. It seems to me the triangle is basic to creativity of all sorts. There always is a threesome: painter; world he paints; and ensuing work of art, the painting. Similarly, intellectual creativity consists of a three-sided unity: knower, the process of knowing, and the known.

Human procreation, as well as creation in general, is in the normal sense a movement through triangles, the child of one mother and father growing up, finding a wife or husband, and establishing a new triangle. But this is, of course, a pilgrimage beset with many vicissitudes. Freud spoke of the four people present at every act of sexual intercourse: yourself, your lover, and your mother and father, who hover over your shoulder. This is a rectangle. The presence of these progenitors on the normal level adds depth and zest to the love-making. But if the presence of the mother and father is pronounced and dominates the situation, then the lover himself may well be impotent or in other ways exhibit a problem that makes it impossible for him to create the new triangle. That is to say, the more implacable the rectangle, the more neurotic the individual is apt to be. Put in technical psychoanalytic terms, the more transference beyond a "normal" point in sexual intercourse, the more problems will be involved. Overcoming neurotic problems, as well as normal life, is a *process of negotiating rectangles to arrive at new triangles.* Hopefully each patient, like Susan here, will ultimately leave parents behind, choose her own man, and actualize the symbol of the pregnancy and baby which she dreams about.

Thus, when here I use such terms as "space," "form," and a form in space such as "triangle," I am not at all talking in abstractions but speaking rather of the immediate processes of living.

Dream 7 / *Session 53*

I was moving into another apartment. It was something appalling to realize that I was renting an apartment, sight unseen, on the basic assumption that it could not be as bad as the present place. I walked in and saw all the plumbing in the middle of the apartment. This turned out O.K. because I had entered the wrong door. Then, from the correct vantage point, the place looked very nice. Then I was disturbed that I did not have enough furniture inside the apartment and had no money to buy more.

I was then visited by someone from the stock market, a securities exchange broker. He was telling me of news of someone who was going to get a divorce, someone I did not know. I was feeling glad to hear of the news of the divorce, but this was a sweet kind of pleasure which I could not express openly. I felt guilty about my pleasure.

The visitor stretched out on a couch as if he owned it. I did not know him, and yet I stroked his testicles. I don't know why. It happened without any conversation and as if it was expected of me.

The search goes on: Susan keeps moving, now into a new apartment. But the motive is not to get *to* something, but *away* from her previous world. Nothing could be as bad as the present place; the movement is a leap in the dark, which understandably scares her. The plumbing in the middle of the floor I take to be the ever present sexual, excretory symbols which she uses as the content of her particular conflicts. It is fascinating how she again "tries on for size": she enters the stage from another door—ah, now it looks nice. But if she does leap from her old world, precipitously and without sufficient inner development, she won't be able to "furnish" the new place. The motif of breaking apart relationships (divorce) reappears: she was pulling marriages apart in the triangles of her previous two dreams. Though it was her ex-husband in the first and her "friend" in the second, in this dream they are unknown: "*someone I did not know.*" This blocking off of awareness seems to be a way of avoiding her own guilt in her pleasure at breaking up these couples. In any case, the securities broker seems to be the therapist entering the picture: she is engaged in *exchanging* (apartments, marriage partners, roles) in the therapy, and she wants a special security in the process, the security of someone else taking charge and doing it for her. He stretches out on the couch (which presumably he actually *does* own). What is most dramatic in this episode is that she *denies knowing* this man, the therapist. This is like a scene from Ionesco's plays, in which people who are most intimate, such as husband and wife, do not know each other when they meet. The act of stroking the testicles is so specific that it must be saying something equally concrete, to be discovered presumably in her associations. (Does she want the testicles? Or must she give him gratification, or seduce him, to get from him—the securities broker—what she wants?) She denies knowing why she does this; her action is again a passive response to an expectation she projects into the mind of the other person—the passivity now looking like an only half-successful guise for her own blocking off of awareness.

This active blocking off of awareness, this effortful resistance to seeing what she is doing, presages some sort of climax.

Dream 8 / *Session 60*

I had a discussion with a man about investing in the stock market. I gave him all my money for this. Then I searched for a woman to clean my apartment. My next-door neighbor, a man, took over to find one. I came home and found my neighbor in my apartment, asleep.

The cleaning woman came in and started to act in a very disturbed manner. She wanted me to give her my sweater. I was afraid of her. She threw me on the floor. Then I pulled off my green sweater. At one point, as the cleaning woman paced, she straddled my body. As she was walking over my head, she said, "You're lucky I didn't piss all over you." But I did not ask her to return the key to my apartment or not to come again, because I was afraid.

Then I remembered that stocks were bad and they were about to go into a depression, and I wanted to make some arrangements. Oh yes, the woman had already taken another sweater while I was not there.

Ann, a policeman, and I were seated. The policeman said I should get the key back and not to worry about anything the woman stole because the government would reimburse me. Just then the madwoman walked in at that point and just sat down in a very relaxed manner. She had a small round case with a key. In her presence the policeman insisted that I give him the details about the sweaters. I told the policeman but I stuttered because I feared the madwoman. As I gave the description of the green sweater, the policeman asked the woman if she stole it. She casually said yes, that she intended to return the sweater. As she took out the sweater, she took out a gun, too, and aimed it at the policeman. She pulled the trigger but there was no ammunition. As the madwoman and the policeman wrestled, I woke up. I was in a cold sweat.

A mood of desperation is now apparent. This dream seems to me to be the central climax in the whole drama so far. The patient has been like a rat in a maze, trying this door and that passageway, searching here and there, commanding, imploring this person and that, but to no avail. The seriousness of the struggle now in process is shown in the presence of the mad-woman, the patient calling on the ultimate civil authorities, policeman and government; but though the policeman fights with the madwoman, the madwoman is the stronger, command-ing figure. The dream ends in their wrestling, with no resolu-tion.

Once we have grasped this struggling, wrestling theme (which might be peopled in many different ways and still reflect the same main motif of desperation and anxiety), we can turn to what Susan makes of the specific characters. She "gives" all her money to a man to invest, a handing of herself over to the therapist (the securities broker of the previous dream). The search for a woman to clean her apartment is a similar action; it is getting someone to do something for her (again, the "clean-ing" sounds like therapy). The neighbor who goes to sleep in her apartment I take to be a minor picture of the therapist, and the policeman a major one. The fact that the therapist is supposed to find her a cleaning woman suggests the subsidiary role of associating him with mother, at least saying the man (father) is supposed to make the mother work for her.

We could go into this symbolic figure of the cleaning woman in considerable detail—its relation to her mother; the sweater symbol as the clothing which covers and protects the breasts (possibly here an indication that the mother deprived her of the breasts in early infancy); the "straddling" (a word which first came up in relation to intercourse with the father); the ostensi-ble look upward at the genitals; and the humiliation she suffers in the madwoman's power to "piss over her." Susan is com-pletely cowed by this woman, so afraid that she cannot even ask for the key to her own apartment. She seems to be saying: "Mother has the key to my world, and I dare not take it." Here latent elements from the earlier dreams emerge. Susan is telling us that the reason she cannot move toward her own identity, find her own world, is her conflict with her mother. If we ask whether this madwoman is also the patient herself, the answer is obviously yes. The presence of Ann, who seems to have elements both of Susan and of her mother, also suggests this. If such a female figure (the madwoman seems so powerful and profound a figure it approaches archetypal dimensions) appears in Susan's dream, it is a profoundly significant element in her world and is *both* her mother and herself in varying degrees, depending on the particular situation.[7]

Susan is convinced the madwoman is more powerful than the therapist, who merely "tells" her she should get the key back —move toward her own life and world—but the trouble is the mother has the "key"; and the patient stutters, cannot communicate because of her pronounced anxiety. She has the therapist reassuring her, telling her "not to worry" because the authorities will reimburse her, and asking her to report the details of the difficulty, that is, the therapist is fiddling in the dream while Rome burns (how many satirical references to therapy Susan puts in!). *She* knows how anxious and desperate she is, but she thinks the therapist doesn't.

The "stocks were bad," she says: a predictive statement that her assets (and she) are about to go into a depression.

We find latent material now coming into the open concerning Susan's passivity. Her getting the man to "invest" for her (she cannot "invest herself") and the woman to clean for her

---

[7] * Here I was building up in hypothesis an impression of Susan's background, though at the time I was making these notes I knew nothing about it: that she must have been given a great deal of affect ("spoiled") by the mother—an only child? probably not, because she is so competitive; but rather the favored one—and then later she experienced radical rejection, either real or fantasied as a function of her great demands; that the mother rather than the father must be the powerful figure in the family; and that her underlying problem is not with men but with her mother.

are parallel motifs. She gives over to these figures the power over herself (money, sweater, apartment); she does not experience herself as the active agent of her destiny, even though she is at the same time a highly active person (*vide* how much action there is in these dreams). In previous dreams we have seen her passivity as a strategy, a technique for controlling others. In this dream her passivity emerges in a deeper dimension as a function of her fundamental helplessness, her desperation and anxiety. I might have assumed this theoretically to begin with; but as the material which was latent comes into the fore, she herself convincingly tells us.

Dream 9   /   *Session 64*

I had a dream while I was visiting home. I dreamed I was living with my girl friend. Two distant relatives on my mother's side, my aunt and cousin, visited. I always felt a discomfort with them as a child. I had the same discomfort in the dream. I was worried about how they would interact with other friends of mine due a little later, that the relatives might not accept them. After my friends arrived, I was panicked how things would go, what my relatives would think of me. I was afraid my friends would just not be acceptable to them.

There have been no dreams for four sessions after the desperate, climactic dream of the madwoman. What is Susan doing with her anxiety?

One motif for dealing with her anxiety is indicated in this dream. She is trying to make everybody fit in the home scene, via mother's relatives; anxiously trying to see whether they can accept each other under one roof. Here is the mirror symbol again: Would the little girl Susan, via her friends, be acceptable? It's a matriarchal world, though slightly removed in that she makes the figures mother's *relatives*. Though she feels anxiety, "discomfort," and "panicky," these don't sound so severe; has she succeeded in making everybody acceptable, or has the pronounced anxiety of the last dream been repressed?

Dream 10 / *Session 67*

I had a dream last night. I was listening to the radio, to an old soap opera. Suddenly, at the end of the program, at a crucial point, the announcer said: the program will be set "x" years from now. I realized that the now children would be adults—a tremendous gap. I realized that this would be dishonest, an avoidance of the real problems.

Yes, she carries on the childhood theme. These last two dreams seem to me "flashbacks" to her earlier life, in which the basic conflicts underlying the climactic dream got started. In the guise of the soap opera, again satirically, she says that she must talk about her childhood. She encounters resistance and would like to avoid this, and feels the therapist, in the person of the announcer, wants to skip it, but she is aware that leaving that gap would be dishonest.

The great anxiety of dream 8 seems to have dropped in this "gap." (Whether something went on in the therapy "at a crucial point" that fits in with her avoidance desire is a question which can be asked but not answered now.) The dream seems to me a little gem of communication. She's saying that she needs to talk about her childhood, and if she goes from infancy (in which mother *is* all-powerful as the breast and cleaning woman) to adulthood, her life will be a phony soap opera.

Dream 11 / *Session 72*
[She was graying.
She was relating to a married man.]

And if the soap opera continues, she will get "old and gray" without ever having lived; life itself will be a great gap. The hair symbol comes back, now bespeaking a sense of urgency. I take it quite specifically: if she does not fill the "gap" of her childhood, she will stagnate before her time, grow old but not mature, like an apple that withers without having gotten full and ripe.

The relation to the married man seems to me to be saying the same thing—a short-circuiting of life rather than a full living of it in complete relation. The married man may also of course be the therapist.

Dream 12 / *Session 85*
It involved a dog that jumped on me. He showed his teeth and I was not afraid of him.

This looks like a frequently seen sexual dream, with the man's sexuality viewed as hostile, dangerous. Man is a dog, and sex has teeth. She has herself in the dream being unafraid; but why not? In the context this seems clearly a whistling in the dark, or an assertion of will power, a trial of strength to show her implacability in front of the dog.

Something is obviously going on sexually in this woman's life which makes her anxious but which so far she denies.

Dream 13 / *Session 109*
For some reason I was thinking of that dream where my father has intercourse with me. I had these feelings there, too. You know, I remember more of that dream that I had forgotten. My father comes in and sees me necking with the boy. My father says nothing and stalks out. The boy then opens his fly and takes out his penis. My father comes back and sees this. My father gets furious and orders the boy out of the house. "So that is what you want," he said furiously. He made me have intercourse with him and I protested. But he exerted his authority. I remained dressed in the dream. He plunked me down in the chair on his lap and had me straddle him. I protested all the time. But I felt compelled to obey his command. Then I woke up while having intercourse in the dream, feeling miserable. But I had the same feelings of victory, pain, and surprise.

Now the latent meaning of the adolescent dream, reported in session 3, comes into the open. This is a nice illustration of how the originally repressed material later comes out in the phenomenological movement on the stage. The new elements, repressed in the previous telling, are: first, the father sees her necking with the boy, says nothing, and stalks out. When the boy takes out his penis, the father orders the boy out of the house. The father, thus, far from being the angry violator of his daughter as in the first rendering, is now shown to be a protective man, acting like the father of any adolescent girl. This emergence of latency substantiates our hypothesis that the unconscious is what cannot or will not be activated. The principle is true that "it was there all the time," but it is also true that it could not have been told earlier.

The second new element is the father's sentence: "So that is what you want." I believe we can take this for just what it says in her own words, put in the father's mouth—that *is* what she wants. From then on in the dream she has him commanding, furious; I believe this to be a strategy. Our earlier assumption that this was *her* mood, however completely projected on the father, is borne out in this dream as not only plausible but obvious. (We cannot assume the father *is* an angry, hostile man; we simply don't know. My hunch, in the total constellation, is that he probably is not, but rather is a weak, inept, indecisive man, and that the anger and aggression are really hers.) I take her putting the anger and aggression on him as indicative of her own inability so far to see what she does to men. What does it mean when someone sets up another person in the dream as giving the command, then being herself in the position of obeying it, particularly when the dream already says *she wants* it? I think this is more complex than a social censorship, as it was in Victorian days: the conflict is not between her and society in our day when everybody dreams Oedipal dreams, but between elements in herself—specifically, it seems to me, in her inability or unwillingness to face what she does to men. She still has herself straddling the man, as the madwoman straddled her. She is dressed, she does not uncover or bare herself; she gets his penis, in the act of straddling him, but otherwise doesn't participate. This seeing herself *acted upon* now seems more and more to be a cover for her own aggression.

There is a note in the transcript of the sessions that Susan started an affair with Morris, the husband of her friend Leah, a month before this dream. A long gap is present here—twenty-five sessions—between dream 12, the one about the dog jumping, and dream 13. We can now answer on two different levels our earlier question: where has the anxiety and despair shown in the climactic dream of the madwoman gone? She is evading her anxiety and despair by plunging into sexuality. On another level, her anxiety and despair have "fallen into the gap" created by the repression of her childhood, as indicated in the soap-opera dream. These seem to be active and passive methods of dealing with anxiety: but they amount to the same thing; namely, Susan's saying, when faced with a basic conflict like that in the madwoman dream: "I cannot yet let myself become aware of what this conflict was or what it now is." The implication is that what she is doing in sex will turn out to be a neurotic "acting out" of the conflict with the madwoman mother.

Dream 14 / *Session 114*

My apartment was very filthy. I was on the floor, nude. When I got up, there was about an inch of dirt—no, it was clean sawdust—clinging all over me. I was nude. Suddenly Morris was with me. Then we were dressed and walking along the street, then riding in a taxi. He put his hand on my breast. I felt disturbed. I moaned, "It's too soon; it's too soon; I'm not ready yet." I awoke feeling anxious.

Her personal world is filthy when she lets herself become bare (she says twice she is "nude") to experience it; the guilt is obvious, even to the "sawdust trail." It is important to note that this guilty scene takes place *before* Morris enters; thus we cannot draw the too easy conclusion that the guilt is caused by the sex with him. It is guilt in her, in her apartment, in her world.

I am strongly struck by the moaning sentence: "It's too soon; it's too soon; I'm not ready yet." I take it as a revealing statement of fact; she is not ready for sex, and not just in this particular instance, but all along. The sexuality has not been sexual relationship with men, but something else. The sex fills the "gap"; it is the easiest means at hand for swallowing up her anxiety. Morris's reaching for her breast is more than a chance sexual gesture of the male; in a drama we would see it as a pointing gesture, an indication *to* the breast. I think that the issue all along in these sessions is not sex itself but sex in the service of filling the gap, sex as an avoiding of the core problem, namely the breast and mother. Susan is apparently an attractive woman, and for such a woman, in our culture, sex is the most acceptable avoidance mechanism; sex covers up her conflict, transforms the conflict into a contest with males, and turns her shame into victory. But it's all a pseudo-battle, for her shame and her rivalry hinge on the breast and mother; and by the pseudo-battle, she still can cling to these.

There are no dreams for thirty-three sessions. What is going on in *this* gap?

Dream 15 / *Session 147*
David and I were having intercourse. I wanted intercourse with David in the chair facing him. I initiated and we had intercourse. I recall the adolescent dream of intercourse with my father. That had a feeling of punishment and of terror. This dream was less terrifying. Actually, it was pleasant and a relief. I see the dream ties in with my fantasies before I fell asleep. Maybe I'm saying that I want to initiate when I want to, to express what I feel without fear.

For the second time, a latency dimension of the adolescent dream comes out. She is still straddling the man. But the element newly admitted into her consciousness, and spoken, is that *she* specifically takes the *initiative*. This bears out our earlier hypothesis that she was the one who wanted, she was the asserting one, in the previous two truncated versions of this dream as well, and only now can it be spoken out. I don't think the fact that the man here is David and not her father changes this, since the dream is so clearly a reenactment of the adolescent dream.

Dream 16   /   *Session 153*

[At this point Susan recalled the adolescent dream of intercourse with her father. She felt that more than the idea of sex
was involved there.] Rather than sex, I wanted my mother
out of the picture and my father to be with me on a loving
basis, that somehow I did not have the closeness with my
father and sex was my idea of having closeness with a man.

In these further comments on the original dream (dream 16,)
she interprets the dreams as an expression of her need for closeness with her father and man. But if it is closeness, why the
straddling position and the original rage, the "forcing," "in-
sisting" ?

I find myself dubious about this word "closeness," and especially dubious of verbalizations to the effect of wanting "closeness." Obviously, Susan has a considerable problem in intimacy,
in loving, in *mitsein*. But people can be close without intimacy,
without tenderness or love, as two prize fighters or wrestlers
(as in her previous dream) are "close" in a clinch.

The general aggression, anger, fury of these dreams says to
me that the "closeness" she refers to is of the latter kind, the
closeness of contenders, of one person asserting, triumphing
over the other.

To be sure, the dream of intercourse with David and the
previous adolescent dream of intercourse with her father are
Oedipal, but the significant and original element is her need to
set it up her way, call the tune. She does not ever lie down, as
most women "give" themselves (the one time she does lie down
she is "straddled" hostilely and aggressively). She sits up in
what looks like a co-position, but straddling is having the
"upper position." She has "put" the movement on the man in
the past dreams—he "forces," he "insists"—but we now see the
dramatic, efficient movement comes from her, which she calls,
disarmingly, "initiative." [8]

[8] * Her statement at the end of the dream with David, that the dream
says: "I want to initiate when I want to, to express what I feel without
fear," seems to me to gloss over the dynamic structure of the dream. I

Dream 17 / *Session 154*

[Susan reported that she had two dreams that did not awaken her. These were:]

I was wearing a necklace of a string of beads. I kept fingering them until it broke. It was a new string of beads. I felt upset. My friends were vaguely present. I don't know what it means.

Another night, I was dreaming about sexual intercourse. Several doctors were present. One of them was Ann's doctor. The experiment concerned me and my own family doctor. This doctor and his wife were asleep in one room. In the course of this experiment, this doctor and I were to have some sexual relations but through some mechanical device, since he did not physically leave his wife. I felt uneasy about doing wrong and being unfaithful to David. It was also important that my doctor find his sex with me satisfactory. There was this mechanical gadget that went from me to the doctor, something like a cystoscope. The next morning, I saw the doctor come out of his bedroom in pajama tops and no bottoms. I noticed his penis was abnormally small. I did not feel disturbed when I awoke and remembered the dream.

The necklace continues the sexual theme, a supposition borne out by the fact that the subsequent dream the same night is

---

feel, on later reading of her associations and discussions through here, that many of her "interpretations" and formulations about the dreams, which she generally gives right after reporting the dream, are intellectualized psychoanalytic jargon that serve to cover up what the dream is trying to say. It is only later, in subsequent dreams, that there is genuine insight. For example, dreams 15 and 16, to which she gives intellectualized, relatively superficial, albeit comforting interpretations, are followed by dreams 17 and 18, which give penetrating insight into her despair and hostility, not at all in line with her previous interpretations. This is a good example of how a person is "wiser" and more "serious" on the dream level than in conscious life. Despite the anxiety-allaying banalities she gets off in "explaining" the dreams, her dream life goes right on trying to tackle the issues. This also shows how the level on which therapy is taking place is "below," of a more significant, meaningful quality, than the things either therapist or patient are saying *about* the therapy.

about sex.[9] More explicitly, the symbolism of the necklace suggests to me the vaginal circle, and the use of sex to attract others (which beads, as well as pretty hair, do). The fact that a necklace is worn between the body and the head reminds me of the earlier subtheme in Susan's conflict; namely, the separation between animal body and human head, a body and head which she, an intellectualizing person, has great difficulty bringing together.

But the important element again is the action, the movement. Here it is her breaking this circular form by her fingering, use of the hand—*manus*—which echoes the manipulating element in earlier dreams. She does this herself; no other person is present; it is not the aggression of "furious" males—all of which reflects a new dimension of insight, a previously latent level, coming into the open.

In the second part we are given further evidence that sex is not sexuality for its own sake but a detour, an acting out, an assuagement for and bypassing of the anxiety so vividly pictured in the madwoman-policeman dream, an anxiety that is still present. We hear the echo of her earlier cries: "I am not ready," "It is a soap opera," "The child is not grown up," "A void has been left."

When sexuality is in the service of a flight from anxiety and desperation, we would expect it to become mechanical, like all neurotic mechanisms. Surely enough, Susan then proceeds to dramatize it more eloquently than we could verbalize it: sex is an "experiment," a mechanical device which is painful, an instrument pushed not only into the vagina but up into her inner body. She can only try to please, an old, scarcely serviceable defense; and we can permit her own compensatory satisfaction in making the doctor's penis small, a triumph which at least

---

[9] The point was made by Freud, and so far as I know is borne out as an empirical fact in the work of analysts of all sorts, that the dreams of the same night are on the same general theme. The rationale for this is that dreams do not come hit-and-miss but come because the person is struggling with some issue, some conflict, is in some way or other encountering what is going on in her life at that time. This fact, that the dreams the same night tend to be on the same theme, bears out our hypothesis about the unity of dream life.

releases her from anxiety ("I wasn't disturbed"). We could ask, of course, why wasn't she? For were we to see such a drama on the stage, we would feel this is indeed something to be disturbed about.

Susan keeps the wife of the doctor (whom we may take to be the therapist) securely there. She does not want to put the other figure in the Oedipal triangle out of the way. Thus, another latent element emerges to correct her earlier rationalized interpretations of her father dream with the cliché that she wanted her mother out of the picture.

Through many of these dreams I found myself, as already suggested, thinking that Susan experiences herself like a rat in a maze, trying this role and that, seeking this way and that to find who and what she is, exploring this world and that one—the different doors in her apartment dream being almost literally a rat-in-a-maze picture. Nothing seems to work; she becomes more and more desperate (along with gaining insight, which she seems to grow into, rather than becoming aware of), working up to the climax of the wrestling-madwoman dream. Where shall she go? There is a great gap, her childhood, that needs to be dealt with. In this desperation, what way is open? Sexuality is the one frontier to which we still can go in our culture, as Riesman and Sykes have told us, the one green thing that can occupy us; and so sexuality is a perpetual motion, a never-ending running to escape anxiety. Psychotherapy is perhaps a world in which we do not need to run forever, but in which, when we collapse with fatigue, or hopefully earlier, we can get some insight into what the futile race is all about.

In treating Susan's sexuality as an anxiety-escaping device ("experiment," in her terms), I do not mean to imply that it is necessarily unproductive of insight. There would be insight potentially in it, if only to show her that she ends up in the cul-de-sac of mechanization. More than that, the sexuality does represent a genuine struggle; it has enabled her to gain some insight into her own hostility, and possibly the beginning of insight into how her "passivity" is a cover for her aggression. If the way we have been seeing the theme of her life is correct, we should expect, as happens in the next dream, that the frustrating cul-de-sac of sexuality would push her to discovering and experiencing what keeps her from loving as a woman. This begins to happen in the further discussion of the dream before that (dream 18), and then emerges outright in the next dream.

Dream Material[10] 18 / *Session 155*

There is much hostility I have to David that I have been trying to ignore. (*Silence.*) And yet, he is so understanding. I do enjoy being with him. (*Silence.*) For some reason, the dream, the one with the beads, comes to mind. I think I'm saying that if I look carefully, if I finger the beads, the relationship will go up in smoke, maybe. That I haven't taken an honest look at what my feelings are. (*Silence.*) Maybe I'm afraid that if I look, I will tear the beads, the relationship apart."

Now insight begins to come. Some latent meaning of the dream of the beads emerges, a new way of seeing the drama of that dream after Susan has dwelt on the mechanization of the sex dream. The insight may seem obvious to us but seems to come to her with an authentic newness: something is wrong in what is going on between her and David, and if she does look carefully at what is going on, she will see something very different, namely a "breaking." It is interesting that she keeps the dream on the less esteem-threatening basis of looking-at-feelings, whereas the *act* really involved in the previous dream is "fingering," manipulating; this, not looking, is what breaks the beads. More accurately stated, "If I take an honest look at what I am doing, I will see I am tearing the relationship apart."

Dream 19 / *Session 156*

Janet and I were in my mother's living room. Janet is an old, good friend who acts maternally toward me. I felt that some conflict arose between what David wanted and Janet wanted. It had something to do with David and me going

[10] At several places Dr. Caligor included as dreams Susan's discussion and new insight into a dream in the past. I will designate this as "Dream Material."

some place. But Janet already had reservations for her and me. I felt disturbed, torn inside.

A new scene of the relation to her mother: she sets it in her "mother's living room," with Janet, who "acts maternally toward me." There re-emerges, with new meaning which was previously latent, the triangle of her, the man, and mother, and the issue of whom she shall stand with. She sides with the woman. She states the problem outright and with great clarity (another example of latency of meaning): *My mother has reserved me for her.* Certainly the symptom of feeling disturbed, torn inside, is entirely appropriate to such an insight. The whole dream bears out our earlier assumption that Susan's most fundamental problem is with her mother and women, not with men and her father.

Dream 20 / *Session 159*

I remember a dream I had last night. I remember biting into something and something came loose in the upper right part of my mouth. I asked my mother if I had false teeth in my mouth. She said no. Then I realized all my fillings had come loose and lumped together. I asked my mother if they were gold or silver fillings. My mother said silver. I thought, it will cost a lot because it will be replaced by gold. I felt no sensation, no feeling, no anxiety. The only feeling I had was relief when my mother told me that I did not have false teeth.

On the direct level, this seems to be an endeavor to make sure she is not irreparably "false," but can achieve some authenticity, can be "filled" with something better than what she got from mother.

But now to look at the dream more intensively. "*Biting* into something" is a phrase with several different implications: putting one's self sharply into a task, like biting into a problem in analysis; also it is a time-honored expression of aggression, as in animals getting food and in "oral aggression" in human beings; and/or it may refer to the "love bite" at the climax of sexual intercourse. In any case, she needs to have her assertive, aggressive organs in good shape. It is significant that she goes to *mother* to ask if these teeth are false, mother who outfits her with her tools for campaigning, especially against men, mother from whom she got aggressive tools but apparently not the nourishment she feels she needs. The "fillings becoming loose" suggests the loosening of defenses in the analysis, and getting them replaced seems to refer to the analysis also (with Susan's customary not-so-subtle satire concerning the cost). But we must ask whether she is saying she wants the analysis to reoutfit her with better defenses, better tools for aggression—and she has the therapist now in the position of the mother to do this. The affect of "relief, no anxiety or other sensation," does bear out the supposition that she is partially after new defenses and expects the analysis to give them to her.

Through these last dreams Susan is struggling with genuine problems, and each of the dreams not only joins issue but comes up with its partial insight. Regardless of whether the teeth are defensive, her concern here with not having *false* teeth bespeaks some honest concern for insight.

Dream 21 / *Session 167*
There was a man vaguely involved. Somehow, I had to take off my shoes, grit my teeth, and step into a foot bath, like at a swimming pool. The foot bath was full of snot, spit, slime.

The man comes back on the stage, albeit "vaguely." Her "gritting her teeth and stepping into a foot bath" is a scene full of insight, enacting vividly the way she experiences sex with men, even to the fact of only partially undressing, taking off her shoes; and all the while the man is only a vague accessory somewhere about. Again a latent element comes into the open: sex is "bathing," a rite of cleansing; but in her world the cleansing rite does not cleanse at all; it is a bath of "snot, spit, and slime." Certainly there is guilt and shame indicated by these last words, but I believe the guilt and shame arise from her conflict of motives in this gritting her teeth and stepping in. On this issue we are helped by our principle of holding close to the *significant movement* in the dream: sex as such does not enter except indirectly, and the man as male is almost irrelevant.

Dream 22 / *Session 168*

I had a dream before the weekend. I don't remember too much except it involved a relationship with a man I met several times but did not particularly like. He was married in the dream, just as in reality. He and I were arranging appointments. I don't know what interest I had in him, but I felt flattered. He was aroused sexually and could not wait until the next appointment. Then it became apparent that he was losing enthusiasm; and I knew that I would not see him because he would not keep his appointment. He was off with his wife. Basically, I did not care, but was concerned with a loss of face. I don't know if anyone knew of these appointments or not, but I really didn't care for him as a person. One reason the notion of the appointments gave me pleasure was because other women did not have men, and this indicated that I was very desirable. Actually, he and I planned the appointment, but he never came back. It was evident that the future appointments would have been of a sexual nature. (*Silence.*) It was not a disturbing dream.

Now the man is a central actor. The sexual content comes completely into the open as something she is not interested in. He is "married" (in the dream, as "in reality") ; she has no "interest" in him, she does not "care"—which is stated over again: "I did not care for him as a person." What she is concerned with is status: "I was flattered"; she is concerned with "loss of face." Sex is a competitive struggle not with men but with women: "Other women did not have men, and this indicated that I was very desirable." It is as clear a statement as we could wish that the sexual game is not desire for sex and intimacy on her part or the man's, but one long and involved struggle for status and prestige—like the dyeing of the hair, a manipulatory contest, concerned with the "mirror" situation: how she rates in relation to other women. Her "losing face" is interesting in relation to the earlier "mirror" symbol: there *is* something to the belief that one loses one's face literally, as is feared by primitive tribes, if one's face is merely an image in a mirror. That she has the initiative coming from the man, his aroused desire, and she has herself responding to the man's need is, as we have seen earlier, her passive way of making the motion come from the other person to mask her own activity. The man doesn't particularly count in her competitive struggle with other women. The dream resolves the situation with some insight. She has him fail to appear; she sends him "off with his wife."

Appointments are something you make with the therapist: and we must not omit the probability that this is explicitly the therapist in the dream (he is married "in reality"). She wants the therapist to be sexually aroused toward her—perhaps she feels that's the only guarantee that he will be interested in her; but she does "not like him particularly." This session would be an excellent one in which to draw off negative transference toward the therapist. My belief is that these pronounced negative, hostile feelings toward the therapist are her reaction to her progress, her experience of humiliation that a man (contemptible breed!) is helping her. Her negative feelings may also be an expression of her anxiety at her insight, with consequent need to put distance between herself and the therapist." [11]

Dream 23   /   *Session 171*

I was pregnant. Would it be a baby? Or was it some malignancy, a cancer, a tumor? I don't recall more. I was anxious, and continued to sleep.

I marvel at how eloquently the struggle goes on as she follows the same theme from dream to dream! She is pregnant, indeed; but is it a baby—the symbol par excellence of a procre-

[11] * After reading the notes on the session, in which she tells of having had a "wonderful weekend with David": she may be attacking the therapist precisely *because* she is getting on well with David. In any case, I feel the issue is not a new way of relating to men, but a statement of real hostility and antagonism toward the therapist, and men in general, because women and competition with them are what counts.

ative experience—or it is a malignancy? To be realistic, we must assume she is trying to tell us of the presence of a malignancy; otherwise, why would she have the dream? She is communicating her anxiety (and insight) that her sex-mechanical-competition-driven pattern is a malignancy in her organs of feminine creativity and productivity. As is her tendency, she makes it an either-or issue which she joins. But the phrase after the statement of her anxiety, "I continued to sleep," makes me wonder whether she will cover over the problem, sleep through the issue.

She is probably also telling us (with a despair that makes the above resignation understandable) that since the pregnancy is felt as a foreign body, a cancer or tumor, to be a grown-up woman capable of procreating itself constitutes a malignancy, a being sick. It is not infrequent that women tied to hostile, destructive mothers find it safer to remain children than to be grown-up women, in which case they would have to compete with the mother, and also, out of their identification with the mother, they would experience womanhood itself as a destructive thing and a sickness.

Dream 24   /   *Session 173*

I had an abortion. I had conflicting feelings about getting it. The person who did the abortion also did an oophorectomy [removal of an ovary]. David had been at the operation and he did not like some of the things the surgeon did. When I came out of the operation, I was disturbed that the surgeon had done more than he was supposed to. I think in that dream David wasn't David but you. It was the question of cutting back too soon, is it the right thing to do, am I going to make the analysis an abortive experience? Today I haven't got the doubts. I feel that cutting back from three to two times a week isn't really ending the analysis. (*Silence.*) (*Tearful and upset.*) The question of my graying hair came up at the end of last hour. I think I have a tendency to think of my hair in terms of time pressure—a perfect sign of the passing years. (*Silence.*) The surgeon applied the pressure to the abdomen to make things come out. He did not cut me open; he did everything vaginally. When he did apply the pressure to the abdomen, a lot of blood came spurting out. He wanted this; he thought it was the right thing to do.

She gets rid of the pregnancy; she has an abortion. (Again, what a consistent sequence!) But in ridding herself of the malignancy, would she also lose the organ, the ovary, which makes procreation possible in the future for her as a woman? She places the choice and responsibility on the surgeon (thera- pist) and sets herself as passive between David and him. The dream shows profound despair and conflict: if she gets rid of what she has associated with sex and being a woman, learned from mother—i.e., the manipulation-aggression-status pattern —will there be anything left, will there be any genuine femi- nine potentiality?

It is interesting that the symbol of hair comes back—the years are passing, and will life itself be an abortive affair? The bleeding and so on, which the surgeon is causing, are the way something actually is born. There is a real question at this stage of basic conflict whether she will make the analysis abortive.

Dream 25 / Session 179

I had a dream Monday morning. I took this job as a coun- selor but I did not want to take it. I was talked into it by my parents, who were counselors at the same camp. One of the things that influenced me was that a man—I think David, though I'm not sure—was a nature counselor at the camp. David, my mother and father worked at the boys' camp; I, in the girls' camp. In the dream I was looking for David and having a hard time finding my way. I was lost in a valley with steep sides and could not find him. I was in some kind of recreation room and I did not quite get to see David. But I'm not sure it was David, though he was meant to be. I was quite anxious.

She searches for the man, her man, and is "having a hard time finding my way . . . lost in a valley . . . and could not find him." But the stage is set in the context of her parents; she goes along with them because they "talk her into it" (*vide* the passive-active system). This is an accurate, insightful picture of her stage of development—a girl still in the kingdom of her parents, though at least the possibility is present in this kingdom that she may search for her man, her peer, with whom a relationship might be possible. The state at the end—"I was quite anxious"—is a healthy sign, indicating the issue is to some extent joined.

The triangle now is a rectangle with four persons: mother, father, she, and David. David is the one "meant to be," though who he is is left open in this "recreation [re-creation] room," and he is "nature counselor," the man who stands for *her* nature, her development, in contrast to her staying in the mother-father-daughter triangle.

Dream 26 / *Session 182*

I had a dream the other night. It involved two diaphragms. One was in poor condition, the other a new one. I got them mixed up. It took place in my mother's house. Dr. Morgan [Susan's boss] was there. I was aware I had left both diaphragms out so that Dr. Morgan would see them. David was the only man around. Dr. Morgan took me by surprise. He would have to infer a relationship between David and me. When he did see the diaphragms, I did not feel uncomfortable. Dr. Morgan picked up the poor diaphragm and said, "You're blushing." I said, "I'm not." He teased me and said, "Your face is as red as this shirt," and he pointed to his red shirt he was wearing. Then the ash fell from my cigarette and landed on his shirtsleeve. It nearly burned a hole, it melted the fabric, which was synthetic. It melted the fabric but it did not burn through. I felt bad. The hole stood out in the white fabric.

The scene is still set in the mother's house, the world in which Susan is trying to work out something with men. The two diaphragms give us a graphic picture of ambivalence, choice, which she repeats in two fascinating juxtapositions, in her statement that Dr. Morgan would *see* and *not see* them, and in the curious statement that "David was the only man around," though Dr. Morgan is obviously there. The choice of two men suggests immediately the father and the potential lover, a supposition that we have to keep for the moment in abeyance. But she immediately makes it concrete: two men are present, one of them her boss, older (presumably, the "poor" diaphragm is older than the "new" one), in a role of boss-father and probably therapist; and the fact that she has him teasing her may bear out a fatherly role. The triangle consists now of two men and of her as the woman, with the issue of choice woven in and out. At least, she indicates, some differentiation is possible.

It is interesting that she takes as the central symbol of the two men the appliance, a diaphragm, which keeps out the man's sperm, *prevents* conception and procreation; and we can expect the aggressive counterattack with the cigarette in her burning a hole in *his* shirt. (There are, of course, several phallic and female genital references—the white and red colors?—which might come out in her associations, and would bear out our structural analysis above.)

Dream Material 27   /   *Session 187*
I recall the dream of dyeing my hair two times and fearing that I might not be able to find my own hair color. I was saying I wanted to change, yet was very much afraid of what a change would be like. I had a need to hang on to all of my problems even though I was dissatisfied with the way I lived. Yet I was afraid that giving them up would be even worse. The feeling of being caught.

So! At this fairly climactic stage, the symbol of hair comes back into the picture. Again I wonder, listening to her concern about whether she could find her own hair color—as I wondered about this same sort of dream before—what keeps her from seeing that hair *is* its own color; why must it be manipulated, *made* into something? Susan sees change as manipulating the world and yourself on a stage where everything must be forced—which, of course, is exactly why she can never find (or *be*) her own hair color. Identity is for her something to be gotten only by forceful manipulation—which destroys one's identity in the process. She is also saying that she experiences herself as a self by virtue of her problems; to be "sick" at least gives some reality; and, as I indicated earlier, the one woman she had to identify with, her mother, gave her the example that a woman is a woman only as she dominates and manipulates.

Dream 28   /   *Session 188*
Last night I had another dream about going gray. I was pleased that instead of a few gray hairs there were several gray spots that were really right because it looked more attractive than several sporadic gray hairs. I felt good on awakening.

And now *gray* hair, and liking it: she feels good on awakening. But this is much too easy; I do not buy such a simple solution to the difficult problems Susan has been struggling with. The dream, coming at this particular point in the analysis, I take to be a wish fulfillment, playing ostrich, a dream that serves to cover up her anxiety arising from the fact that the problem with men remains entirely unsolved.

If I may apply Paul Tillich's formulation of anxiety, this dream seems to be her choosing "nonbeing to escape the anxiety of being." Perhaps it is better to give up than to struggle endlessly with a seemingly unresolvable conflict; at least if Susan were "old and gray," she would never have to commit herself to a man; she would have preserved the "gap" forever, mother's little girl still playing at being attractive. Tillich's formulation is on the ontological level, but we can translate it into clear experiential terms: to choose nonbeing (old age, conformism, death) *does* relieve the anxiety of living, and heaven knows Susan has as much anxiety as one can bear at the moment. My point here raises interesting questions about wish-fulfillment dreams. Are they always to some extent a going backwards, a gratifying of needs by playing ostrich, a way of choosing a less differentiated "being" in order to avoid the anxiety of actualizing one's potentialities in the present and in the future?[12]

Dream 29 / *Session 195*

There are three sections in the dream, one of which is hazy. I was visiting my parents, and David was there, too. There was something I was concerned about, money, but I'm not sure. And it had something to do with others evaluating what I was doing—like making a train on time.

Then the next section of the dream. I was in a store, there was a shoe counter. I was looking at shoes that were on sale, reduced, sports shoes, reduced from $5.90 to $3. Mr. Lambert, my office manager, was standing there, looking at me. I began to be concerned whether I was extravagant, would he see me as extravagant. I felt I didn't have the right to indulge myself. Mr. Lambert is a man who has had strong feelings against the project for which I was hired. I feel he has unfriendly feelings toward me. I also feel he may be anti-Semitic.

In the last section of the dream, I was in the office. I was rushed and David said he would like to help me. He didn't ask me what to do and he did some computations for me. He knew we based this on a 10 per cent sample. He went about it scientifically and I felt that he was so sweet. But he had data originally a sample, so that instead of a 10 per cent sample, he ended up with a 1 per cent sample. I hated to tell

---

[12] * After I had written these comments on her hair symbol, I came across, in her discussion in this session, her saying that she had considered, on entering analysis the first time in Albany—as in the original dream on entering this analysis—dyeing her hair red, and *her mother dyed her hair red*. This fact makes explicit and concrete what we have been saying, that Susan sees her identity as a woman as manipulating herself into her mother's pattern, and this presents a terrifying and insoluble contradiction to her.

She also, in this hour, refers to the "many occasions before and during the first year of analysis when I very sincerely felt that I would just as soon be dead as alive." In this hour, then, when she is talking specifically about gray hair, she says in her own words what we deduced before, that the issue is the "being/nonbeing" conflict.

him because he was so helpful. In trying to describe the feeling I had—like a little girl who helps mother by making muffins that do not taste good, yet everyone valiantly eats them. At one point David says, "You're keeping something from me!" That notion made me uncomfortable because I had been feeling so able to say anything to him. He also said, "Maybe you're hiding something from yourself." Then he said something that I found very disturbing. He said my conceptualization in the dream was of him as a child, not mature.

She does not give up, however, but comes back to the main conflict.

On the stage now the triangle is enlarged again to a foursome, as in recent dreams, to include her parents, herself, and David. This is a sort of prelude to the main part of the dream, saying that it will present the issue of how to bring a peer, *her* man, into the family triangle. The most eloquent statement is in the last section; she makes David a sweet little child who tries to be helpful though he is fairly stupid. (These phrases, "I hated to tell him," etc., which come up often in Susan's dreams, I take as the usual censorship of her own hostile, contemptuous feelings, which, being blows to her image of herself as a nice, sweet girl, are difficult to admit.) David speaks just like a therapist, telling her she is hiding something from herself, and then proceeds to formulate exactly what the dream is saying, namely that she treats him (and the therapist) as a child. She can let her man into the original triangle if she derogates him to childhood status, makes him indeed her "little boy" as she was mother's "helpful little girl." [13]

[13] * On later reading, I see that what cued off this dream was her seeing the therapist's wife and child in the elevator, and the competitive feelings which resulted. This is significant with respect to what we had said about her playing ostrich in the wish-fulfillment dream. She cannot rest in choosing "nonbeing," because, though such a defense gives temporary comfort, it does not protect her from competitiveness, envy, and her unsatisfied yearning. In this sense, envy is the expression of "unlived life," and I would add that competitiveness is, too. Seen from this angle, Susan's *competitiveness and envy are positive signs,* reflecting her own

Dream 31   /   *Session 205* [14]

In the dream I was in Alaska, I was running away from some kind of danger, trouble. At one point I saw or was seen by two men who were doing manual labor. I heard their conversation but they did not know I was there. I knew they were desperate in some way. They were talking in a fairly calm way about their situation. Their manual labor—digging, I think—I don't really know what it was, but there were huge pipes on either side. I was frightened that they could kill me. I don't remember the details of their problem, but their killing me would help to solve it for them. I went on and found a woman in this relatively small community who was going to be joined later by her husband—a doctor. She was scouting to find some facilities for him; he was going to set up practice. I associate this woman with Ann, or a gym teacher I had in high school. I felt that if I joined forces with her I would be much safer. I don't think she was too happy about it. But we did form the alliance. (*Pause.*) Then the scene is in a restaurant. There was a large round table. This woman and I and others—men and women—were there. I said something about our cooperative effort; I somehow referred to this woman's and my relationship in terms of marriage. And as soon as I said it, it sounded as though she and I were in a homosexual relationship. I tried to say they must not misinterpret my words; I tried to retract the word marriage. But they kept looking at each other knowingly. I

---

vitality and the potentialities in her which will not be satisfied by playing ostrich forever. Her yearning, as well as her specific neurotic symptoms, are constructive indications that she cannot choose nonbeing and stay resigned, or at least cannot without getting a good deal sicker. With this kind of patient, I would very early in the therapy, and then all the way through, try to help her admit and experience her competitiveness, envy, hostility, aggression, try to help her see these as indications of constructive potentialities in her—warped and gone awry, to be sure, but potentially sources of vitality. Susan must probably retain her competitiveness and envy as the closest she can get to strength so long as she has to remain "mother's little girl."

[14] * Dream 30, a further discussion of the previous dream, is omitted here.

was disturbed. (*Pause.*) Then the scene changes. I was in a bathroom. I didn't have clothes on and was washing my body. This same woman came in and said, "Aha, I see someone is going to have a baby." I knew I was pregnant. I looked and saw that I was pregnant and realized it was visible to others for the first time. Also, that the pregnancy that was not visible when I had my clothes on was visible when I was nude. The dream was upsetting, very much so.

As in the play *Hamlet* on the stage, in this dream all the characters have been delineated, the issues set up; toward what climax will the drama move? There is certainly movement toward some climax.

She is in danger, running away, specifically from two men (David and the therapist?). The element that connects her with the two men on the stage in this opening scene is *hostility*, with many battle phrases to follow, such as "alliance," "force." We shall put aside for the moment the question whether the hostility is theirs or hers. Killing her would solve *their* problem, she says—a reversal: killing them would solve *her* problem? The important thing is that hostility is the dominant element. She joins the *woman*, for reasons of safety, and assumes the helping role again, because, strategically, it is safer. She thus tells us again that the woman is the significant figure, the strong one, the one to be allied with in danger, the woman in this case being the "wife figure" in the basic triangle, possibly the wife of the therapist. This siding with the woman is confirmed emphatically in the "marriage" and, amazingly enough, in the impregnation, assumedly by the woman, a pregnancy which is visible if she becomes nude (she did not take off her clothes in the early dreams of intercourse with men). Just as the woman is the only one who can have a baby, the man is the only one who can impregnate her; but on her dream stage, Susan flouts reality simply enough, for the reality of impregnation by a man probably means a subordination to men which she cannot or does not wish to make. In any case, the men, having been run away from, are made irrelevant.[15]

[15] Some therapists would center on this "homosexual" theme. It is

Dream 32 / *Session 206*

I had another dream Sunday night. I don't remember too much of it. I think it had the same feeling. The dream was about detection, X rays to be read. I don't remember much about it, except to say that what went on in the other dream was somehow repeated.

An appealing statement that something more needs to be seen, and to be seen in the way a doctor sees inside a patient. In my experience, Susan's repeating her previous dream is her way of calling the therapist's attention to the fact that they missed the full meaning of that dream. What is she saying she wants, yet is afraid to see? My feeling at the moment is that it is the same thing: her hostility to men, which she has run away from, and her strategic method of doing this, "marrying" the woman, a safety she purchases at too great a price in self-destructiveness.

Dream 33 / *Session 207*

You know, I just remembered a dream I had. I recalled it while coming here. The frames of my glasses, in the dream, were broken by someone else; I think a man, but I'm not sure.

Here we have another statement of not being able to *see* something, for which she makes a man, presumably the therapist, responsible. She makes it the frame, not the glasses, which is broken; strictly speaking, one might still see, though with difficulty. She has conflicting desires, indications of which we have noticed earlier, "to see or not to see," and the responsibility for this can, of course, be put nicely, if vaguely, on "a man."

---

present, clearly, but in my judgment the dynamics of the dream indicate it not as the central theme. We could analyze Susan's homosexual tendencies at length, but I think they would not help us get at the central problem, which is stated directly in the dream: flight from anxiety, hostility in relation to men, and allying herself with her mother. In therapy with a patient who has such dreams, I would be very interested in seeing whether associations or further dreams indicate some sexual contact between mother and patient when she was a child.

Dreams 34 and 35 / *Session 208*

I had a dream Saturday night. This was, the narcotics squad of the Treasury Department was using Riker's Island. They were holding parties for narcotics addicts, to gradually wean them from drugs by gradual reduction. And the F.B.I. felt this was making their work more difficult, they were furious they were not told of the parties.

I had a peculiar dream Sunday night; only this time the people were not strangers to me. It was about David. In the dream, David was some other kind of doctor. He had invented a machine that had a blanket cover on it; it was used to treat cancer, and it emitted rays of some sort. And these rays could penetrate to the primary sites of the cancer and get at them like no other technique could. There was this machine in use, and another one that he had developed that he was reluctant to use. I may have been in this, but I can't remember the part I played. But there was a certain amount of anxiety whether or not the newest machine would be successful and when David would use it.

These two dreams continue like chords of a passage in Beethoven, replete with his dissonance, pointing toward some climactic statement to come. In the first, two powerful authority groups—doctors vs. F.B.I.—are in conflict about how to treat a sickness, presumably hers. The structural form of the dream gives its meaning, but I also wonder about the specific content, i.e., whether the Treasury Squad is the alliance of her mother and her (her mother is the source of nourishment, money) in keeping her narcotized; and the F.B.I. represents those who investigate, who give "insight," and whose work is made more difficult by the narcotizing.

The second dream repeats the X-ray theme, with latent meaning more forcefully stated. David (or the therapist) has a mechanical, highly technical device which can penetrate into and treat her illness. With trepidation, she permits the man to use his instruments, despite her ambivalence ("I can't remember the part I played," "anxiety," "would it be successful," and "when would he use it"). What she is doing in giving the power and initiative to the man is a moot question therapeutically; she may be trying to "play the female" in this lopsided way in which she is passive, so much so that she becomes involved only as an object in the dream.

Dream 36 / *Session 217*

In the dream, I went to visit someone who lived in an apartment house. There was a revolving mechanism where there usually is a revolving door to the building. This mechanism, which revolved constantly, was like a huge revolving plate that had another turning mechanism on it; you had to contort to get on; like crawling through tubes, as soldiers would in basic training. You had to maneuver through to get into the building. I was afraid but noticed others jumped on the gadget. So I jumped on, too.

I don't know if I knew the man I was visiting or not. In the apartment there was only one man there—an Indian I had never met before. He was very tall and heavy-set. I liked him. There were four of us in the apartment: the Indian, me, another woman, and another man. We were all going to an exposition or exhibit. It was like in Boston in that we took a streetcar.

I don't remember what happened at the exposition, but something happened to the Indian. He was killed and I felt bad about it. I think there was a time interval between meeting the Indian and going to the exposition. And I think that I had some kind of relationship—not sexual—with him.

Then I'm at the exposition. There was some question of wanting to have sex with the Indian and being hesitant. In some way I injected myself with his semen, and after that, found out he was dead. I suddenly knew I was pregnant. And I wondered how I would feel about having his child now that he was dead.

There was a lapse of time.

Then I was in my apartment alone. The contrast between my apartment and the other was important. Then a woman visited me. She was very tall and had dark hair—no one I knew in reality, but in the dream I knew her. I think she was the fourth person in the apartment. I was surprised to see she was very pregnant. She seemed to have expanded in all ways physically since I last saw her. She said she could not stay long because Ben, some sort of person of authority, had planned for her to make a large dinner for eight or ten, despite the fact that she was pregnant. Ben was responsible for my going to the apartment in the first place.

Then I awoke and felt confused. (*Silence.*) I had another dream last night; I do not remember except that it was something competitive.

The drama moves indeed toward a climax, and practically every important symbol brought up comes back here to be united in the whole and given new meaning. The apartment to which she goes, with the revolving mechanism on a revolving plate, makes me think of her coming for analysis. The "crawling through tubes" like the birth process, and her maneuvering, contorting, but finally just jumping on the mechanism, also sounds like the way she sees the analysis. How revealing for her problems that a birth process is seen by her as a symbol which combines a mechanized gadget and training for soldiers and requires contorting and maneuvering!

In the apartment there are four people. The original group remains the foursome, which we may still take as the basic four Freud speaks of, out of which the rectangle develops: one's self, one's lover, and one's parents. The "exposition" to which they are going sounds like the therapy, and the patient's exhibitionistic tendencies in it: in any case, something is "to be exhibited."

The Indian, whom she likes, she now has killed off. We may take him as one aspect of men, including David and the therapist; namely, the primitive, strong, elemental aspect of the male (*vide* the animals in the early dreams).

The act now of impregnating herself with this semen seems to me profoundly significant. It is a symbolic motif which brings together in one powerful act many of the themes we have already seen: her ambivalence about sex ("some kind of relationship—not sexual—with him"), her competitiveness with men (particularly with the therapist), her yearning to be pregnant (to have the therapy productive, to have a birth which is hers), but her inability to subordinate herself to the man in the way she interprets as required for impregnation by the man. This is latent meaning coming out with vivid clarity and united form. The host of biological symbols of this act come to mind: the queen bee being impregnated by the male, who then dies; the female praying mantis who bites off the head of the male, who then, in his death throes, copulates with special zest as he impregnates her. Susan will carry the child after the analyst is killed off; she wants the therapy to be productive, procreative, but she cannot let the therapist be alive to do his part in making her productive.

Then, in the third scene in this important dream, she again has only two women on the stage, herself and a tall woman, who was the one previously present, with *dark* hair. This is presumably the color of Susan's hair, and I think the first time in any dream that this frequent symbol actually appears in the color of her hair. She tells us by these positions on stage that the significant issue is with women, and the male is a vague, off-stage accessory. He is made some sort of authority, who requires the work of a large dinner to be done by the woman and is responsible for her coming to the apartment in the first place, and has a name beginning with the same letter as the therapist's —all suggesting another representation of the therapist. A woman, unfortunately, has to work for these men who throw their weight around; but the women are the significant ones, who can be pregnant. I take the tall dark-haired woman to be both Susan and her mother, of whose pregnancies she seems to have been partly envious but with whom mainly she identifies. Then, as if to confirm our assumption of the competitive elements through this climactic dream, she adds a footnote about another dream of "something competitive" which she still needs to keep covered.

Dream 37 / *Session 219*

I had a dream Tuesday night after this happened. I don't remember the dream, except a part where my coat was ripped across the shoulder so that one quarter of my body was exposed to the cold. Someone told me about it, then I noticed it. The coat in the dream was similar to a coat I bought in 1946. The thought was: "Now I have to go out and buy a new coat." It wasn't anxiety but "Oh, dear, now I have to buy another coat."

She is "exposed," cold, in her body, the elemental aspect. I take this as a brief reference to her anxiety at having exposed herself so much in the last dream, given the "exposition of herself," to use the same word as in the previous dream. Exposed here means nudeness, bareness, which she has assiduously avoided with men in the past. She must hurry out to find a new cover for herself.

Dreams 38 and 39 / *Session 222*

I had a dream Saturday or Sunday night in which some lines from a play came back to me: "At your high tide, come to low tide." High Tide is a private sanatorium I had heard about from a patient who had been treated there. In the dream, I was talking to the person who runs High Tide; he was talking directly to me about some commitments he was making for doing research in working with patients for their benefit without enriching himself in any way. He said, "I can't just run this private hospital where everything is centered in just bringing the money in." In the dream, this had a very real quality.

I had another dream the other night. I was in the kitchen of an apartment I lived in, though it was not my present apartment. There were some high cupboards that were filthy and crawling with ants, maybe even a couple of roaches. I felt that the housekeeper was not keeping the place clean, was not doing her job. And I realized that I would have to do it myself. I did not relish the notion; and I felt terrible that I should be slob enough to have bugs. But I knew I would do it and clean it up. The bugs were there. I knew I would go away and leave them for a while, but come back and clean them up. In the dream I was not happy that the bugs were there. But I knew they were there and that I had to do a job to clean them up.

Here we have two interlude scenes having to do with how she is doing her analytic work. The first, a satire on psycho-therapists, is given a special twist that makes it a compliment and a statement of confidence in the present therapist. We must ask, however, why a satire comes up at all, unless she is con-cerned with satirizing the present therapy.

The second dream also suggests a criticism of the therapist: "the housekeeper was not keeping the place clean," so the patient would have to. Since this is set in the woman's room (kitchen) and the persons are female, I wonder again whether she puts the therapist now in a mother role and struggles back and forth with him in this context. Apparently she sees therapy as "cleaning things up," rather than as insight into what makes things dirty, rather than as a working out of the "bugs" in her life.

Dreams 40 and 41   /   *Session 224*

I had a dream over the weekend which involved Irwin and his second wife. There was a lot of chasing about; but I'm not clear and I was terribly concerned about what they would think of me. [All she could recall beyond that was that the wife was a blonde and that she (Susan) was anxious.]

I had another dream. I realized my menstrual period had begun. Nothing else. I think that to me indicates that maybe I'm becoming a woman. [As to the feeling tone of the dream] None. Just a recognition. Just a fact. I was not happy; I was not sad. I accepted it. Somehow, it was the acceptance of me as a woman.

A return to the old triangle and an old theme: two women, both on the level of wife, and one man, her ex-husband, and she preoccupied "terribly" with the mirror situation, what would they think of her. The new wife, who now has her place, is *blonde*, the color which she was trying to dye her hair in the first dream at the outset of analysis. The tenor of the dream seems to be either rivalry with the other woman, the "blonde" new wife, or her position as child in the old triangle—or both.

Her menstrual period had begun (dream 41); she gives this an unambiguously positive interpretation, that she is becoming a woman. On the contrary, I experience a note of wish fulfillment and desperation in this dream,[16] and also desperation in the dream about Irwin and his wife. To me, there is a current of despair continuing since the climactic dream of the semen from the dead man, a desperation covered up by her adeptness at whistling in the dark ("Somehow it was the acceptance of me as a woman").[17] Other data from the therapeutic hours and

---

[16] * The presence of this repressed desperation was substantiated by the "wave of anxiety" she reported she felt when the therapist mentioned her being "alone, unfulfilled, deadening her feeling."

[17] Some therapists, reading this section, will say the patient should be accepted at her word—that it is "positive," etc.—and will reproach me with being too negative and reading negative interpretations into her hopeful statements. This hinges on the whole problem of repression. Those who don't believe in repression, who don't believe the unpleasant, despairing element will tend to be repressed, will hold that the patient grows "naturally" toward health if given the right soil, security, etc. I believe this viewpoint oversimplifies human nature, and that Freud's belief in repression is here closer to the truth.

To me, repression is one aspect of the phenomenon of consciousness. The tendency to repress, or deny, truths or aspects of the truth which, if faced, would cause anxiety and lowered self-esteem is an expression of the relation of one's self to one's self, the phenomenon of consciousness.

The possibility of making something unconscious, of denying it, I take as one of the capacities of consciousness. To paraphrase Nietzsche: "Man is the only animal who can lie to himself." Rank's idea of conflict of wills, Jung's concept of the compensatory element in unconsciousness, etc., relate to this point. In my judgment, the critical issues of psychoanalysis lie precisely in the phenomenon that the human being can deny, repress, "lie" to himself, and indeed *has* to do so to survive unbearable threats to his security, self-system in childhood, and so on. I see psychotherapy as affording a relationship in which this process of progressive denial of "knowing what we know," the progressive denial of consciousness, is reversed. But this does not take place automatically.

from what is going on in her outside life might shed light on whether my interpretation or her more positive one is correct.

A note (which I did read) inserted by the therapist in the dream material indicates that David ended the relationship with Susan at about the time of the session following these two dreams. This casts a clear light on this last group of dreams. Susan, an intelligent woman, must certainly have been aware at some level that the relationship was going to pieces. This would indicate without any doubt that the above dreams are wish fulfillment and mask a sense of desperation, the "blonde" business probably a clutching at an old hope that if she were a blonde she would get her man, the "menstrual" element an insightful despair that she is not a woman, that she failed to get pregnant (now with its positive symbolism of procreative love). That David ended the relationship eight sessions after she reported the "dead Indian's semen" dream is dramatic indeed. It is not too much, or too melodramatic, to say that she killed David off. This indicates how powerfully and profoundly the dream life can and does reflect Susan's stand in real life. To say she killed him is not to impute any "blame," of course: she may have needed to do it to protect herself in the face of the sensed threat that he was himself pulling out; or it may involve needs for revenge on her part; or because of her own despair about herself, it may be that, in line with the old adage, "The only good Indian is a dead Indian," the only man who can or would inseminate her is a dead man. In any case, all these last dreams can now be read as being her reaction on the dream dimension to the impending breakup of the relationship.

In the therapist's note about the breakup, I find it poignant that she reacts with the statements that she "felt more ready for and capable of a relationship . . . but feared it might be too late. . . . She felt 'like a hothouse flower, blooming in the desert all alone.'" Perhaps she needs to be a "hothouse flower" and that is just the trouble.

The error in the concept of repression is not in the concept itself but in the use of it as an excuse for applying the dogma of the analyst as a "blank check" on which can be written any cause-and-effect explanation of the patient's problems, by simply saying "the patient represses this or that."

Dream 42 / *Session 228*

The dream that, that I had that, that woke me up on Sunday night was about David. And I, I had been seeing him over a period of time and things looked hopeless for marriage. And I loved him but, but I felt that the situation would never come to fruition. And I married somebody else. I married Fred Lerner, that's the fellow who works under me. And although I married him in the dream, I just seemed to forget about it after it took place. I was seeing David again, and finally David and I decided to get married. And I don't know whether I asked him or well, I, I look at the notes I had made and I see that I have here that we finally got married at my suggestion and I didn't remember whether it was a direct suggestion or whether I had been trying to manipulate him into this move. And it was a ceremony that wasn't attended by anyone. It was performed by a judge, it was very quiet and it wasn't until after we were married that I remember that I was already married. And I was, I felt terrible and I felt very much afraid to tell David. And I, I decided and to have the name on the marriage certificate, the first marriage certificate, changed from Lerner to David's name, and David agreed, although—this is kind of cockeyed —although I still hadn't told him that I was married to Fred. And after we were married, right after we were married, no period of time, suddenly I had a child and I know it was David's child, but at that time the pressure of the two marriages began to build up and I think that I just felt like a rat caught in a trap, and, and I began to compare David and Fred. And there was just no comparison, none whatsoever, and one of the things that bothered me about being married to Fred was that he would always remain a relatively poorly paid worker and that living would be very difficult for us, and even though Fred was trying, Fred was trying very hard because apparently he had published a book. It was a humorous book describing his experiences in this country and describing humorously his life with me and with my parents. Apparently we were living with my parents, and, and I think

that in the dream that it wasn't until, that I had been feeling
that I could get away with this deception by just changing
the names on the marriage certificates. But when I saw the
book that had been published, I knew that, that the jig was
up and I felt the pressure on me again and then I, I, I talked
to everyone in the family about going along with me on the
question of changing husbands and there was still a lot of fear
of David's reaction and I didn't know what to tell him but I
knew I must face him and I was afraid that he would leave
me and at the same time I was afraid that he was the only
man that I would ever love. And caught in that dilemma, I
woke up.

This dream is remarkable in the clarity with which it deals
with the issues, again bringing together symbols from previous
dreams and putting them into a drama in which previously
latent meaning is made explicit. She is aware, now, of how
much she manipulates men: as a substitute for David she marries
(the verb is active, not "is married to," and she is the *subject* of
it throughout) the man *under* her. The game that ensues, after
she causes David to marry her, "forgetting" she was married,
and the changing of names on the license, is an amazing symbolic action: *who* the man is doesn't matter. This game of
musical chairs in which wife and husband do not know each
other, is a striking picture of transference in its original sense:
she goes through life simply changing the men's names. We
note the different triangles in this dream: all are confused, but
they all consist of two men and her. Is the man she forgets her
father? Or the therapist? And is the book that is published the
therapist's book (who presumably knows a good deal about
"life with her and her parents")? The child symbol has reap-
peared, coming out now as competitive with the man; the man
(Fred, David, and therapist—the identities are a mélange) produces his book but she produces her child. When the book is
published, the "jig is up" (referring to the therapist's book, and
her life then being an "open book"?). The theme throughout is
changing names, changing husbands, being married to one but it
is all the same as being married to another, caught in two

marriages at once—a desperate dilemma indeed, in which she appropriately feels "like a rat caught in a trap."

The dream begins with her hopelessness about her own power to love. This, in turn, rests on something that is only later made explicit in the dream: "we were living with my parents . . . and I had the feeling I could get away with this deception by just changing the names on the marriage licenses." So long as it is her parents' world she lives in, the triangles will always be a hopeless kaleidoscope, with never a man of her own in her world.

Dream 43 / *Same Session*

It was a very mixed-up business and I don't have the whole thing in focus, but at one point a person at the office was in the dream, a woman who is, well, I, I don't, she is a woman who had never married and not a very sensitive person and is very abrupt and I don't think she has terribly many human contacts in this world. She was in the dream and I, I think that I got the two of us mixed up. I think that I thought that I was she, and there was another point in the dream when somebody left the office, I guess quit her job, and it may have been Ann, and I tried to take over and I couldn't do the whole job and I, I felt, I felt very anxious. And then, and then there were, there were a lot of scenes involving David and his sister and I wanted something from him, and he really wanted to pull out and I was fighting desperately against that and, and there was an awful lot of conflict about what I should or shouldn't do. And then I was in another situation with both men and women and, and I had a, I was paired off with a man and he, he left me and then I was paired off with somebody else and he left, and people, people kept leaving and gee, I think I, a lot of them reminded me of guys that I had known at one point or another in my life, not necessarily guys who have really meant something to me, but they . . . I had thought them attractive in, in the past. And I, all I know about the situation is, is that there was some question of danger and, and people kept chasing me and then leaving me, chasing me and then leaving me.

Her desperation is expressed more eloquently than we could express it, by the simple picture of movements she presents in a timeless review of her life: "David . . . wanted *to pull out* and I was fighting desperately . . . I was *paired off* with a man and *he left me* and then I was *paired off* with somebody else and *he left*, and people *kept leaving* . . . and I think a lot of them reminded me of guys I had known at one point or another in my life . . . and people kept *chasing* me and *leaving* me . . ."

She now has some insight that she may have something to do with what has happened: she sees herself as an insensitive, abrupt woman, faced with the prospect of never marrying, faced with a task that is too great for her. The triangles here are whirling (with a sister-brother element added); the only thing clear is that she is fighting desperately in a situation of danger, with that gripping refrain of chasing and leaving, leaving and chasing. The use of dramatic *space* is significant: every relationship is aggressive, chasing and leaving, no one being *with* anyone else.

Dream 44 / *Same Session*

There was another dream I had the night after that with another. . . . (*Pause.*) Yeah. A report that we give to one of our clients every three months was completed on time, but nobody delivered it to them. And I called their office and I spoke to someone and I learned that a very important official was going to a meeting that night and I had the feeling that it was crucial that we get that report over to their office that day, and I was very disturbed over the fact that it hadn't been delivered. And I spoke to Dr. Morgan about it and I wanted to send someone over immediately with it. So he said no, you have to talk to Mr. K. about it, and I remember his saying that we have to be diplomatic and not tell Mr. Klein what to do but, you know, ask him what he thinks, and I was, in the dream I remember taking time out to appreciate my boss' operation, and it was decided to get a certain number of copies of the report over to their office and I was to take them over. And I hurried down to the neighborhood in which the office was located, and I met a friend of mine—

I, I think it was a woman and there was a, it was when I met her I realized I didn't have the report with me and there was a big sale going on in the store in which I saw my friend and they were offering tremendous bargains, particularly in books and records and I had a great urge to browse in the book section and I did and I was torn between a desire to buy a lot of the books and a worry about the money that I would be spending, a real fear of spending the money, and at the same time there was also a feeling of, even if I buy these books I may never get to read them. And I was, I wonder what happened after that. Oh, I was more, I was worrying again about going back to the office for the report. And also that same night there was a lot of driving back and forth to Boston and there were a lot of torn-up streets and here again there was a situation that I felt was dangerous. And right now it seems to me as if tearing around in Boston, this just chasing in a car in the torn-up streets for some reason makes me think of that business the night before, involving the men chasing me and leaving me, chasing me and leaving me. It's almost like a purposeless activity, purposeless activity. (*Silence.*) And I think that I was also warning myself that I can't think of myself as somebody who is omnipotent in terms of doing the whole job, doing everybody's job. And I think that when you get right down to it, a lot of the feeling that I have about the possible future of a relationship with David, there's no other word for it, but feelings of omnipotence on my part.

The arena is shifted to work, but the same "purposeless activity" of chasing and leaving goes on. We see on the stage a frantic running, now not merely a rat in a maze but a rat in panic, "chasing in a car in torn-up streets." (What is Boston, which came up also in the exposition in the Indian dream—does this city have some significance in her childhood?) In content, the dream has her needing to deliver a "report" (probably in the therapy) in the context of "the office."

A woman hovers on the corner of the stage, and leads Susan

to books and records, a temptress holding up the easy, "bar-gain" evasion of intellectualizing, "browsing" through life in a world where you can exist in your childhood omnipotence of contradictory fantasies and don't have to choose yourself or commit yourself to a man. There is insight in the dream in her seeing her need to be omnipotent, and how this relates to her power problem with David.

Dream 45 / *Session 231*

I dreamed about David. I dreamed I went to him several times to try to get him to resume our relationship, and he always said no. And after leaving him, I had to go home by myself, and it was very late. And it was a dangerous situa-tion, and I felt an incredible amount of anxiety in going home by myself. And in the next section of the dream I was with someone, attending some kind of committee or subcom-mittee meeting. And I was on this committee with someone else from my own particular group, and this other person may have been my mother, and I think I wasn't paying very good attention to what was being said, and I wasn't taking notes. And then at the end of the meeting we were going to have to report on the matters that were discussed to a much larger group, and I was told by this person who I think was my mother that I was going to have to make a report on this area where I was totally unprepared. I think I may have even missed part of the meeting when this was taken up, and I said "no, no," that I refused to do it. I was very anxious. And then suddenly I decided to try to get my notes together, to try to get some notes together so that I could make the report to the larger group. Suddenly I was a little less afraid than I had been. And despite the fact that I was less afraid, I remember waking up in the middle of the night in quite a state of anxiety. I don't remember if I woke up in between the two sections or at the end of the second section, but despite awakening in the midst of an acute attack of anxiety, I was getting ready to do what I was so afraid to do in that dream.

David having left her, she has to go home alone. It is late and dangerous and she is incredibly anxious—to my mind, because of what is to happen next. There is no man, neither father nor David, to protect her; this is a journey *home* which everyone has to make *alone*, to use her two words.[18] The critical element here is the entrance of the woman, who I believe is the same woman who hovered at the edge of the stage in the last dream, and is now identified outright as her mother. Here Susan tries to repress: she says in the very same sentence which introduces her mother: "I wasn't paying very good attention" (I wasn't taking *note*). The "no, no" is a vivid picture of her ambivalence about the repressing, containing both the positive element of standing against her mother and the negative element of not wishing to see what is going on. The person, however, to whom she reports is the therapist: it seems she now has him in a role of mother authority. But despite great anxiety, Susan decides in the dream to get her notes together to make her report, and suddenly she—like anyone who's decided to break through—is less anxious. This last part predicts that she will tell us in due time—and I would expect in the dreams in the not too distant future—what the report and the conflict are, and when she does tell us, it will be centrally about mother and home.

In all her anxiety dreams about her relations with men, it is significant that only in part of one dream (the Alaska one) is the man the enemy. Other than that, she is never afraid of the man, he is never the threatening one; he is a relatively innoc-

[18] I do not mean to leave this in fuzzy, semi-poetic language. What I mean to say is something very concrete: that the patient in therapy must sooner or later confront and experience the basic conflicts in his childhood family constellation, out of which he came. To say this is not to propose a rigid genetic determinism, but only to emphasize the depth dimensions of experience which we all carry with us, dimensions that began at birth. And my hypothesis of consistency in the pattern of character and personality, which has come out clearly in this dream study, has as one aspect a consistency with childhood. Now, when it comes to facing these fundamental conflicts, Susan cannot ride on David's back, or hide behind the "transferences," or even get the therapist to drain off her anxiety. She must face these alone in the sense that *she* faces them. Therapy gives a world of trust and understanding in which confronting the conflicts becomes possible, but the therapist cannot protect her from this kind of aloneness.

uous accessory, someone to fit into a larger drama, and he is important only in whether he leaves or stays, or, more specifically, in what she can do with him on the chessboard of her problem of security. It is her own security pattern which is threatened, her strategies of establishing herself, her patterns of coping and power. And as we have seen, the woman in the form of the mother enters (at these points in the dreams) as the real adversary.

Therapeutically speaking, when a patient like Susan is facing her anxiety fairly directly, not much needs to be said by us as therapists: we need only watch what she does with her anxiety. The anxiety now coming out into the open in Susan's dreams represents a critical stage in the drama. In retrospect, her preoccupation with sex, which began shortly after the climax dream with the madwoman, appears mainly to be an escape, and the love for David, while not devoid of genuine elements, was premature and a defensive "flight into health," as any relation with a man would be for her these days. The sex-love defense has now collapsed: this is the point she is at. The questions are how will she take her anxiety: will she experience it, will she gain insight and change thereby; or will she cope with it by covering it up, whistling in the dark, and grabbing for some new techniques? Those are the questions in principle. In practice she seems in this last dream to be telling us that she will do the former, not the latter.

Dream 46 / *Session 232*

I was going up to the White Mountains, where I spent last weekend with Lois and Bob, and I was talking and thinking about my birthday and, and what day of the week it fell on in 1950 and the day of the week it falls on this year, and I was trying to find some kind of pattern, you know, portents of the future. And in the dream a real feeling of, and at the same time, that I was carrying on like this, I felt very ashamed of even thinking along these lines of superstition, but I was doing it anyway. And somehow at the end of the dream I had a feeling of optimism about this year, and it was, it was, some of it was based on patterns I had picked out. But the rest of the feeling of optimism was based on the way I was functioning.

She looks into the future of her life, from the mountains' height, trying to feel optimism. She knows this is partly a magical endeavor to reassure herself, but partly she believes it has to do with her functioning. This term "functioning" strikes me, as it has several times in the way she uses it, as connoting that she sees the answers to life in ways you *do* something, which may come close to manipulating, like changing herself by dyeing her hair. Her way in the past of dealing with anxiety is to fly into activity; and this is what has been breaking down in the frantic, panicky activity of the last dreams. The symbol of "birthday" is interesting: a birthday *does* (quite apart from superstition) portend old age and death, and here for her it might also refer to her own birth as an infant, or be a hope of birth in the therapy.

Dream 47 / *Session 233*
This dream I had Sunday was not too clear, but it involved going to a wedding. I think I may have been invited by David, and I was, I went to the wedding with June Brandt, a friend of mine from college. And June, I think, also has problems with closeness. But she did get married a year and a half ago, and she's going to have a baby any—well, next month. And, but she wasn't pregnant and she was a guest at the wedding and I was sitting at her table and I saw David when I came in. I don't remember what his relationship to the bride was, but I wanted to be sitting at the same table that he was, and I wasn't, and I felt, I guess, disappointed, a little anxious. And then when the ceremony began, and this was a very peculiar ceremony, and after the first exchange of words the bride turned and tore out of the room. She really ran as, quickly enough to win a race. And I thought I had to go after her to tell her something, how lovely she looked, and how much I admired something that she had done. And I came back into the room where the ceremony, after dashing off and telling her that, I came back into the room that the

ceremony was being held in and it was dark and I couldn't find June. And I was pulled down, apparently we were seated at the tables. Somebody reached up and pulled me down into the seat, and it wasn't June. It was not someone I knew, it was a man. And I felt terribly anxious. I think I felt that I had made some kind of blunder in dashing off after the bride, and I started to say no, no, no, I have to get back, I have to get back to the table where I'm seated, and I, I just felt that I was in a desperate situation. (*Silence.*) And then I woke up.

Here Susan dramatizes her ambivalence toward marriage. On the one hand she wants it, though not for motives of love of a man. She has David invite her just as a guest to the wedding; she sits with her friend, with whom she partly identifies, who now is married and pregnant, but she is very much on the edge of things, pulled between David and the pregnant girl. Having the bride turn and "tear" out of the room is a strong use of space to break up the marriage—which suggests both her own ambivalence about marriage and her competitiveness with the bride (note the word *race*, and the word *tear*, meaning "to pull things apart," and *dash* as breaking, like dashing hopes). Ah, now the mirror comes in to reassure and cover over her anxiety: she runs after the bride to compliment her on her looks, but, more profoundly, to tell her *"how much I admired something she had done."* Though the word "something" is left vague, the action she is admiring is completely clear, namely, that the bride ran out on the marriage. The triangle now is that she cannot find her girl friend, and a man pulls her down beside him—the first time, so far as I recall, that a man asserts himself in a normally masculine way. He does not rape her, he is not hostile, he only wants her to be beside him—and she is terrified. She does not "know" a man. She tells us that she has given away something ("blunder") in her symbolic act of doing the same thing as the bride, i.e., dashing out. The cat is out of the bag: she does not really want to get married at all. She wants to be a *guest* at weddings, and she wants in the future to be preg-nant (the therapy to be productive). But the most compelling want at this time is in her cry to get "back," back to the table where I'm seated, back to her "earlier" life, back to the woman and to mother; something hasn't been worked through with women, and she is thus in a "desperate situation." Whether the man pulling her down (for the first time, some genuine fear of intimacy with a man is present) is the therapist is a question we must ask, if not answer at the moment.

This whole dream could be understood—and perhaps best understood—in spatial terms, that is, as a pantomime of movements. She is *with* David, she *leaves him* to go *to the girl friend*, she has the bride *tear off* the stage, she *dashes off* after her, and when she returns, the possibility of her *being with* a man is nicely acted, but she *runs back* to the original seat with the woman.

Dream 48 / *Session 236*

You know, I have been having a number of dreams in the last week, and most of the time I just can't remember what they were, except that I do know the night before last a very important part of this, of the dream that I did have, was an effort on my part to have someone else stop using euphemism, and I was, I was struggling against this other person to call a spade a spade.

Ah, what a relief! A cry of blunt and elemental honesty, to end the euphemisms and to call a spade a spade, a cry directed manifestly against the therapist. But as we have seen often with Susan, she projects a great deal, she struggles against somebody else on a problem which she also has in herself.

Dream 49 / *Same Session*

In this dream two animals, one belonging to me and one belonging to somebody else—the other person might have been my boss, the other animal owner—were being kept at my parents' house. My dog or cat, I don't know which, was smaller than the other, and it, it cost less to provide for somebody to tend to the removal of, of the feces of these animals. And one reason that it cost less was because I guess I must have had a cat. Because in the dream my animal could use a pan and Kitty Litter. And at one point I was having a discussion, it may have been my mother, on the cost of providing this service. And also involved was the cost of taking the bus three times a day to go back and forth between my parents' home and the school or office where I had to be. And I, I had a feeling that, that I was extravagant, that I was spending too much time on the animal and on the carfare. And I think that my parents might have been helping me. And part of this feeling of extravagance on my part also had to do with playing cards and, and with cosmetics. It must have, I guess maybe I was spending money gambling and devoting a lot of, too much money to appearance. And I, I had the feeling that I could do all the things that were involved more cheaply and I felt guilty because my parents were helping me and they shouldn't be. And I, I was talking to my boss about making some kind of a change and he told me to write to a friend. He, as a matter of fact, was setting off to visit this friend. He was going to give a lecture at a college and while he was giving this lecture he was going to stay with this friend, who had a non-academic, an administrative position at the college. And I don't remember his last name, but his first name was Jet, the friend who was the administrator. And my boss felt that Jet, or whatever his name was, could help me by giving me information about a possibility of changing my situation. And what I have down here is a scholarship, that may have been part of it, I don't know. (*Silence.*) But the worry about the money and three times a week and paying somebody to take the feces away. (*Laughing.*)

Animals return again, for the first time since the second dream, albeit only to have their dirt hauled away. I have missed references to animals; presumably she, in her preoccupation with controlling her "animal-sexual" nature, keeps this elemental side pretty well under the cover of her security strategies. What seems to me most significant in this dream is the interplay on the stage between her attachment to her home and parents on the one side and the therapy on the other, she the actress who moves between them. Therapy she sees as hauling the defecation and dirt of her life away (identifying herself, appropriately, with the cat); she discusses with "my mother" whether this process costs too much; she takes the bus "three times" a day between home and office (a conventional number of times a week one goes to therapy); her parents are "helping her," while she spends too much time and money on removing the dirt of this cat (herself).

The mirror theme comes in for a nice touch; the implication is that she came originally to therapy (*vide* the first dream of dyeing the hair) for "cosmetic" reasons, to change her appearance; and there is an element of gambling (a not unperspicacious observation) to therapy.

Dream 50 / *Session 237*

I remember the last [of the dream], I remember the end, the last sequence. And I don't remember much that occurred before that, except that I was with a man. And he and I were walking together, there were some other people involved, people to whom there was some social obligation, and we were all going to a public place. And there, although we had to be with these people, we didn't care for them particularly. And we were walking slowly into a large room, public room in a hotel, must have been a restaurant, and two of the people we knew sat down at a table for four. And I think that this particular couple was a couple we liked less than some of the other people in this large group. And I said, "I guess we have to sit down with them." He said, "I guess we do," implying that I shouldn't even have mentioned this in a doubtful way. And I associated him with David, and with some of the social situations that we were in with people who were not particularly compatible. Particularly, the people we went to Williamsburg with, and they had a party in May that was a perfectly terrible party. I think I mentioned it here. And we both wanted to leave as early as possible, because we both reacted to the party in the same way. And ah, we waited a decent interval, we weren't the first to go, we were about the third couple to go. But the hostess said, "Oh, I wish you'd stay for coffee." But we couldn't. David had the feeling that we should have stayed. And I thought of that when I remember this very dim business about the other couple. But the last sequence was much more vivid. I don't know if we were still in the public room, or if we were in a smaller room; the new handbag that I had just acquired as a gift was on the table. And my mother picked it up, she wanted to see it, she wanted to look at it. And she was handling it very roughly, and I was afraid of what would happen to the bag as a result of this rough handling, and I asked her to put it down and she didn't. And I began to get indignant. It was my handbag. I began to get very angry, and the way in which I said "Put it down" began to change. From a request, it got more and more angry and more and more heated. And finally I picked up her handbag and said, "Put it down, or I'm going to do something to your bag, and something destructive." And I was standing in a doorway or near a door jamb and I heard a loud clank, and I realized I had taken my mother's bag and banged it against the door jamb. This infuriated her and she threw my bag down on the floor. And then the man was standing and looking on. I think that he may have tried to say something to my mother that was very ineffectual. It was really as though he was looking on passively. And I think that's when I woke up in this rage at my mother. And mixed with the rage at my mother for what she was doing to my possession was a feeling of a great deal of discomfort that I had behaved so childishly to deliberately destroy something, just because it's hers. The first thing that comes to mind now, and maybe it did dimly right after the dream, what really comes to mind with full force now is the dream of the sweater and the maid.

Therapeutically speaking, I regard this dream as the most important in the whole analysis. In the prologue, it places on the stage the significant foursome: herself, her man, and the "other couple," whom she "did not like." We would hypothesize, in line with this structural form as we have discussed it before, that the other man and woman are her father and mother (the woman she wants to get away from is called, specifically, the "hostess," which sounds like mother). But whether or not we make this assumption, Susan goes on in the main scene to draw the conflict line as powerfully and clearly as is possible. Her mother and she engage in an Armageddon, a knock-down-and-drag-out struggle. Susan is so engaged that she is *beside* herself—she hears a loud clang and only then is aware of how she has banged her mother's handbag, i.e., aware of the extent of her rage against her mother. This fight, when each (the mother first) tries to destroy the other's handbag, and the overt rage and gathering fury (Susan's) that go with it mark, to my mind, the healthiest moment in the whole dream sequence and the moment most indicative of favorable change in Susan's life.

What are these handbags? The patient speaks of hers as a "recent gift"; a handbag is what a woman carries her "gold" in, and her other possessions, particularly her feminine possessions. A bag also opens like a vagina. And here I shall introduce an out-and-out specific symbol. I have found in my therapeutic experience that for many women in our culture one symbol that does turn up in free associations to have specific meaning is the handbag as vagina. Freud first made this connection.

We have reason, theoretically as well as empirically, for being dubious about Freud's tendency to make a number of specific correlations in dream symbols: feces equaling gold, horses equaling sex, etc. Whether or not a specific symbol always stands for a specific psychological experience depends, in my judgment, on cultural factors, among others. Some symbols approach the archetypal—symbols having to do with elemental processes in the universe, like fire and water, which may have relationship to universal human experiences such as birth, death, bipolar nature, conflict. And there may well be processes that exist in all cultures and historical periods (as Jung claims he has found the cross and circle symbol in the mandala). But specific items as symbols, like the handbag, would seem to be much more cultural. I have, therefore, often asked myself why the handbag seems to have this relationship to sex for contemporary women. Is it because of the marketing orientation in our culture (which we share with the Victorians) that the woman's "possession" is thought of as her vagina—this is what she "puts out," to use an ugly vernacularism, or her money, with which she buys her man? There is certainly a marketing orientation in Susan; she is highly concerned about her possessions and about men as possessions. In the dream, she refers to her bag as a "recent gift"; and, apparently, pleasure in sexuality is a recent acquisition for her. In any case, if a specific item like handbag, in contrast to a form like mandala, does seem to have specific meaning, this must have to do with special cultural congruences at the time. I think that if what Freud called symbols are taken this way, we do not have to throw out the baby of his contribution in symbolism with the bath water of the fact that his symbols become too literalized and too much identified with symptoms.

Whether we make this specific interpretation or not, the essential meaning of the dream is the same: Susan fights with her mother for her intimate possession, her feminine selfhood. The implication is that the angry mother was destructive of Susan's femininity and sexuality in early childhood. Another implication is a sado-masochistic, sexual attachment to the mother.

Present on the edge of the stage is the man, brilliantly characterized in simple words: "the man was standing and looking on . . . he may have tried to say something to my mother that was very ineffectual . . . he was looking on passively." No man has ever helped Susan in her struggle. Indeed, she even feels the man (the therapist) is vaguely on the side of the mother ("David had the feeling we should have stayed" with "the hostess").

The impression is given in these dreams that the father never gave her a point on which to stand to gain some independence from her mother; Susan was left at the mercy of mother, helpless and alone in a destructive, not constructive, sense. No wonder she became so competitive and manipulative; by these means she at least survived.

I take her "discomfort" at the end at "behaving so child-ishly" to be self-censorship and an expression of her guilt at having dared to stand against mother.

Dream 51 / *Session 238*

A man, and possibly the father of a friend of mine, I wasn't sure, who was an employee of the market where I shop for food spoke to me in the dream about my mother. I don't remember what he spoke to me about, but she was in difficulty. It was either nonpayment of a bill or possibly theft, and I realized that my mother needed psychiatric help. And I began to do something, to take some kind of action, to straighten out the difficulty. And then I got a call on the phone from Janet, a gal who was my closest friend when I was in college. And she called to tell me that her father wanted to speak with me. And I had a feeling that it was related to this difficulty of my mother's. And she was anxious to end the conversation and hang up, but I insisted on talking to her anyway. And I began to tell her about what I had discovered, and to, to also to tell her that I didn't have to talk to her father about it. And then I go to the store where my mother has the difficulty and I continue to, along these lines of talking to the people who were involved with the diffi-culty there and to try to straighten things out. Then I was with my mother and she and I were shopping together and I was feeling that I was extravagant and that she shouldn't be helping me by buying me things. But I was easing my con-science by stressing the, by thinking of the fact that we were visiting sales, and we were getting good buys and things were really much cheaper than they might have been. Then I, apparently I wasn't with my mother any more, I met Claire, another former friend, and I, I was talking to her about my own troubles, my mother's troubles, and I do this despite Claire's attempt to snub me. And then I found myself with Steven, and here too there was some connection with my mother's difficulty. And he wants me to have a drink with him, he wants to take me to dinner, a wonderful sea-food restaurant he knows, and he mentioned a name that I, I had never heard of, and I felt that it probably wouldn't be such a good place after all. And, but there was a feeling that I, that I should go, and I don't remember whether Claire was still there or not. I may even have invited her to join us. I don't know. But then I was, I don't know what happened at that point, but I do remember next there was a telephone call from a policeman who wanted to know—apparently my mother has had difficulties like this in the past—he wanted to know if my mother has had any further trouble. And I told him of the situation, pointing out that I am taking steps to resolve this problem. I think that there was some question about whether to go into this with him or not. But as soon as he established the fact that he was the policeman, that he did know about her past difficulties, then I went into it with him. And as I was looking at all these pieces, I began to wonder what I really was saying.

That Susan would feel anxiety and guilt after the Armageddon dream is understandable and to be expected; this dream seems to come out of her anxiety and guilt at having fought her mother. The question is how she copes with them. In this dream, below its complexities, she seems to be trying to return to a role of "mother's good little girl."

The family triangle comes back in a number of variations, but each with her mother and a father figure—Janet's father, the policeman, possibly Steven; and presumably Susan is the child in the triangle. As "mother's helper" (*vide* the earlier dream about David), she is actively and responsibly concerning herself with mother's troubles. These troubles with mother are also hers, as shown by the use of these phrases in apposition as though to tell us they are the same thing: "My own troubles, my mother's troubles." I take Janet and Claire to be aspects of her own ambivalence, the side of herself that urges her to hang up on her own awareness, to block off, repress consciousness of her "troubles with mother." These women, who want her to repress the whole business, are probably also mother's stand-ins: Janet has been put in a "maternal" role before, and later in this dream Susan considers inviting Claire to go along with her to dinner with Steven, which, on this hypothesis, would keep the family triangle going nicely.

Her marketing orientation comes out quite overtly here: "market," nonpayment of bills, "theft," "food." It is in the market that mother has such a hold on her, for by giving her breasts to suck in infancy—food, special attention, even gifts later, and whatever else led to Susan's preoccupation with shopping—mother seems to have "bought" her. The fact that the manifest problem in the dream is that the *mother* needs psychiatric treatment is more than a projection: the mother-in-the-girl is precisely Susan's problem. More specifically stated, it is her morbid relationship with her mother that prevents her developing in her own sexual, feminine way, having and *going with* her man (here going to dinner and eating *with* Steven, rather than *from* mother). Her mother's specific influence comes out in her subtle depreciation of Steven ("I felt that it [Steven's restaurant] probably wouldn't be such a good place after all.") It is her mother-in-her which brings her to therapy.

The role of the ineffectual male, ever present at the edge of the stage, is again fascinating; this male needs to be taken as including reference to the therapist. She may be telling us that therapy had originally been seen by her as having a drink and a "wonderful dinner" (Steven), but more certainly the therapist is seen as the now well-known figure of the policeman, who "knew about her mother's *past* difficulties." She ends the dream with that charming aside, like an actor in a mystery drama: "As I was looking at all these pieces, I began to wonder what I really was saying." This is one of those not uncommon instances of a patient's telling us: "I knew and did not know what I was saying," bespeaking the presence of conscious and unconscious dimensions simultaneously.

Dream 52 / Session 244

In the dream I was talking on the phone with Florence Bernstein. There had been some kind of a misunderstanding, I don't know if it was between Florence and her husband, Marvin, or possibly between Florence and me. But the effect of this call was to help and iron out this misunderstanding, and it seemed to be successful from that point of view. She and I made a date to have lunch and it involved considerable planning and negotiating on her part, and I was thinking of a place to eat on my way to meet her, and I was very worried about money; and now the first time being worried about money and thinking of a place to go, for the first time I realized that a lot of the problem that I've been talking about in here for the past weeks is—I don't know where I'm going; and I'm also worried about money. I'm also worried about the fact that I put so much time, not money, into it—so much time in the past, been wasted, frittered away, and I still don't know where I'm going. But before I left, I left with a suitcase. I was carrying a small train case, but before I left to go and meet Florence, I remember looking at a pair of shoes that were in very bad condition. They were comfortable shoes, but they'd gotten banged up because I had fallen, and I had hurt my feet when I fell. And I remember the way I looked in the dream, I had a slight mark on my nose, and I had some Mercurochrome on it or some medication on it. And at one point in the dream I realized that I must have broken the skin on my face when I fell also. But I was looking for the place to eat, and because after I left Florence I was going away on a weekend trip with a man; and at one point Ann was with me and she looked in this case and she pointed out that I had to be very thorough and remember everything that I would need. But I had not packed my diaphragm and I remember her going down the list, you care about A.,B.,C. I, I don't remember all the items now, except the last item on the list was you care about, as she pointed to the deodorant, she said something like you care about not smelling but you don't care about having a baby as a result of this and there was no time. For some reason, I could not go home and get the diaphragm and I was worried about how to get another without a prescription and then I remembered the druggist in my neighborhood who would give me one. I thought about my friend Ellen, who got a diaphragm from him by just asking for it when she was having an affair with a guy with whom she worked. She was married at the time. I don't know why I brought that up, either in the dream or after I woke up. It doesn't make any difference. Why should I think about her having an extramarital affair. What does that mean to me now?

Here Susan tries to get rid of the anxiety and guilt following in the wake of the battle with her mother, by crawling back into old holes. She retrenches to the simple triangle—man, woman, and herself; cements the relationship with the woman so she can be "fed" again (lunch); immediately associates this with money (as indicated in the preceding dream); and proceeds to turn sharply against the therapist with the challenge that she has wasted, frittered away so much time and money and still doesn't know where she is going, a conflict brought out by the fact that she has just gone back to the woman. ("I don't know where I'm going"—to the women or to the men?) Her hostility toward the therapist both comes out of and covers up her anxiety.

I take the next main portion of the dream as a struggling back and forth with old psychological defenses: she has fallen, hurt herself and her possessions (the shoes); her "mirror" status is not too good (the mark on the nose from the fall, the torn skin, and the reference to "not smelling"). The old defenses are pretty well banged up after the fight with mother; she can't go home again, at least in the old, comfortable, secure sense. This to-do about the diaphragm, whatever it may say about the object as such (a diaphragm both *permits* sexual intercourse and *prohibits* full procreativeness, conception), surely bespeaks her very active ambivalence about her relations with men.

Dream 53 / *Session 249*

And I cannot remember much about the dream, except that at one point I fell down the steps. But it, it, I didn't go bump, bump, bump all the way down. I fell so that I had the experience of falling through the air. But I landed on my two feet. And they smarted a bit. But I did land on my own two feet.

Another anxiety dream, but with anxiety not confronted but controlled and "managed" all too well. This falling nicely through the air and landing on her feet is what we all can do in a dream, propelled as we are by the dream world's extraterrestrial power. In life, "sad to say, it never has been so," as *The Threepenny Opera* puts it; we fall down steps in the way she graphically pictures in order to deny, namely "bump-bump-bump." Coming just after the session in which she cut down the therapy to one session a week,[19] this dream seems a clear wish fulfillment, a whistling in the dark to cover up anxiety.

Dream 54 / *Session 250*

"There, as, as, as I remember it, the, ah, in the beginning I was, ah, one of a group. And it was a social occasion, and oh, we were talking, drinks were being served. There was a radio or a record player in operation; and a man came to take either the radio or the record player because of nonpayment of the installments that were due. And, ah, this wasn't a very happy situation. Nobody was really distressed; it seemed like a very, very familiar situation. And I, I'm not sure whether I actually participated in this, in the dream, or whether this was a movie I saw as a spectator. And because there was some talk in the dream at one point about my having seen a particular movie, it was a short picture that was not a feature attraction, but there was some talk about my having seen a specific picture about four times. Next I was involved with my boss and a man. A man who wasn't particularly attractive, but somebody else referred to him as someone who had won a certain amount of fame by acting. And I think he was acting in the movies. And it was he, I think it was he, gave me some kind of a viewer, some device that I looked through. And this was a device that had the effect of making the moon seem to come closer and then to recede. And, as I was looking through this viewer, I began to have a very queasy feeling, at, ah, at seeing the moon come closer and then recede. It was the kind of thing I think people experience when they're seasick. And I attributed this to a recent change

[19] I read this in a footnote.

of glasses. I was having trouble with my eyes. And I thought that that's why this was happening. This man, I think his name was Scotch, or very much like that, was going to England with my boss. They were just going for the day, on business. They were going to discuss a research project with someone in England. And there was much talk about this remarkable jet age when it did become practical to go to England and return on the same day. And, before they left, there was some business about getting into a car. There were four people, no, there were five people. There was a woman in the back seat, and my boss was driving, and there was the man who was going to England with them. I was getting in the car, and there was another man who was getting in the car. And my boss started to drive before we were all inside. I got into the back seat, and I remember calling to the other man to hurry and jump in because the car was moving. And apparently while this difficulty with the car was taking place, I was confused and I, at, at my boss driving off before all of the passengers were in. At that time I didn't know he was off to England. Somehow, when I learned his destination, it made me feel better, perhaps because I could, ah, understand why he was in a hurry. And in the next sequence, I was entering my parents' home, and they had just come back from the country, apparently they had had some difficulty in getting transportation. On my way, in, I dropped some wrappings, either candy wrappings or cigarette wrappings, on the lawn. And I felt guilty when I went inside and I saw that my father carried his trash in the house, and he commented on my carelessness, my sloppiness. And I felt very guilty about it, and I didn't know whether to go out and pick it up from the lawn or not. That was last night. And of course, this, it was only much later that I remembered what it felt like going under when, the one and only time that I've been given gas as an anesthetic. And I also thought of the relationship with David, which seemed very much like that. This coming closer, going back, coming closer, going back.

A confusion with all kinds of *movement*, but very little

insight. The very fact that she has to dream in such a complex carousel form bespeaks both her anxiety and her flight from it. The last sentence gives the theme, a "coming closer, going back, coming closer, going back." She is now using the spatial metaphor we have used often in understanding her dreams. The "relationship with David seemed like that," and "like going under anesthesia." I think in this and in the figure of the boss she is talking of her relationship with the therapist; the boss's name was Scotch—Caligor?—and he was off to talk to someone about research. The record player, seeing the moon through a viewing device, seeing a moving picture "four times," the car starting before they were all inside (she *is* anxious about the approaching end of the analysis)—all suggest references to therapy. Is she bringing out satire, criticism of the therapy, now that it is going to end shortly? Partly so. She is also confessing the hopes she had to begin with, of a magical solution; she wanted to "see the moon." I think she is doing a third thing, too—the most significant of all: she is trying to make her therapy unreal, to deny here at the end that it really happened, or rather to make it a happening several degrees removed from reality like a movie or looking through a telescope, in order to avoid the anxiety that would be entailed if she takes it, her broken defenses, and her insights for real.[20] Her going back to her parents' home at the end of the dream bespeaks this same kind of anxiety. And her excessive guilt over such a little sin against her father as dropping cigarette wrappings on the lawn makes us ask, on the simple level: Is she guilty about dirtying the therapist's front yard with her hostility? To which we answer: Of course. But we hasten to add that the *excessive amount* of guilt is related to something much more profound. I believe it is her own guilt at what she is doing to herself in these escapist, self-confusing dreams.

[20] This is not an unusual development as therapy nears its end. The patient both needs to be angry at the therapist that he did not work magic and also needs to cry out that he, the patient, cannot assume the burden of his own life in the world of reality, of taking himself as the driver now, rather than having the boss drive, to reverse the scene in Susan's dream.

Dream 55 / *Session 250*

And I had a dream Tuesday night, too. At, in the early part of the dream I was with a man. And I think it's either a man that I know, or a man that I did know. Maybe it was David, I'm not sure, and I was very surprised to find myself with him. And at the same time that I was surprised I was pleased that he was interested in me. And I went to visit Leah. Sara and another friend of hers, Mildred, were there. And, I hadn't seen either of these people for a long time, and I was embarrassed when I saw them, and I didn't know what to say to them. And I didn't exclaim about "Oh, it's been such a long time since I've seen you." I sat down and, and was very calmly asking Mildred questions about herself, and what had been happening to her family. Ah, I say Mildred, because at this point Sara went out of the room. And this was a very uncomfortable situation for me. I think that, ah, I felt embarrassed primarily because of Sara, a gal I used to see from time to time, and then I dropped her. I dropped her pretty consciously and pretty deliberately. I didn't want to hurt her feelings, but she's a very aggressive female, and I didn't enjoy her, and I just stopped seeing her. And the embarrassment that I was feeling in the dream was not apparent, but I felt uncomfortable inside.

It is significant that this dream, reported after the previous dream, actually came before it. If she had told this before, the picture would have been less confused. For here is clear movement on the stage; she starts with the man, leaves him to go to the women, and then she ends up with the issue which has been a central theme all along: the aggressive female. The embarrassment sounds very rational in the dream, one doesn't like to hurt someone; but if it is that rational, why dream it? Being "rationally nice" is an old defense of Susan's. On the contrary, is it not elementary that this "very aggressive female," Sara whom Susan "dropped," is in fact the aggressive element in herself? Sara goes out of the room in the dream—out of sight, out of awareness. But when you repress the problem, you get some symptoms, such as embarrassment. Her embarrassment is over her own aggressiveness, the self-betrayal involved in leaving David, and her fond hope that she can just "drop" this aspect of herself "pretty consciously and pretty deliberately."

Dream 56 / Session 251

As closely as I could remember it, there was one sequence relatively early when I was upstairs in a house. I don't know whose house. And I think I wasn't well, but I needed something downstairs which I couldn't get and which David agreed to get for me. And he went downstairs and he didn't come back. And after a while I went downstairs and I saw him enjoying himself with a group of people. And as I came down the steps, somebody was pouring a drink for him and I realized that he had forgotten all about me. And that's . . . the next thing that I remember, I was a member of a group. I was with my mother and two sisters who were fairly young. And we were going to stay with someone, a friend, ah, I think possibly the friends were Eve and Lester, very old friends of the family, while my father was out of town. I, I guess this was late afternoon, and I knew I had a date with Donald in the evening. He was due to return from a trip that day. And as I was in the group, I was talking to Carl. Carl is someone who works in the office. He's a filing clerk. I was talking to him about a play that was being produced by a group that he and I were associated with. I am not sure if this was at the office or not. And the female lead in the play was ill; and Carl suggested Leona, another gal who works in our office, as a substitute. And he pointed out that she could pretend to be married to the male lead and live with him a while before the show to get publicity. Ah now both Carl and Leona are Negroes, and I, ah, I thought this was a difficult situation. And I said to Carl: "Gee, in the eyes of the public, ah, pretending su-, such a marriage would be, ah, considered almost as bad as marrying a Jew." And as soon as I said what I did say, I got very embarrassed, and Carl reacted, and I, I felt that I had blundered; that I had, ah, in effect made some statements to him that indicated anti-Negro feeling on my part that just wasn't there. I was, I was planning to have dinner with someone who was in this group before meeting Donald. And as we were all sitting there, my little sister began to entertain the group. Oh, she was a little girl, possibly about three or four. And she was singing and using standard gestures, and I was surprised at the performance because obviously someone had been coaching her, she didn't pick this kind of thing up herself. I didn't know she could sing. And, ah, the fact that she used the typical gestures to punctuate the popular ballad that she was singing bothered me. Of course, that's what I was talking about earlier in the hour in terms of my own reaction to the way I sounded on the tape recorder. At that point Donald appeared. He was dressed very sloppily, and he was with a friend, or his brother, who was also dressed in a very slovenly fashion, and they were both unshaven. Donald has come to pick me up, and I was very annoyed. Ah, we had said nothing about dinner and I didn't want to go with him yet, I, I, I wasn't ready. I didn't say so directly. Yeah, I did say that we had said nothing about dinner. But I didn't say, I don't, that I didn't want to go with him. But I expressed my annoyance by withdrawal, and I was cool and distant. And I had the feeling that he had absolutely no consideration, that he didn't care what I want. And he was talking, he began to talk to my mother and to others about me. They turned from me and this made me furious, though I did not say anything. And I was very annoyed that he was drawing them into the situation.

It would be easy for us to be confused in this dream, for again she must, in her anxiety, make it complex. And it is not only a dream in itself but a play within a play in that Susan sees herself as acting.

Let us, therefore, take it in its simple, basic elements. She is with David; he leaves her (she has of course forgotten that in the last dream *she* left *him*), and the relationship is for the moment erased ("he had forgotten all about me"). She now is home, and the drama is shifted to an earlier period ("two sisters fairly young"). Then comes this give-and-take about marriage and identity, with more misplaced embarrassment (my hypothesis is that it is her embarrassment about "pretending" to be married to the therapist, and "performing" in the therapy). The next scene, that of the little girl of three or four, is to me the important one. Even if she had not explicitly identified this girl with herself (*via* the tape recorder), we would have been justified in making the identification. She is telling us that her problems, particularly her experience of her identity as a woman, have their seat in exhibitionism, her "performance" as a little girl, her need to be the center of the stage in rivalry with her sisters. Even if she went out to dinner now with Donald, it would be a little girl in grown-up woman's clothing. We hear the refrain that came up previously with Morris: "I wasn't ready, it's too soon, too soon." She stands there, at the end of the dream, the little girl who experiences adults talking about her over her head; and though she feels furious, she remains "nice."

I wish to put in a note at this point with reference to what patients typically do in the last weeks before terminating therapy. Frieda Fromm-Reichmann points out that the patient often regresses, and all the old problems come up again—a fact that, as she well says, may be understandably disconcerting to the therapist. My experience bears out Dr. Fromm-Reichmann's statement; and it seems that this is what Susan is doing. She brings up the seminal problems again, now in a kind of capsule, condensed form, as though saying, "We must run through the beginnings again."

It occurred to me, while studying Susan's next dream, that something else may also happen. That is, the dreams at the end of analysis, as at the beginning, may take on a *summary* character. Like the first dream typically in therapy—Susan's first dream was an excellent example—the final dreams may tend to bring the essential elements together, as does the following dream.

Dream 57 / *Session 252*

I have a baby in my arms. It wasn't my baby. Maybe it was related to me in some way, but the baby was an infant. It had very little hair, was very young, maybe six months old. And I said something to the baby. I think I asked the baby a question. The baby's name was Hilda, and I was quite surprised when the baby answered me in perfectly articulated speech that—"I think you will find something about it in the apartment upstairs" and I was startled and I started to tell someone, maybe it was the baby's mother, that the baby could talk. No one had ever heard her talk before. No one knew she could.

The baby, which presumably was in all those symbols of pregnancies throughout the dreams, is at last born. Susan holds it, though she still is of two minds about whether to accept it as her own, as the infant in herself. Now "hair," set up as a main symbol in the first dream, comes back into the picture; it is possible to begin life again, without the aggressive tool that can be manipulated this way and that in playing the woman's role with men. The patient is surprised that the baby can talk in perfectly articulated speech. The surprise may be her way of telling us that she knows more than she admits to knowing. In any case, Susan's ability to talk has always been far ahead of her capacity to use insights for emotional growth (intellectualizing is one of her prime defenses), and also she (the baby) actually does have insights she is not "old" enough to be able to accept and assimilate. I assume the "apartment upstairs" refers to the office of the analyst. The dream has for me an aura of over-simplification. Whether, or how, this is true, we shall have to wait to see.

Dream 58 / *Session 256*

The man in my dream was a young man, ah, I will be meeting tomorrow night. I've, I've never seen him. Ah, apparently it was, I guess it was Gale who told him that I was thirty or thirty-one. And he said something about the fact that I didn't look my age. And, gee, at this point I don't remember whether I told him that I'm, I'm not thirty-one but thirty-six. I guess, well, I don't know whether I told him or not. I don't think I knew when I woke up. But I do remember that I had a conflict about telling him the truth. (*Silence.*) I felt I should but I don't know whether I did or not.

The symbol of hair is implicit, if not mentioned explicitly: Shall she tell her age, which is shown typically by graying hair, as she brought out in an early dream of her hair getting gray? In the earlier dream she whistled furiously in the dark, telling herself that "gray hair looked fine." The context in which this dream occurs is more realistic—she ages slowly—but also more constructive in that it involves centrally not how she looks but rather whether she can be honest in relation to a new man.

Dream 59 / *Session 258*

On Friday night I had a dream and it was not a dream that aroused any feelings of anxiety. It was something, it was a dream about which I had no feeling. I don't remember too much about it. I remember it involved Irwin, and Irwin was coming to see me, and I don't remember if he was coming to see me at my own home or at my parent's home. Er, as in reality, he was married, but his wife wasn't with him. And I was very surprised when he visited me. And I don't remember what we talked about, but I do remember at one point we were in bed together and, er, I reacted, I responded physically in a way that I don't remember responding to Irwin when we were married. And I began to feel that the situation is not right but he is married and, and I began to want to withdraw from the situation and I think that I had this feeling before there was actual intercourse but I am not at all sure.

She needs to reassure herself and deny to us at the outset that this dream "aroused any feelings of anxiety." The old triangle is there, but she has the wife out of it and she herself takes that place with her old husband. The more passionate response is obvious, and the rejection of the choice of the man already married. But these points are difficult to evaluate, for reasons I shall mention a few pages hence. Is she talking here about "withdrawing" from the analyst, and is she anxious to get out before her involvement becomes too great, or before the man-woman problem of her life comes inescapably to the fore? The fact that she has to repress the feeling ("I had no feeling") would substantiate such a hypothesis.

Dream 60 / *Session 258*

And the next night I had another dream that didn't seem to be an anxiety dream at all. You were involved in this dream. At one point I remember, sitting around a large, round table. There were a lot of people present. Some, there, there was a woman in the dream who was identified as your wife, but it's not someone who looked like your wife at all. It was a woman with dyed black hair, jet-black hair. And at one point I was very surprised that your wife would have dyed hair. I think that at first there might have been some feeling of discomfort in connection with being in a social situation with you. But it, it, it was very soon dissipated. I had to leave the group. I, I had to complete some preparations for a trip to Europe that I was taking. Apparently, this was a business trip. It was not just a vacation. I was going, I remember that there was something that I had to do in northern Italy.

Again, hair comes back as a central symbol, indeed used in precisely the same way as in the opening dream—dyeing the hair—except that now it is shifted to the therapist's wife! Well, we can allow Susan this last parting shot, competitive as it is. In reality, the therapist's wife, whom Susan met on the elevator, was a *blonde*, which must have been fairly hard for Susan in the early days of the therapy. We can only hope she is able to take the insight back into herself—I assume her hair is black— for her own self-acceptance as she takes off on her trip to Europe. This dream is the first, I believe, in which the therapist is present as himself. Susan may be saying that her self-acceptance has increased, insofar as she can conceive of the therapist being married to her.

Every one of the concluding dreams of the therapy, including the following one, Susan has introduced with almost exactly the same phrase: "It wasn't an anxiety dream." The lady doth protest too much: Freud's idea is surely applicable, that if this were so, the patient would have no need to bring it up. Susan is very anxious about ending therapy and is telling us this by bringing up "anxiety" in order to deny it.

Dream 61 / *Session 259*

And I went to sleep and I had a dream that involved a continuation of the evening. It wasn't an anxiety dream. I dreamed that Todd came back to my apartment with my parents and in the course of the conversation he referred to his twelve-year-old daughter. I was very surprised, but I made an effort to accept this without appearing startled in any way. And, ah, I had the impression in the dream that Todd had wanted to startle me, surprise me, and, in some fashion. And I remember thinking that it seemed very strange that he had been able to make a marriage re-, re-, regardless of the fact that the marriage didn't last. And he, he commented on my lack of violent reaction, in an undertone. And I said something to the effect that, that this, this lack of shock is pretty amazing, wasn't it. And then I don't quite remember what happened. I don't remember what all four of us were talking about. But at, at, at some point later on, Alfred and Gale either told me about or showed me . . . About a telegram they had gotten from Todd to the effect that Susan is not shocked at learning that I have a twelve-year-old daughter—and that was the dream.

My difficulty in evaluating these last dreams stems chiefly from the fact that Susan is engaged in a fairly broad campaign of suppressing her feelings. This is shown by the overt denial of anxiety in each one. More specifically, in the dream about Irwin, she takes pains to emphasize that it was a dream "about which I had no feeling." This last dream denies her emotions about as emphatically as one can: she was surprised and shocked in the dream, but she has herself studiously deny this *in the dream itself*—which indicates a deeper dimension of repression. She gets pride out of impressing Todd with how successfully she can cover up her emotions, Todd surely being the therapist here. "I made an effort . . . not to appear startled in any way." The device of having the telegram sent is as graphic (and satirical) a way as one could imagine of emphasizing both the fact of her strong emotional involvement and her denial of it. (We have the satirical expression in our culture when talking to a friend who doesn't get the message: "I'll send you a telegram.") In fact, this last dream as a whole is presented as an exercise in *revealing how much she can prevent herself from revealing*.

Thus I believe these last four dreams must be seen in the light of what Susan is doing in terminating the therapy. What is she denying, holding back? Certainly a great deal of anxiety. It must be fairly clear in what I have written in the last third of this study that I believe she is saying in her dreams that she is not ready to terminate, just as she was not ready to cut down on the sessions some time back, and that cutting down and terminating—whatever else they may also be—are in the service of her need to keep the problem with men encapsulated. The positive aspects of these last dreams must, therefore, be kept in abeyance for the moment, since in this denial of anxiety and feeling Susan is entirely capable of making things come out as befits her plans. She is an old hand at this kind of strategy, especially in her relations to men (and to the therapist), and she has in this series of dreams *temporarily* succeeded in this a number of times. I say temporarily advisedly: later dreams in the sequence, generally following a week or so after the strategic denial, have shown her turning to "call a spade a spade"; then she gets to her real anxiety.

In the light of these limitations in how we can take these last dreams, I may give my interpretation of this final one. To me, the structure of the dream itself (i.e., before we read Susan's associative material and the discussion of it) tells us that she sees herself as a twelve-year-old girl and that she is in a daughter relation to the therapist—Todd, who again is made a mildly ineffectual father who was lucky to have been able to make any marriage at all, let alone one that lasted. The shock and surprise are in what Susan is doing to and with the therapist. I do not know whether she sees it as *his* shock if he knew she was making him Todd—father—and terminating at the age of twelve, or *her* shock at the realization of what she is doing to herself in staying at the age of twelve (or both), and an admission that all along she had "planned" (I use the word to refer to unconscious orientation) not to get beyond the age of twelve and become a woman relating to men.

After writing this, I read the other material in the last part of the record since the Irwin dream. Susan's associations and the discussion largely bear out what I said above on the basis of the structure of the dream. Todd turns out in reality to be a psychologist, which indicates more directly that she associates him with the therapist. In her associations, she makes Todd a figure of dubious maturity, a "little behind David" (toward whom she is consistently hostile at this time), and she gives the therapist's marriage the same number of years she was married to Irwin, which is a satire of the therapist as well as a comment on her "divorcing" him. She bargains with the therapist about dates for her payments, when he is trying to get her to consider the shock in the dream, which seems to be a way of covering up her own anxiety at the strident message. She tries then to interpret this shock as related to her surprise that Todd could have gotten married, since in the dream it is clearly shock at the existence of the twelve-year-old daughter. When the therapist proposes that the daughter is herself, she cries, "No, no, no," when one "no" would have been sufficient if something weren't being denied. She is unable to make anything out of the dream and its shock when the therapist urges her, because, she concludes, "there was so little involvement for me." She mentions several times "trying to detach myself from it," "not the vaguest notion of what it means," and repeats to us again that what the last dreams have in common is that they are "not anxiety dreams." She reveals her conscious pride in her "strategy of denial" in the last dream—"a certain amount of pride that I was able to hold back some of the surprise because I just didn't think it would be appropriate." This word "appropriate" appears several times: it wouldn't be "appropriate" to have intercourse with Irwin (whom she makes the therapist); it wouldn't be "appropriate" to seduce Todd. Is not the word "appropriate" in these connections an intellectualized way of making things rationally fit a preconceived plan?

The upshot of my feeling, based particularly on what Susan is telling us in this last dream, is that she is at a twelve-year-old stage of development; that she has made progress and gained insight in the therapy, but it is chiefly insight related to self-feelings and problems of identity which occur in a child of twelve. She has stopped at puberty and has not dealt consistently and deeply with, or negotiated, her problem of being a woman in relation to men. I believe she has made real progress with respect to the attitudes and patterns we could expect in a child of twelve (pre-pubertal, pre-Oedipal). I also believe that her problem with her mother, which would seem to be what has to be negotiated before a girl can go through puberty emotionally and become a woman in her own right, was her major problem. On this issue, some real confrontation occurred, which we saw in the changes of myths and symbols (like hair dyeing, impregnation, and the triangles) in the dreams. I would expect that Susan does function better in her practical life after therapy. But I would question, at the same time, how much of this is due to her having taken on new intellectualized defenses in place of the old, battered ones. In the last dreams there are indications that some of her intellectualized defenses have been solidified. This becomes a problem in that such defenses, often called, euphemistically, "better ways of functioning," may actually shut off a person, in this case Susan, from future feelings and experience. I would rather have seen more overt anxiety at the end, despite the fact that it would be less comfortable. I think it would have meant a more fertile, flexible, future openness to her own potentialities and interpersonal experience.

The question this leaves us with is: What about her future relations with men? In these last dreams I do not see her prepared for enduring relationships with the opposite sex, to use one of Sullivan's criteria. The last dreams show her not only not dealing with the problem but retaining her contempt and need to belittle and satirize men, and priding herself on the retaining of these "skills." I am not making a cultural value judgment here: it is perfectly possible for a woman or a man to choose not to be prepared for relations with the opposite sex, and I leave out of the question at the moment whether she is capable of going further at this stage in her development (though I believe she is). I only want to call "a spade a spade," to use her refreshing phrase. This last point leads us to a further question: Does Susan's "planning" to retain these patterns of relating to men which she learned from her mother (which is suggested by her being "proud" of them) mean itself a continuing of the morbid attachment to her mother? In short, that Susan will keep a room in her life where, to quote her earlier dream, she is always "reserved for mother"?

3

Susan in
Retrospect

This chapter was written after I had read, for the first time, the entire case track—Susan's association and her dreams, the dialogues and transactions between her and the therapist, and the events which transpired in her life outside the consulting room. I shall here offer some summary impressions by relating what I originally said about the symbols in Susan's dreams to the other bodies of data from her life experience.[1] We shall take several soundings, checking some of her symbols against the actual dialogue and transactions in the sessions, and also against what is happening at the time in her actual life. Does what goes on in the case material prove or disprove the validity of our approach to symbols, both as a general principle and with respect to the specific symbols we drew out of her dreams? And what can we predict about her actual life from the symbols in the dreams?

We shall begin with our simple but ubiquitous symbol of "hair," then move on to a very different kind of symbol, the triangle. Does the case data throw any new light on the meaning of symbols in dreams itself? We shall keep in mind the similarities and differences which come up in the symbolic approach to the dreams and the approach of the therapist in the actual sessions.

---

[1] One approach would be to select out of the total case material each reference to a given symbol, interpret its meaning, and then try to collate these meanings. But there is obviously such an infinitely large amount of data in every case, including this one, that that approach is manifestly impossible.

It is possible, however, for any student to set up certain hypotheses, and to draw out the data of the case on the particular theses he wishes to study.

Dyeing and Dying

When I was so struck by what Susan did with her hair in the first dream, I had no way of knowing whether, or how, hair would come up as a symbol in later sessions. I only knew that it had been boldly expressed in the first dream. Actually, it comes up in twelve of the subsequent dreams—almost one out of five—and is discussed in several other sessions. More significant than this sheer number, however, is the fact that *hair appears at the critical junctures in Susan's therapy and life.*

We can expect that if a dream symbol is of critical significance to the dreamer, it will turn up in especially critical conflicts, i.e., anxiety situations. This does indeed turn out to be true in Susan's case. In her own words, anxiety amounting to "desperation" marked the first dream. In the twelve times hair comes up in dreams and in the discussion, every instance is a situation of immediate and more or less pronounced anxiety, except one, the dream of the six-months-old baby and its "new" hair near the end of the therapy.

I hypothesized that in the first dream the dyeing of the hair was related to Susan's rivalry with her mother, and that Susan's denial of her own being (hair in her "own color") was part of this rivalry. It comes out in the case material, with respect to this dream of dyeing her hair red, that Susan had dyed her hair red on entering therapy once before, and that when Susan was a child, her *mother dyed her own hair red.*

Hair appears again in the second dream ("people whose faces were covered with hair"), the *oppositional* dream. This oppositional pattern turns out to be very important in Susan's character and behavior—opposition to mother, opposition to herself, i.e., her feminine potentialities, and (a fact which I saw more clearly retrospectively than at the time she told the dream) opposition to the therapist.

Hair then becomes a symbol of a *particular kind* of anxiety, a "short-circuiting of life," as I phrased it earlier; and as she put it more touchingly, "getting old before my time." For when it occurs next, in dream 11, it expresses anxiety about "graying," and comes the same night as a dream in which she is "relating" (oh, innocuous word!) to a married man. What I did not know was that shortly before these dreams Susan, motivated, as she herself put it (again supporting our clinical hypothesis), by rivalry and competition with women, had begun an affair with the husband of her friend. The fourth mention is again of gray hair, with a similar anxiety that life for her may be an "abortive" experience, and comes *at the time when she is considering cutting down the therapy from three sessions to two.* In my judgment, this cutting down *was* an act of abortion. "My graying hair . . . a perfect sign of the passing years." [2] Again, when she is anxious about cutting down the sessions, she recalls the first dream, of "dyeing my hair two times and fearing I might not be able to find my own hair color." [3]

What light do these things throw on symbols as such? Susan's long discussion of the significance for her of graying hair shows how a biological event which could be simply a literal, *objective fact* for a person of sixty or seventy takes on a genuine *symbolic* quality for her, a woman of thirty-three. She has most of her life ahead of her if she can but choose to live it. It is not just "My hair is graying and I don't like the fact," but "I am 'deathly' afraid that some way I am living will result in my getting old before my time"—for which anxiety gray hair is a most fitting quintessential, symbolic communiqué. I assume it will be accepted as obvious by readers that Susan's several valiant attempts to reassure herself in this discussion that she is not afraid of gray hair ("David doesn't object to it," etc.) are the speeches of a very anxious woman.

Here she also brings out aspects of the *genetic* origin of the hair symbol. When she was a little girl, she relates, not only did her mother dye her hair red but she was so afraid of aging hair that she persuaded the father and little Susan to pull out her gray hairs. This puts more content into our hypothesis, made on the basis of the symbol, that the hair was related to rivalry

[2] Session 173, page 169.
[3] Page 177.

with mother. Apparently Susan begins every therapy experience with the same prologue, consisting of re-enactment of her
identification and rivalry with her mother; as we have mentioned, she said that when she began previous therapy in Wash-
ington she dyed her hair red.

What is clinically important, I repeat, is that all this comes up
at the time the sessions are to be reduced—which indeed may
be for Susan a short-circuiting of life; it may mean that she is
letting herself get old before her time. The next mention of
dyeing her hair (dream 40) comes just before her breakup with
David, and in it she sees the wife of Irwin, her previous
husband, as a blonde, bringing up the rivalry element now, with
the "other woman" winning. In the next to the last dream in
the therapy (dream 60), Susan has the wife of the therapist
dyeing her hair, presumably the color of Susan's; thus Susan at
least does not "lose out" in the contest.

This one symbol, then, is like a compass taking us on a
strange and meaningful pilgrimage through a previously un-
charted land: dependence on and rivalry with mother → a denial of her own identity → aborting life and the therapy → to
a condition where dyeing is indeed dying. Then there occurs at
least a partial turn of the direction of the pilgrimage when Susan
brings the rivalry more into consciousness and into the real
world by associating it with Irwin's wife and the therapist's
wife. The pilgrimage continues, until a baby is born with only a
little hair (but its own!), and in the therapist's wife Susan at
last affirms the color of her own hair.

The Triangle: Sex and Its Symbolism
When Sex Is Not Sex

We found the symbol of the triangle coming up often in our
discussion of Susan. The triangle as a symbol, however, seems
to be on a very different level from hair: The first is almost

wholly a form, as in mathematics, whereas the second, hair, consists almost entirely of content.

Before going further, we need to make a distinction between content and form in symbols. Hair is a bodily material which is seen and touched, serves as padding and protection, especially for the head and genitals in civilized man,[4] and its symbolic quality depends only secondarily on its form.[5] Triangle, on the other hand, is almost purely form, as in geometry. I want to propose that every symbol has *both form and content*, that these are inseparable, and that each symbol is somewhere on a continuum between the two poles of content and form.

Let me try to make this clear by looking further into the symbolic meaning of triangle. A triangle may be thought of as pure form when it is a sign, as in mathematics, but once it is given *symbolic meaning* in a person's experience, it takes on content. Our whole body in its motion participates in this seemingly abstract mathematical form. Take, for example, the *balance* with which we walk, which contains lines of force in relationship to each other that are not entirely dissimilar to lines of force holding the stars in their constellations. Walking itself is a series of triangles, the feet, as they touch the earth, making the two points (and constantly changing as we walk), and the legs meeting the torso of the body making the third corner of the triangle. We make progress, "cover ground" in walking, by this quite remarkable balancing device of the constantly shifting triangle.

Painting illustrates this inseparability of form and content best of all. Van Gogh painted himself striding out to the fields in Southern France with his easel in a famous triangular stride

[4] It may not be irrelevant that in our society people in therapy associate head and genitals: the head of the penis is spoken of as the "little head," and the woman's genitals (by men who are afraid of women) as a "mouth" which could eat them up. On a sociological level also, the head (thinking, talking) and the genitals (sex, pleasure) are the two most "valued" aspects of experience. My colleague, Dr. Robert Beck, points out that the body references in Susan's dreams are almost exclusively to sex and the head, with the head being referred to considerably more.

[5] On second thought, it does seem that the beatnik's bushy hair, the virgin's long hair in some countries of Europe, the modern tomboy's crew cut, do show the *form* of hair as its symbolic power.

that is a classical example of the triangular form in human walking. Let us say I paint you walking. I can reproduce on a canvas all I see of your legs, arms, and body—that is, I can put in plenty of content. I can also simplify that content into lines for the movement of arms and legs, making your legs almost pure force and motion, until I have an abstract painting of pristine mathematical form, like Mondrian's paintings. If, after painting you both ways, I ask where *you* are in the canvas, you may point to the more realistic rendering. But I think you would be wrong: the motion, the way you carry yourself, the dance and gesture by which you "come on," communicate more of what and who you are than your static appearance as a substance.

The problem of any artist is not to copy your body (a camera can do that better) but to uncover the essence of motion which is the essence of "you" walking, and to put in the content not as a "thing" but as motion, vitality, power, tension. Thus one great importance of the abstract movement in art is this dedication to finding the essential forms, which may be shown in the vitality of the slashing lines in a de Kooning, or in the tension of spaces in a Motherwell.

I speak of the "essence" of walking as being in the form, and I have similarly spoken of symbol as the essence of meaning. That is to say, the dance, the gesture, the way you carry yourself reveal the symbolic quality, which is the *meaningful form*, of yourself. I hope I have here demonstrated that in human experience form and content are inseparable, and this holds particularly for the symbols by which men live.

Susan's symbol of pregnancy, which we shall refer to again, illustrates a symbol more obviously participating in both form and content—it is on one side the triangle experience, i.e., form; and it has the obvious content of a fundamental biological event, i.e., the production of a new being. Susan uses this biological phenomenon to refer to something which has particular meaning for her; namely, the birth of new potentialities in her own psyche.

We can now see more clearly how hair and triangle, though seemingly on very different levels, can merge into the same symbolic pattern. We have seen in Susan's dreams that hair is full of all kinds of *content*, particularly related to how men see her, and that the color of hair is a means of attracting them sexually. And we have seen how this content moves immediately into the power lines of the triangle by which she can get the "ascendancy" over other women, gain the "victory," as she puts it. We have seen a number of other things too, which refer to power positions chiefly, and only very peripherally to the actual content of hair.

The hair symbol led very quickly in Susan's dreams to what I call the symbol of the triangle. It was at the end of dream 6 that I developed the triangle as a theme. But apparently not soon enough, for as we look back we find it present emphatically in dream 3—her boy friend, her father, and herself; in dream 4—herself, a girl, and a fellow, with the action being whether she will go to the male or the female; and in dream 5—herself, her former husband, and his fiancée. Indeed, it is very difficult to find a dream in Susan's whole series which is *not* set up in triangular form.[6] There is almost always a man and another woman somewhere, and the question is whom is Susan going to be with. Practically never does Susan have a dream in which she looks at her life or world as a person in her own right, able to survey and act. The only one I think of is the one in which she makes different entrances into an apartment to see how she likes it best. But this turns immediately into the triangle when she hears gossip of the divorce of her friends and has a "sweet feeling" about someone else's marriage breaking up.

We note that this triangle, as we noted it about hair, always comes up at the *climactic* points in her experience. This is substantiation for our hypothesis that it is an important symbol and communicates crucial aspects of her character pattern. The early series of triangle dreams, through "Leah and her husband" (dream 6) and the dream about the divorce (dream 7),[7] lead

---

[6] That is, a dream that contains other persons and is not merely stage directions.

[7] In retrospect, it would seem that her stroking the testicles of the man (therapist?) in dream 7 is a way of getting him on her side for the

up to—and I believe set the stage for—the climactic madwoman dream (dream 8). The climactic nature of this dream is indicated from one aspect by how constantly she refers back to it (e.g., pp. 157, 171, 185, 248).

The most interesting light the triangle symbol gives us is on the meaning of sex for Susan. If we keep this symbol clearly in mind, we note some significant things. One is that there are never dreams of a twosome, never herself and a man in his own right. Practically every dream has somebody taking away, or wanting, someone else's partner. Interpersonal "relations" do not seem to exist for Susan; we find only "ascendancies," rivalries, tests, and contests. There is a great deal of talk of sex throughout the case and many dreams presumably about sex; but there is only one dream in which she is alone with a man: and here the man is only "vaguely involved." She follows this opening scene with a most troubled view of sex: "I had to take off my shoes, grit my teeth, and step into a foot bath . . . full of snot, spit, and slime" (dream 21).

I want to quote some sections [8] from a session in the therapy which occurred just after Susan began an affair with Morris, the husband of her friend. These extracts illustrate how the important symbols and themes come together at climactic junctures in therapy, and also it tells more vividly than I can what sex means to Susan.

> *Susan:* I saw Morris last night. And I'm becoming aware that sex is getting better, that I feel more. This is quite different from the first time Morris and I went to bed. (*Silence.*) I have often thought of that night and there is something frightening about it. (*Silence.*)
>
> *Dr. C.:* In what way frightening?
>
> *Susan (hesitantly):* I've often thought just what happened or how it happened and I can't remember any of the details. All I can recall is being in bed with Morris; I have no awareness of our getting undressed, or what was said or if anything

---

madwoman dream; i.e., is an expression of her anxiety in anticipation of what is about to occur.

[8] Pages 155–157 (Italics mine).

was said, or how long we stayed in bed. I don't recall any sensation other than pain. Pain and a feeling of victory, as if I strove for this and brought it off. Morris did not stay the whole night. The next morning I felt ashamed and even thought it was a dream, it had so little reality for me. *During the intercourse, I kept worrying about the pain, of not being able to experience pleasure, of being frigid. Yet there was this intense feeling of victory; of surprise, pain, victory.*

Dr. C.: Surprise, pain, victory. Anything come to mind?
Susan: (Silence.) (Is embarrassed and squirms.)
Dr. C.: Any thoughts?
Susan: I feel uncomfortable. For some reason I was thinking of that dream where my father has intercourse with me. I had these feelings there, too. (*Silence.*) You know, I remember more of that dream that I had forgotten. My father comes in and sees me necking with the boy. My father says nothing and stalks out. The boy then opens his fly and takes out his penis. My father comes back and sees this. My father gets furious and orders the boy out of the house. "So that is what you want," he said furiously. He made me have intercourse with him and I protested. But he exerted his authority. I remained dressed in the dream. He plunked me down in the chair on his lap and had me straddle him. I protested all the time. But I felt compelled to obey his command. Then I woke up while having intercourse in the dream, feeling miserable. But I had the same feelings of victory, pain, and surprise. (*Silence.*) It's the same thing with Morris and the dream: of my being the chosen one, the desired one, whether over Leah or my mother. (*Silence.*)

Dr. C.: What about the chair position?
Susan: I knew two people would lie down to have intercourse. The way he had me straddle him on the chair was the correct position for chair intercourse. I must have seen something somewhere. I must be blotting out something just as I did the first contact with Morris. (*Silence.*) Sitting up, straddling with my legs apart, has always been a favorite position. (*Silence.*) I used to have intercourse in a chair with Irwin, using that position, before we were married. (*Silence.*) . . .

I recall the dream with my mother standing over me with her legs spread and saying, "You're lucky I don't pee all over you." (*Silence*.) I'm aware of going through life repressing a lot of hostility. (*Silence*.) Funny, I also think of when I found out about intercourse. When I asked my mother, I was seated on the toilet seat. I was shocked. I thought intercourse horrible and a punishment. As a child I always thought of sex as urination, slimy, terrible. (*Silence*.) I guess in some way I still feel this way. Otherwise, I would feel more pleasure, less pain. (*Silence*.) . . .

Dr. C.: (*Hour is near end.*) . . . And in the first telling of the dream, as with Morris the first night, you shut out how you had helped set up the situation. The parts you did recall involved things happening to you without your having an active part in them.

Susan: I never thought of that. (*Silence*.) It's true.

This section shows us immediately how the important symbols come together into the same pattern. Having seen Morris the night before takes Susan back to the first night with him, which then brings to her memory a new aspect of the adolescent dream of intercourse with her father, which goes then to the symbol of straddling, which leads to mother and the madwoman dream.

The hour ends with some insight. It also shows how hard Susan tries to cover up her anxiety by proclaiming "sex is getting better." But what she actually tells us is sex is "pain and victory." She cannot let herself have dreams of the fun of flirting, of being in bed with a man naked (she is never undressed), of intercourse, of the pleasure of having the man on top (it is almost always straddling). I think this substantiates my hypothesis that Susan's is a situation in which sex is not sex but is a flight from anxiety in life which she can't yet bear and is also in the service of a more fundamental struggle. It is understandable that the dream of the dog jumping up on her and showing its teeth should occur exactly at the time she begins her affair with her friend's husband—which I learned of from the transcript of the therapy sessions. But it is unfortunate indeed that with David, the man she says (and apparently with reason) she loved more than any other man in her life, she still continues "feeling sexually constricted." [9]

It has been clear in my interpretation of the symbols that I believe Susan's involvement with her mother is the fundamental problem which makes the sexual problem insoluble. We know in our therapeutic practice that women who have special rivalries with their mothers (i.e., rivalries that weren't negotiable because either there was no father present, as in divorced families, or the father was present but not a source of strength or not a man with whom the child can have the normal "practice in flirting") tend to be frigid.

I believe both the transcript of the therapy and Susan's life as it is developing at this time substantiate my hypothesis that so long as the triangle involved is rivalry with another woman for a man, sex will not be sex but a method of allaying anxiety and of taking flight from problems. It may well be that Susan's *preserving of the triangle in itself* is a flight from actual sexuality, because it protects her from ever having to be with her own man as a twosome.

Pregnancy as Cancer

There is one place, I realize as I study the whole case, where I did not have the courage of my own convictions. That is in the pregnancy-cancer problem. This goes on in Susan's dreams, particularly from number 23 through the dead Indian dream, number 39, and roughly covers most of her love relationship with David. I believe now that she was trying to get across a clear and strong message in her symbols in these dreams, and as I look back on my interpretation, I am convinced that if I had taken the symbols more directly, I would have heard her meaning more clearly. Perhaps one of the reasons I did not keep an entirely clear perspective is that I got too interested in

[9] Page 203.

the psychodynamics of the dreams through that section—
admittedly seductive and intriguing in their own right, what
with the Alaska adventure (coming after the tiff about her
"competitiveness with the therapist's wife") and pregnancy by
a woman and fancy machines for abortions and X rays. I lost
sight of the fact that, interesting and useful as psychodynamics
are for our own understanding and the patient's, they have
their significance only *within the context of the symbolic,
mythic form* in which the patient is setting up his life at that
point in his life.

In short, Susan is telling us something very specific; namely,
that pregnancy is tantamount to having cancer. A pregnancy
by a man is a malignancy. Let us note how this is said.

The fantasies of pregnancy appear first after she has "the
nicest" weekend with David, and she already sees these fantasies
as a reflection of her tendency to manipulate him.[10] Directly
after that comes the eloquent dream: "I was pregnant. Would it
be a baby? Or was it a malignancy, a cancer, a tumor?" And
though she was anxious, she is not ready to confront the issue
that night: "I continued sleeping."

In the very next dream (24) she has the abortion. Immediately, too, comes the pressure to get away from men: she cuts
down the sessions with the therapist at that point from three a
week to two.[11] There occurs her teary and fitful imprecation
against the therapist, that he wants to go too far with her: "I
bargained for just so much. You must not make me feel I must
go beyond that."[12] But the real fight here is not with the
therapist, who if anything is too permissive; it is a fight within
herself that we sense between her tearful outbursts. For she
knows the abortion also means losing her ovary, losing her
female procreativity. Pregnancy by a man, cancer, and the positive function of the ovaries are hopelessly confused in Susan.
She knows this on some inchoate level (and *I* would have
known it on a more choate level if I had taken the symbols more
directly). For she, in the same breath as she tells the dream,

[10] Pages 165–166.
[11] Page 169.
[12] Page 170.

brings up her anxiety that cutting down her hours in therapy may serve to make the therapy also an abortive affair. And now there reappears on the stage our old friend, *hair*, in the form of nemesis, a warning of the passing years.[13] But she senses also, with some consternation and inability to understand why, that she is pulling out of the relation with David, whom she is later to speak of as the only man she ever loved. Nevertheless, she does cut down the therapy, whistling the while to drown out her anxiety of the day before: "Today I haven't got the doubts." [14] It is a strange and gripping contradiction enacted before us, this crying, pleading, imploring girl trying to throw back her shoulders and march ahead without any doubts.

Immediately afterwards she dreams of being "lost in a valley" (dream 25) and not being able to find David, and then the two dreams of diaphragms (dream 26). The sequence is fantastically consistent here when we look at it, for next (dream 27) comes back the old dream about dyeing her hair and not being able to find her own true color, then (dream 28) a dream of her hair going gray—and she has herself liking it! Well, to grow old before one's time, to forfeit one's feminine procreativity, may not be a good fate, but at least it's better than dying of cancer.

The drama line permits a little time out for a satire of men, presumably David and the therapist (they are only "sweet," well-meaning children). Then she gets down to the serious fear of men in the Alaska dream,[15] in which she does permit herself to be impregnated. By a man? Not on your—or rather, *her*—life. By a woman! The dramatic sequence (note that these dreams are strictly consecutive) moves through an X ray (dream 32), a scene about broken glasses (dream 33), which,

[13] We note, again, that at critical points in the therapy the central symbols come together to show a kind of core of Susan's character. Not only does hair come back into the picture, but also the direct struggle with mother, as Susan refers back to the critical dream 8, in which the madwoman straddles her.

[14] And she is soon to be talking about cutting down from two to one session, though she doesn't actually do that till later.

[15] This is the only dream in the whole analysis in which she is definitely afraid of men as men. What is she afraid of? They can kill her—chiefly by giving her cancer (impregnating her). But if she can put them back in *her* womb (the great tubes), she might be safe.

like X ray, for her often signify a problem of seeing "inside," and further dreams of X ray and cancer together (dreams 34, 35).

We surge up now to the climax, dream 36, the dead Indian dream. She lets herself, at last, be impregnated by a man. But to do so, she has to kill him off.

The upshot of my narration here is that if we take the simple sequence of the symbol, pregnancy—cancer, we get a clearer, more consistent picture of what is going on in Susan than we do either by analyzing the psychodynamics or by centering our attention on the dialogue between her and the therapist. This sequence gives emphatic support to my hypothesis in the earlier part of this book that she herself killed off the relationship with David. It supports also my hypothesis that she cannot at this stage in life permit herself to love a man, or even beyond a certain point to be *helped* by a man. For therapy also is an impregnation.

If we ask what is the source of this anxiety about pregnancy and why does she identify it with cancer, we cannot give an answer on the basis of the symbolic structure alone. But we do find some answer in the content of her dialogue with the therapist (which demonstrates that I am not, of course, arguing at all that content be omitted). "There was this anxiety about pregnancy," says Susan. . . . "I remember having the association of the monster that would turn on its maker." [16] At another point she states, "The person you create will assert and turn on you and destroy you, like Frankenstein. And that ties in with having children: the person who you create will destroy you." [17] Thus, while we can conclude from the symbolic elements alone that *pregnancy involves cancer*, i.e., *the fetus you bear in your womb is malignant*, we get more specific content from her added associations in the dialogue: the malignancy is a monster; babies are monsters. She seems to be seeing herself as a monster who could turn on her mother and kill her. She goes on immediately in her talk about the monster to associate the destructiveness with her unhealthy relation to her

[16] Page 194.
[17] Page 188.

mother: "I needed my mother's love. If I wasn't what she wanted me to be, I could be destroyed," [18] and she rightly then says the reason she is afraid of "closeness" with David is this relation with her mother. Obviously the malevolence and hatred of her mother is in *her*; if she gets pregnant, her baby will also be a monster and rise up and destroy her. Small wonder she is anxious about it. We often find in psychotherapy that girls who hate their mothers tend to be sterile: they understandably assume that if they have a baby, the child will also be filled with hateful feelings and will turn on them. The common pattern running through here is: mother-child relations (the most intimate of relationships) are malignant; to become pregnant is to be cancerous.

Though this dilemma is never fully resolved in the therapy, Susan does permit herself, near the end of the therapy, to experience the positive side of the impregnation symbol. She dreams of holding a baby, who she believes is her own.

Latent Meaning Made Manifest in the Symbol

Some of the doubts in the minds of many therapists concerning symbols arise from the misconception that the symbol is a fixed, once-and-for-all, abstract statement carved in stone like Hammurabi's code. This is another aspect of the impoverishment of the understanding of symbols in our day. If, as I have proposed, the symbol is the dynamic, continuous expression of the union of unconscious with conscious experience, the never ceasing interplay of past with present, the intercourse between biological and cultural, it should grow, change, expand, and yield new and greater meaning as the person himself develops. Such unfolding development hopefully is abetted in cases like Susan's by psychotherapy.[19]

[18] Page 194.
[19] I refer here to "healthy" symbols. Indeed, this expanding, growing quality is a prime distinction between "healthy" and "unhealthy" sym-

Hence another question we must turn our attention to in this summary is that of *latent meaning unfolding into manifest meaning* as the symbol is developed by the dreamer in the series of dreams. We find this is indeed the case with Susan. We have seen it with *hair*, which made its appearance as an object of manipulation, something external she wears and uses primarily to impress and compete with mother (so we hypothesized) and secondarily, since a woman competes with another by running off with her man, to attract men. Hair soon became expanded to carry the significance of *dying* as well as *dyeing*. (The pun is not accidental; as Freud, among others, pointed out, dreams as well as other expressions of unconscious phenomena utilize the pun as one way of expressing meaning.) Hair then became chiefly *graying* hair, as an expression of anxiety and despair, appearing at the times when she was engaging in self-defeating affairs with unavailable men and when she was "aborting" her experience in therapy. This level of anxiety and despair brings in a deeper dimension of her experience, biologically and culturally, and brings in as well an existential awareness of choice and decision. In the second half of the therapy, the color of the hair assumes a more autonomous character: Susan dreams of women having the color of *her* hair, and even—this combines the theme of rivalry with an assertion of her autonomy—has the therapist's wife in a dream dye her hair the same color as Susan's. Finally there is the most obvious emergence of latent into manifest meaning, in the hair of the baby, which Susan identifies with her own possibilities of development, in the last stage of the therapy.

Latent dimensions of meaning come out also in the symbolic actions. The mother "straddles" her in the madwoman dream and pretty well straddles Susan throughout life (and therapy).

---

bols. Symbols can also *shrink* experience, can narrow perception, block growth: this is when symbols become hardened into *dogmas*. A healthy symbol unfolds like a flower in the morning, except that the unfolding in human symbols goes far beyond the mere biological processes. That is, the unfolding does not simply bring out once and for all the plant form, but in human consciousness, which normally expands all through the person's life, the symbols bring out new meaning continuously, as long as the person's consciousness remains vital.

Susan "straddles" her father in the dream of intercourse and *tries* to straddle him throughout therapy and life. At numerous points throughout the therapy she refers back to the mad-woman dream and adds new understanding to it. In session 173 (when she brings in the dream of David and the abortion in which she felt he "took out too much") [20] there takes place the following dialogue, which I quote from the script:

> *Dr. C.:* Any other aspect of the dream come to mind?
> *Susan:* You mean the dream about the sweater [where the washerwoman (madwoman) straddles Susan]?
> *Dr. C.:* No. But why did this come to mind?
> *Susan:* That dream was fraught with the fears of close-ness. I remember cowering on the floor as this aggressive woman wreaked her vengeance on me. (*Silence.*) Sure, that woman was my mother, but also part of *me!*
> *Dr. C.:* Could be!
> *Susan:* (*Laughs.*) Well, I won't say what's happened to that hostile aggressive me, except it's a much less important part of me. I can't tell you why, but I feel that.

Here Susan, misunderstanding the therapist (how productive such misunderstandings often are in therapy!), refers back to this seminal dream and adds the new meaning related to her *own* hostility and aggression. This is the beginning of genuine insight, despite the fact that Susan uses it for reassurance to avoid the very problem itself, and that she intellectualizes it. Again in session 196 she returns to this dream with similar unfolding of her own hostility. In session 237, when she relates the dream of the Armageddon fight with her mother, she rightly contrasts it with the early madwoman dream, but says in this one she "wasn't lying supinely on the floor." Not until the Armageddon struggle with the mother (dream 51) does the climactic meaning of that early dream come out.[21]

[20] Pages 168–172.

[21] Those who hold that symbols are "arbitrary" will see that some-thing considerably more than an arbitrary process is demonstrated by the inner consistency in Susan's referring back to these crucial dreams at every critical point in the therapy.

The most interesting unfolding of latent meaning into manifest meaning is in the "triangle" theme, particularly related to the Oedipal situation. In the section of the transcript quoted earlier, we observed how the affair with Morris brought out both the latent meaning of sex for Susan and her relation to her father.

Those who were concerned that in taking this approach I was dealing too much with the manifest symbols and that therefore the repressed meaning would escape us will have seen, I trust, with a clarity that leaves no doubt, how the latent meaning is revealed in the series of Oedipal dreams with her father. This is introduced in the dream she recalls from adolescence, dream 3, which she reviews in the passage quoted. Then in dream 13 [22] she brings out something she says she "forgot" before; namely, that the father cries out that *she* wanted it, and she is aware of her own feeling, not at all of fear, as she first told us, but of victory. In dream 15 [23] she goes through a replay of the original Oedipal dream with David in her father's role and now *she herself* demands the intercourse and the straddling. There are numerous other references in this emerging series which I have earlier touched on. Thus, from "I am the poor, helpless victim," there unfolds out of the very same chrysalis, I am the woman who controls you, and I have the God-given right to "do what I want when I want to." [24]

Mirror, Mirror on the Wall

In Susan's first dream a mirror appears. If I were doing the interpretation of Susan's dream symbols over again, or if I had read the whole case to start with, I would have made a good deal more of this mirror. As I look back on my first reading of that dream, I believe I had the feeling that the mirror—such an

[22] Page 156.
[23] Page 159.
[24] Page 159.

obvious symbol—was a bit too "easy"; I was allured more by the element which is much harder to form into a cogent symbol, namely, the banal hair. Be that as it may, the mirror calls for more of our attention.

This mirror, I propose, ties together a number of threads; it forms into a consistent pattern a number of elements in Susan's character structure. These elements center chiefly around her narcissism. To begin with, the mirror, in the first scene of the hair dyeing, was "how do I impress." We subsequently see in dream after dream that Susan is concerned not with liking but with being liked, not with seeing but with being seen. This is shown particularly in dream 5,[25] concerning her former husband and his fiancée: "It was important to me that he think well of me. . . . I tried very hard to be sweet to both. . . . I wanted Irwin's fiancée to have a good opinion of me." Susan's concern with being liked is the more interesting because she was going to Irwin's (and her old) apartment, she tells us, to get "something that belonged to me." Could it be the self she left there, the self she never knew or realized in the marriage, the self that she, like Narcissus in the myth, never recognized? We shall come back to this point after reviewing some other examples of Susan's narcissism.

She indefatigably tries to be the "nice little girl" to the therapist. Her concern with glasses throughout, beginning in the dream in which she breaks the frames of her glasses (dream 33), is not *to see*, but to *be seen*: the frames matter, not the contents; she buys glasses for their fancy exteriors, not because she needs them. Her "extravagance," which comes up again and again, chiefly connected with cosmetics and buying clothes, and is a puzzle and a source of concern to her, seems to me to make sense as part of the mirror pattern. When she is anxious, as after several of the big battles with her mother, she goes to stores in her dream (and in reality) to buy herself some things. People in our society—children perhaps more obviously, but certainly adults as well—acquire possessions as a means of assuaging anxiety. This has good neurological rationale in the fact that the parasympathetic division of the autonomic nervous system,

25 Page 146.

which has to do with eating and digestion and relaxation, works in opposition to the sympathetic division, which is the media for the activation of anxiety. If you can eat actual food or acquire some possession or have your narcissism fed, your anxiety tends to retreat. After the madwoman dream (8), which obviously leaves Susan with a great deal of anxiety, we find her hurrying to have dreams concerned with being liked, specifically whether she is "acceptable," what her mother's relatives "would think of us."

So far, I have been using the term narcissism in its conventional sense. Narcissus in the myth is thought of popularly as the figure who looked in the mirror of a pool and fell in love with himself; and clinically the term is applied to the person who is too preoccupied with himself, has too much "love" for himself. If we look more closely at the myth, however, we see that this is not what happened; he did not fall in love with himself. Rather, *he did not recognize himself.* The image seemed to him to be someone else; what occurred is actually much closer to Susan's predicament. As the Greeks tell the story, Narcissus had refused to fall in love with the likely candidate, the lovely maiden Echo; and the spurned girl, in her resentment, prayed that the gods punish him. Venus then decreed that Narcissus look in the watery mirror, misperceive his own reflection as a beautiful maiden, and fall in love with her.

> Down near the pebbly bottom he saw a face so passing fair, that he immediately lost his heart, for he thought it belonged to some water nymph gazing up at him through the transparent flood. . . . With sudden passion he caught at the beautiful apparition; but, the moment his arms touched the water, the nymph withdrew.[26]

He kept up this romantically Sisyphus-like treadmill of trying to surprise her, only to find she disappeared whenever he disturbed the smooth pool by grabbing for her.

[26] H. A. Guerber, *The Myths of Greece and Rome: Their Stories, Signification and Origin* (London: Harrap & Co., 1907), p. 97.

There Narcissus lingered day and night, without eating or drinking, until he died, little suspecting that the fancied nymph was but his own image reflected in the clear waters.[27]

Narcissus indeed died before his time, not of the cancer of which Susan is afraid, but of not being able to distinguish between himself and the world or between himself and the other person. *The myth portrays the problem of failure of self-recognition.*

Susan is caught in this predicament. She is hunting for herself in her old apartment but is so preoccupied with what others think of her that she never sees herself *as herself* at all. She sees someone else in the mirror; she doesn't love herself enough, in Sullivan's sense. The Greek myth presents young Narcissus as so alienated that he does not know his own sex, but sees himself as a woman; and similarly, though Susan never becomes a full-fledged Lesbian, she never succeeds in recognizing herself as fully female. The mirror symbol is "reflected appraisal" with a vengeance. She not only has no experience of herself except what is reflected from others; she does not even take this as the self which is her and which she can affirm and build upon. "I still think buried in me is the desire to be the belle of the ball." [28] "When I was a little kid, I had to work very hard to get my mother's approval." [29]

This last sentence puts us on the scent of the source of the problem. (We have to ask why a child cannot experience himself as himself; and with the adolescent, what has gone on with this youth Narcissus that he is not free enough to let himself love the beautiful maiden of the woods, Echo?) Susan tells us the motive for looking in the mirror in the first place is not to find herself but to get mother's approval. And we recall now the whole couplet from Snow White, of which I quoted only part as the heading of this section:

> Mirror, mirror on the wall
> Who is the fairest one of all?

[27] *Ibid.*, p. 98.
[28] Page 197.
[29] Page 197.

I am aware that the evil Queen who says this is not Snow White's blood mother, but she does represent the mother's generation as against the daughter's age group. Susan was apparently made into a little model doll by the mother, her neurotic "narcissism" fed by mother's holding her up as a model to the cousins; and she is literally fed and bought things (the sweater) by the mother, whom she must then fight to keep even these possessions (as in the madwoman dream, when the mother figure tries to take the sweater away). The dream of the fight with mother for the handbag as a symbol of feminine sexuality assumes even greater importance now. Susan's difficult bind is that, to establish an identity of her own, she must revolt against the very one who has given her her sense of significance to start with. And ersatz though this identity was, it was about all she had.

The Symbol Resisting Intellectualization

Of prime importance in the consideration of symbols, not only in dreams but in other forms of expression, is the fact that the symbol resists intellectualization. Since the genuine symbol represents unconscious (including biological and historical) elements imbedded in the individual's experience, it cannot be intellectualized without being destroyed. When we, or Susan, do succeed in intellectualizing a symbol, we find ourselves left with merely a collection of words; the meaning has disappeared like sea foam on our palms, leaving us empty-handed.

All through Susan's therapy we see this struggle between intellectualizing and the symbol. She intellectualizes a great deal indeed. Directly after almost every dream, Susan gives an "interpretation of what the dream means," often followed by the implication, "Well, that's that." When reading the transcript of her sessions, I found that I was bracing myself at the end of every dream for the almost inevitable set of psychoanalytic clichés she would throw over the dream like a smothering blanket. Making a "rational explanation" is of course modern Western man's chief and most effective means of defense against the anxiety of irrationalism, and Susan has learned well the lessons of her society. I do not argue that her "interpretations" are necessarily wrong; Susan is not stupid. Indeed, the therapeutic problem is more difficult with patients like Susan who, immediately following some irrational experience or expression, give the *right* interpretation. For the immediate rational interpretation serves to defend the person from the anxiety-creating experience of living out the irrational, troubling communication of the dream.

The important point is that this process never completely works, in any real sense, with Susan. And the reason it doesn't is the vitality of her symbols.

Before we get to that, however, let us review a few of Susan's ready intellectualizations. The first dream, Susan says, refers to the fact that "going back into analysis [means] wanting a change . . . but being afraid," and "becoming a redhead [is] an ascendant action." This interpretation is not necessarily wrong, but to accept it as such is to cover up the real source of anxiety in the dream, her manipulating herself in dyeing her hair and her despair and panic at losing her identity. The third dream—the powerful one of her father forcing her to have intercourse with him—she relates innocuously, if vaguely, to her "never having associated sex with pleasure." The fifth dream—that interesting search in her old apartment—she is recorded as simply saying indicates "her need for acceptance by others."

In noting how these relatively cliché-like "interpretations" actually castrate the dreams, we might wonder whether the therapist has failed to put down all Susan said. But in the sessions that were recorded on tape, Susan shows the same proclivity for disposing of anxious conflicts in dreams with a nicely turned rationalization. Take the dream at the outset of her affair with her friend's husband (dream 14),[30] which begins with her lying nude in the dirt in her filthy apartment and ends with Morris putting his hand on her breast and her moaning

[30] Pages 157–158.

"too soon . . . too soon." At the conclusion of this dream she says nicely, "I see this as a conflict between the part of me that sees myself as filthy . . . and the other part which wants sex and closeness with Morris. . . . I have been toying with the possibility of entering a relationship without fear of closeness" —which she has difficulty with because "she never experienced it with her father." When the therapist—with obvious perspicacity—asks her how she feels, she answers, "I must admit I feel rather complacent right now. . . . Actually, I feel great and that all is O.K." This after a dream which is desperate and full of conflict! Susan also here lets fall a little flattery on the therapist to disarm him ("The analysis must be taking"). With respect to that oft-repeated phrase "wanting closeness" and sex with Morris, we must say, on the basis of what the dream so clearly shouts at us, "closeness" is actually the last thing in the world she wants at that moment.

The reader may feel I am pushing the point too far, but bear with me a moment longer. Not only is intellectualization Susan's best defense; it is the most used defense in all psychotherapy these days; and the failure of analysts and therapists of all schools to break through it (indeed, the tendency of therapists *themselves to strengthen this defense*) is the chief reason so much therapy fails to change people deeply. So let us clinch our point by referring finally to how Susan manages to escape the conflicts in the dead Indian dream. The symbols in this dream have to do with killing off the Indian, siding with the woman, and the cancer-pregnancy conflict; and the whole dream predicts the killing off of the man she loves, David. A serious situation indeed. But Susan disposes of it easily enough: she regards it as "positive" that she refrains from having intercourse with the Indian, sees herself as killing off an old way of relating to her father and to men in general. "It's like giving back my father . . . to my mother, disengaging myself from their lives. Maybe this is why I felt so good the last few days." [31] Within a couple of weeks the relationship with David is indeed "killed off," and she is plunged into grief and despair.

Now if she does so much intellectualizing, why is it the

[31] Page 206.

therapy moves at all? I give a very simple answer which is not simple at all in its implications: *the symbols in the dream successfully resist the intellectualization.* No matter how much Susan whistles in the dark in her rationalizing talk, the symbols in her dreams keep right on wrestling with her real problems.[32] The dreams march down the road of deeper exploration, pausing only to adjure those present to "call a spade a spade." And when the therapist too gets taken in by the rationalistic talk—as every therapist does at some time—the dream tosses out a beautiful warning that "a soap opera is going on." And after a couple of sessions, Susan is again confronting a real problem and the therapy moves. This is another example of the amazing double life Susan led in the therapy, her talk often trying to smooth over and failing to do justice to the depth and power of the dreams, but the symbols continuing to take their motivation and their form from levels in her experience quite below the smooth chatter.

It is not too much to say that the symbols save Susan from lapsing into mere talk. *And her symbols do this against her own conscious intent; she wants to whistle in the dark, but rarely will the symbols go along with it.* This whole phenomenon in Susan is an interesting illustration of the difference between conscious intention and the deeper, more inclusive state technically called intentionality. Her talk reminded me again that, whereas Aristotle was right when he said that speech makes man the rational animal, Augustine and Sartre and Freud are also right that talking is the way we lie to ourselves and play deceiving games ad infinitum. A corollary follows: if a therapist keeps his ear tuned clearly to the communication from the patient's symbols, he is less apt than otherwise to get drawn off the track of the central issues in the therapy.

[32] My statement should not be taken as an iron-clad rule, but as a principle. Susan has some dreams that ostensibly, at least, take part in the whistling in the dark, e.g., the one of falling down the stairs and landing nicely on her feet. I happen to feel that that dream is so pat it gives itself away (and must have had the "intentionality" to do so). No doubt one could find that many of Susan's dreams go along with the rationalizing. I am speaking about the nature of symbols rather than dreams as such.

PART

II

The Case of Susan

BY

LEOPOLD CALIGOR

Introduction

Susan Berman was a patient in treatment with me while I was in psychoanalytic training.[1] I decided to have intensive supervision of my work with her because her case posed a number of problems that were difficult but representative of the contemporary psychoanalytic patient.

Susan had been in treatment for a number of years with a series of therapists (to which I will refer below) and had made limited progress. She was intelligent, well educated, sophisticated in living experience, and was functioning adequately in a responsible job. Yet she felt frustrated and unhappy: she had been unable to find a satisfactory relationship with a man, suffered intense bursts of anxiety and depression, and had a number of phobic-like fears which she knew were irrational but which she was unable to conquer.

I am presenting every dream Susan reported in the course of her psychoanalysis. I have also included relevant parts of therapy sessions, a brief summary of the patient's developmental history and her previous therapy experience, and a series of figure drawings done by her early in the treatment (shown following page 150).

I want to thank my patient, who at termination of her therapy gave me permission to use these data. They are presented here in disguised form.

[1] I saw this patient during the early 1950s while in training at the William Alanson White Institute of Psychiatry, Psychoanalysis, and Psychology. Dr. Harry Bone was my supervisory analyst at this time. I want to thank him for a meaningful learning experience.

Background Material and Clinical Summarization [2]

Initial Interview

Susan is a thirty-three-year-old woman with dark, quietly styled hair. She wears eyeglasses with inconspicuous rims and uses little makeup. Her efforts to be sexually attractive seem to be expressed through clothes chosen to emphasize her slim, attractive body rather than being focused on the face.

Susan said right off she was ambivalent about starting therapy. She felt she had delayed for some time and was relieved at starting, but she was wary, too, since this was her fifth experience with therapy.

Susan saw her problems as follows. First, since her divorce several years ago, she had "an almost unique ability to seek out a safe, empty, uninvolved relationship." This was true of all relationships with men. Currently it was with a homosexual; this lasted for more than a year. Second, she was aware of her fear of being a woman and having a husband, children, and marriage. Third, there was a feeling of passivity, an inability to compete with other women, and near panic when facing a group. Fourth, she was unable to initiate social contacts and felt socially isolated. "If I do not know anyone, I withdraw and fade into the wallpaper." Fifth, she was afraid of learning to drive a car, of ice-skating, and of dogs. Sixth, "I make impossible demands upon myself to be the most brilliant, not just passable, to prove that I am adequate." Seventh, she experienced irrational bursts of intense anxiety and depression. Eighth, "maybe I have a need for punishment. I saw this fellow [the homosexual] for more than a year and it didn't make any difference to me. That scares me. Maybe I am rubbing my nose in it." Ninth, Susan thought she was perhaps all intellect and no feelings and maybe was incapable of feeling.

Susan asked whether one session a week would be adequate. I told her that at least two a week would be indicated, though

[2] All "Background Material and Clinical Summarization" data are based on sessions 1–62.

three would be optimal, but that it was her decision to make. She decided on two sessions a week because "clothes and a nice apartment are important to me," but she left open the possibility of three sessions at some future date.

She seemed eager to be liked; she smiled ingratiatingly, she struck various poses and moved her arms and body expressively as she talked. Her manner conveyed both narcissism and self-consciousness. Her verbalizations about her problems had a glib and intellectualized quality, though at the same time they seemed to be accurate statements.

Developmental and Descriptive Data from Childhood to the Present [3]

Background

Mother. Susan's first comments about her mother were: "My mother raised me 'à la Watson.' I was completely toilet-trained well before one year. I had just one accident and my mother rubbed my nose in my feces and this relapse never occurred again. . . . I recall having a bowel movement at three, and being so fearful of my mother that I hid the stool. . . . My mother was very rigid. She was determined that I get an education and the cultural advantages she never had. She pinched dollars and gave me dancing and elocution lessons— which I didn't like, but took. She even had my clothes made to order. . . . If I ever crossed her, she could get furious at me."

Susan described her mother as having made all kinds of material sacrifices for her. She saw her mother as having set perfectionist standards for her and as having nagged constantly and destroyed Susan's confidence in her ability to make any but the most meaningless decisions. She adored Susan when Susan

[3] The descriptions of her parents, her developmental history, and her problems are based on Susan's perceptions, and not necessarily on how I saw them.

toed the line. But she hovered over Susan, and Susan experienced her as omniscient and enraged when she was crossed. Mother would say to Susan as a child, "Eat it," and Susan would apathetically obey.

Mother insisted she wanted closeness with Susan and invited confidences. When Susan gave them, her mother was critical and disappointed in her and gave inappropriate advice. This infuriated Susan. Her mother, Susan stated, was a Pollyanna who constantly mouthed platitudes, and many people found her exasperating. Susan felt her mother's relation to her was "shallow and not understanding. I never got the feeling of being able to please my mother." Yet her mother was easily hurt when Susan was short-tempered with her; Susan then felt guilty.

Mother had communicated to Susan her philosophy of "grit your teeth and bear it"; never show your inner feelings, but rather, maintain a stoic façade. A woman must not be too open with a man and should use sex as a way of control.

Father. Susan described her father, who taught at the local college, as always reading his newspaper, and a silent person and unavailable to her. She said with anger that all her life she wanted to get close to him but he related to her in a sarcastic, unpredictable, and avoidant manner. She believed his disapproval of her contributed to her feeling unworthy of love. Susan described a long-standing teasing and explosion-provoking operation between them. She had to perform intellectually to get his approval and experienced any inability to measure up to his standards as anxiety-provoking. She saw her intellectual, unemotional relatedness to men, her feeling unliked—"prove you love me"—as stemming from her feeling unlovable in her father's eyes.

Mother-Father Relationship and Home Atmosphere. The father was depicted as silent, only half-listening, with irritation, as her mother prattled on and on. Both Susan and her father had reactions of intense irritation to her mother. Both parents took a stoic approach to the expression of feelings. As a child, Susan would tell them they never fought and maybe it would be more interesting if they would yell at each other. Susan felt there was no warmth between them. She would beg her parents

to have another child, even adopt one, to diminish her loneliness.

Both parents were so overcontrolled that, upon being notified
of the death of a grandparent, "neither shed a tear or registered
emotion." Susan adopted this pattern, and when her mother
telephoned to tell her her father had been taken seriously ill,
Susan sat surprised, with tears streaming down her cheeks, but
had to control her voice completely and suppress any expression of distress.

Susan described a deep-seated hurt that her father never
chose her and that he invariably was allied with her mother.

Childhood. Susan painted a picture of a shy, overtrained,
overfed girl who apathetically ate all, who felt isolated, was
afraid to initiate socially, and passively followed others. Above
all, she had to be certain not to cross her parents, especially her
mother. She had to keep her feelings under control at all times,
and if she was afraid (e.g., of a running dog, of going to the
dentist and having an abscessed tooth treated), she could not
show these feelings. She depicted herself as a child with diffuse
fears, who did not feel free in body movements, who could not
stand up to other children, and who was constantly afraid that
she would be rejected. There was always a right thing and a
wrong thing to do, defined by what won approval and was
sanctioned. She dared not experience, much less express, hostility to her mother, who is omniscient; if she stuck her tongue
out at her mother behind her back, she would detect it. There
was the wish that her father would understand and befriend
her, but somehow he never did. Yet there was the feeling that
he somehow understood her better than did her mother.

Early in her childhood, Susan would regularly raid the sugar
bowl. From six to sixteen, Susan was overweight from eating
sweets.

Adolescence. There was little that Susan clearly described
about herself. She said she was a somewhat dumpy, shy, compliant adolescent outside of the home. She had no boy friends.
She felt incapable of structuring socially and for the most part
was passively doing nothing or following some girl friend.

Susan told of provoking her father out of his silence with

sarcastic humor; when he exploded at her, which she feared, she would maintain a haughty silence sometimes for weeks on end.

In adolescence, Susan still had her mother hovering over her. She would encourage Susan's "freedom" but then would undermine Susan's confidence. For example, her mother would tell Susan that she could choose her own clothes and then would nag about the choice or the length of the hemline. Susan tried to withstand her mother's nagging and finally reached the point of "If you don't stop pushing, I'll scream."

Menstruation started at thirteen. There was no regularity in the cycle until Susan was sixteen and a half, with long periods elapsing between menstruations.

Susan did have girl friends during adolescence, but she related passively to them.

All in all, it was a lonely time of life.

Young Adulthood. Susan described herself as lonely and incapable of initiating socially. She had a series of dates in which all went well the first evening. However, "I have had many second meetings in my life following wonderful first meetings. In the second meeting I become terribly tied up in knots, I lose all spontaneity. I become dull, I feel uncommunicative. It came to a point where I would get very anxious and jittery at the very idea of a second date."

Susan was always a good student, though she had a fear of being called upon to recite or answer questions.

It was very important to Susan that she be desired by men, but she was afraid that she could not win or compete with other women. There was some necking during her college years, and she went along with it passively; and "somehow I managed to avoid intercourse."

Adulthood to the Present. After college, at about twenty-two, Susan was afraid of men because she anticipated rejection. "I can't stand rejection and have to avoid it at all costs." It was just such a rejection from a boy she liked that initially precipitated her coming into therapy. Susan had a "crying jag" and was treated by a psychiatrist who told her she was heading for a "nervous breakdown"; he recommended that she leave her job and rest in the afternoons and prescribed some medication for her "nerves." Treatment continued for three weeks, at the end of which Susan "snapped out of it." She then got herself another job. Susan believes she was catapulted into therapy because of her fear of and pain at being rejected by her father. "Whenever I tried to get close to my father, he would reject me. I never knew if my father would laugh or explode at what I did. I feared his hostility. . . . When I get close now, I expect hostility to be aimed at me."

Susan met Irwin at a social gathering and was flattered because he was intended for another girl and had preferred her instead. She was terrified on the second date but used alcohol to help her through her anxiety. Irwin was the first man who ever told Susan he loved her, and for this she felt grateful and felt that she should love him in return. They were married when she was twenty-four. Throughout their marriage, which lasted six years, Irwin related to Susan with sarcasm. She constantly set up test situations for him to prove his love by doing what she wanted. The marriage was a constant tug of war. Sex was unsatisfactory and unspontaneous. Susan continued to have severe menstrual cramps throughout the marriage. The day Irwin told her he had decided to break up the marriage, she consummated an affair with a fellow classmate (Susan was then thirty) and for the first time felt complete sexual release. The next day Susan menstruated without cramps for the first time.

From age thirty to the time she entered therapy with me at thirty-three, Susan drifted in various relationships with men who chose her and to whom she felt committed though there was no closeness. "Once I am chosen, I cannot say 'no.' . . . It is most important to me that I be chosen. . . . I'm aware I get involved with men who are hostile and fearful of women. . . . They cannot give me what I want, yet I just drift in these relationships. . . . Sometimes I think the only people in the world with whom I'm saddled are the ones I am not interested in." Yet Susan drifts into these relationships to avoid loneliness. The last one, of more than a year's duration, had been with a homosexual and was characterized by their both drifting. Susan felt exploited and used as a social front. Yet she continued the relationship. When he threatened to reject her, she became very hostile, then very anxious, and finally crawled back and apologized.

Susan's way of relating involves anticipating what others want and giving it to them. "It's as though I am nothing, and if I can make myself into what others want, fine." She would obliterate herself and "blend in" with everyone, getting along by submission (except for her parents and her husband) and avoiding all self-assertion. "Peace at any price and deny all your hostility. You grit your teeth and bear it. You smile on the outside and boil on the inside."

Susan feels she has failed to reach any man, just as she has failed to reach her father, and anticipates the same rejection and attack. She feels she cannot compete as a woman for a man because somehow her father always preferred her mother to her. Susan would "humorously" create situations in which her father would sarcastically plead for her to come to visit.

Susan basically feels that all a man could possibly want from her is sex and her body; that is all she really has to offer. Yet sex does not involve enjoyment; rather, it is a power tool, a commodity to be used to get attention and to provoke a reaction.

Susan has great difficulty in expressing hostility directly and resorts to indirect ways of which she herself is frequently not aware. She does use sex for the expression of hostility. For example, she constantly complained to her husband that he was not spontaneous sexually; and she ended the relationship with her homosexual friend by taking him to bed to make him feel sexually inadequate. Susan is aware she has much pent-up hostility which she fears will come out. There are many fears—of falling, of fast movement, of strange dogs leaping, of fading into the background, of being hurt or somehow torn to shreds.

Susan does have friendships of long standing with women who are usually older than she is and who play a mothering role. These are warm relationships, yet laden with competition for Susan. She fantasies competing with these women for their husbands or boy friends, and, with partial awareness, does flirt with them.

Susan has always been given responsibility on the job and has always feared that she will be found lacking. She is delighted and surprised to be told how well she is performing.

Susan currently lives alone in her own apartment and has a responsible job, with several people working under her. She is aware that she presents a façade of independence and strength to the world. Yet, inwardly, she feels quite the opposite and desires total dependence. "Inwardly, I've always wanted to be taken care of. It was like when I was a child and played ill to get a response of love from my parents which was usually not forthcoming. . . . It's the same feeling now. You want to be dependent. . . . It's like my fantasy of kissing my tubercular friend on the lips . . . to catch TB and be totally taken care of. . . . But you cannot count on anyone and have to do it all for yourself."

It is important to emphasize that Susan does function successfully in the surface social roles and that despite her anxieties about herself she is a going concern.

Previous Treatment. Susan had been in therapy for a cumulative period of more than four years in the past ten years.

Shortly after graduation from college, she had her crying jag, which we have mentioned, at the age of twenty-three and went to see a psychiatrist in Boston. Susan "snapped out of it" in three weeks and went back to work. She got married at the age of twenty-four and moved to Albany.

From the ages of twenty-six through thirty-two, Susan was in treatment with three other therapists for a total of more than four years.

Actually, I was not able to get a clear picture of what transpired in the previous treatment situations, as Susan herself was not too clear. She felt the first two analysts "were of some help." These two treatment situations terminated because, in one instance, Susan moved from Albany to New York City; in the other instance, her analyst left New York City. Susan felt the nine months with her third analyst were confusing, "that we both didn't know what was going on."

Susan started psychoanalysis with me at the age of thirty-three. She pessimistically stated, "I'm reluctant to start because I have had three therapists already."

Susan's Initial Approach to Psychoanalysis and the General Therapeutic Focus

Susan initially approached the therapy situation with glibness, good-natured humor, role-playing, and much intellectualizing. When she was helped to see this mode of relating, considerable anxiety emerged. Susan pleaded with me on several occasions not to let her intellectualize or cut off all feelings and whistle her way out of treatment; in a sense, this was a plea to help her avoid making this analysis another failure.

When Susan was given reassurance that we could work on this together, she relaxed somewhat. In a permissive therapeutic environment, she gradually was able to experience some anxiety and vulnerability without immediate denial.

Outstanding was Susan's way of relating: I smile, I sit, I wait for you the analyst to initiate; I have no thoughts of my own. Even if I do start a topic, do you want me to continue this? I just have no thoughts.

It soon became apparent to both of us that she was so intent on pleasing and accommodating, and so busy picking up cues in her attempt to anticipate my possible reactions, that the flow of her thoughts was interfered with and there was much meaningless verbalizing. We therefore decided, after a few sessions, that she use the couch. This was initially an anxiety-laden experience for her; she would panic when I was out of sight and would turn to me for visual cues. Gradually, over the next ten sessions, Susan became sufficiently comfortable not to need me as a visual prop. At first there was a period of uncomfortable silence; then Susan's affect changed rather abruptly. From considerable body movements, a charming voice, a smiling face, and chit-chat, she went into lethargy and spoke in a flat and slow voice. At first she said there was nothing to talk about because she was "empty." Gradually she began to communicate with affect some of her underlying fears and feelings. These included:

1. Intense feelings of desire for escape (apathy, suicidal ideation of cutting her throat or jumping in front of a train, talk of a violent end: "I'm fascinated by escape and yet afraid of it. At one time I had a fear of becoming a real alcoholic; I would drink in the past when I had to become anesthetized—I've often feared becoming a solitary drinker").

2. Deep-seated, life-long feelings of being unlovable, of somehow setting up exploitation and rejection of herself.

3. Intense anxiety when faced with anger or rejection.

4. Intense feelings of loneliness, of being trapped, with no meaningful relationships.

5. Either too many intolerable feelings or no feelings at all.

6. A feeling that she never chooses, but is chosen. Susan feels caught and drifts in meaningless relationships and does what others want of her, with a total denial of herself.

7. Inability to feel anger. Instead, she experiences hurt and submission.

8. Not knowing who she is, and so playing empty roles.

9. A feeling that if others really knew her, they would reject her all the more; that life is one miserable submission to others wherein "you grit your teeth and bear it and smile—and hope they accept you."

Susan described how in previous therapy she would arrive at a point where she was free of symptoms and have a flight into health. "It was like putting on a new cloak . . . ten years ago I went into therapy because I felt depressed, empty, jittery. . . . I realized that my life was a succession of evenings without a future, that I could not get close to anybody permanently. I got depressed and had the crying jag for which I went into therapy. Now, ten years later, I'm faced with the same problems. I haven't solved anything in ten years."

Susan indicated that in one analytic situation she did not get anywhere for several months because of the fear that her analyst would not approve of her. She therefore intellectualized and covered up her own inner experience.

By the tenth session, Susan was experiencing anxiety and some beginning of hope of success in treatment and decided to try sessions three times a week. By the sixteenth session, she reported beginning to feel vulnerable, as she had when she was a youngster and before she had any therapy. By the fortieth session, Susan stated, "my problems have moved from my brains to my guts."

Some of Susan's Outstanding Patterns

Susan attempts to cut off feelings by denial. This is successful up to a point, after which there is either a breakthrough of intense feeling (anxiety and depression or, less frequently, elation) or an impulsive action. The impulse acted on is frequently partially or totally blocked from consciousness, so that Susan comes out with a vague feeling both of what she has done and of why she has done it.

Basic to Susan's interpersonal functioning is her lack of clear-cut feeling of self. She feels most comfortable in a relationship in which the other person sets the expectations for her, defining a role she can fill. Being without such a relationship provokes anxiety because Susan cannot function if her role is not defined. In addition, without such a relationship, there is no fulfillment of her dependency needs.

In order to find such relationships, Susan approaches people in terms of their needs. Her thinking seems to go: "If successful in winning approval, I am wonderful and to be adored. If I am unsuccessful, I am nothing. I feel anxious and overwhelmed and I will do anything to win your acceptance of me." Once in the relationship, she seems to fear closeness and to set up some distance. Susan does not express feelings or needs directly; rather, she subtly manipulates the relationship. She frequently arranges it so that she is the helpless victim, which justifies her rage and hurt and evokes sympathy and concern from others.

Diagnostically, Susan is best classified as a character neurotic. Her primary defenses are projection, denial, and intellectualization. When these fail, Susan's underlying characterological depression, diffuse anxiety states, and hysteric lability emerge.

Susan spent a total of thirty-two months in this analysis, including three summer vacations. I saw her twice a week for sessions 1–10, three times a week for sessions 11–173, twice a week for sessions 174–248, and once a week for sessions 249–263. Except for the first few sessions, she used the couch through session 215; she sat up for sessions 216–263.

Susan's Continuous Dream Life

The following pages contain the dreams Susan reported during the course of her psychoanalysis, in chronological sequence.

Some of the clinical process of the session within which the dream occurred is given. Unfortunately, I have not been able to provide this consistently, since during the early sessions I recorded verbatim only the dreams. Later I endeavored to make notes of the whole session, which I could do fairly accurately as Susan was a slow and precise talker; interviews 63–227 are based on verbatim written transcripts. Sessions 228–263 are tape-recorded. This is why the early sessions have little clinical material.

The rationale for presenting as much as possible of the clinical process directly relevant to the dreams is that, according to my general assumption, present happenings in the patient's life, and the analytic relationship in particular, strongly influence the dream life.

Dream 1 / *Session 10*
[This is the first dream mentioned in analysis. It occurred two nights before Susan's initial interview, when the decision to start treatment with me had already been made.]
I was in the process of changing the color of my hair. I was trying to be blonde. It looked quite dreadful. Then I tried

to dye it red. When I was nearly through, I looked into the mirror and was horrified. I desperately wanted to revert to my own original hair color but I could not. I awoke frustrated and anxious.

Susan saw the dream as referring to "the idea of going back into analysis. I have a lot of feeling about change, wanting a change, being afraid of anything more than a superficial change . . . being afraid of what the outcome might be . . . deliberately becoming a redhead would be taking an ascendant action. And this I am afraid to do. It would mean pushing myself and this terrifies me. . . . I've never been ascendant in my whole life. I'm afraid to try. For me, the grade is either one hundred or zero."

I was impressed by the pervasive anxiety and feelings of futility that Susan's dream had indicated. She seemed to be trying to tell me that she did not know who she was as a person and was desperate about whether, in the analysis, she could return to or find her original self.

Dream 2 / *Session 32*
[A recurrent childhood nightmare]:
I would have these nightmares of semi-human characters who walked on two legs and had faces covered with hair like animals. They were called "busses." They lived in family units. I would somehow wander into the area of the city they lived in. I would usually have some kind of warning but not heed it. The most frightening thing about these creatures was that they used words that always had an opposite than the usual meaning. I would awaken terrified.

Susan felt the dream reflected that "as a child I lived among people who said one thing and meant another . . . a father who was inconsistent and could get angry or smile for the same reason . . . a mother who said I could get close to her but I could really not."

This lack of directness in communication must be Susan's way of relating. She seemed to me to be concerned with the fear that people are monstrous, only semi-human—including herself.

Dream 3 / *Session 34*
[An adolescent dream recalled from age fifteen]:
I was necking with this boy. I thought my parents were upstairs. My father came in and got angry. He ordered the boy out of the house. Then my father turned to me and was really furious. As a punishment for what I did, he forced me to have intercourse with him. I protested. But he in a fury insisted that I straddle him while he sat on a chair. We had intercourse. I woke up in a cold sweat.

Susan was vague in interpreting the dream. She felt it related to her never having associated sex with pleasure or enjoyment, to her seeing sex as a burdensome act with the primary purpose of begetting children. She felt that somehow feelings about her father strongly influenced how she related to all men.

What struck me was that Susan had only a thin censorship in this Oedipal situation. She seemed to be suggesting that emotional intimacy is unpleasant and she saw herself as the helpless one upon whom this was inflicted.

The question posed is why she was so afraid of her sensuality, vitality, and impulsiveness.

Dream 4 / *Session 37*
[First dream while in analysis]:
It was a mixed-up dream. During the beginning of the dream I was going somewhere with a girl friend, someone I knew in high school. At one point in the dream there was some kind of physical contact—I think a kiss, though I'm not sure—and in the dream I had a real immediate response, a violent physical reaction. This disturbs me because I have never been attracted to women before. In the dream, someone was going to wash my underwear, probably the girl friend. I took off my pants and they were sopping wet with excitement.

Then there was this fellow I knew in college. I didn't

know where we were going or what we were doing. He began to kiss and fondle me on the street and said he would love to have intercourse with me. So we started to take our clothes off in the street—it was dark. We did a weird dance, I following his movements. Then I realized how inappropriate it was to be naked in the street. I tried desperately to get inside, to get away from this public place where I was totally naked. I awoke feeling anxious.

Susan saw this as representing a form of self-love, for the girl friend was also named Susan. It represented also the fact that in sex she is passive, is chosen; that she is guilty about sex; that she tries to relate to men through sex.

After she left, I made some notes of my own questions: Does the woman who washes Susan's underwear represent her mother? Is the gist of the dream that her need for warmth or tenderness from her mother is displaced on these exhibitionistic relationships with men?

I wondered at the deep, unintegrated impulsivity on the one hand, and at Susan's overt façade, her compliant behavior and haste in getting away from being seen, on the other. I noted that the man started doing the weird dance and that Susan followed and patterned herself after him.

Dream 5 / Session 43

The dream involved Irwin, and I was trying to get something that belonged to me from his apartment. We were civil to each other; there was no overt hostility. It was important to me that he think well of me.

Then another woman entered the picture. She was Irwin's fiancée and I wanted her to like me, too. I wanted her to see me as reasonable. I tried very hard to be sweet to both. I was still going through drawers looking for whatever it was when I woke up; I was looking for some information I had left in the apartment.

Most important, I wanted Irwin's fiancée to have a good opinion of me.

Susan saw this dream as indicating her need for acceptance by others; to feel safe by making certain the other person is not angry at her.

And, I added to myself, a denial of her own needs, and feelings in order to win approval. Susan defines herself by the way she relates to others; for example, Irwin and his fiancée. (They probably represented her parents.) This reminded me of the child's desire to please so as to gain security, and the confusion about what this is or how to get it.

Dream 6 / Session 46

Susan had a vague dream about Leah and Morris, who are married, breaking off, and Susan was glad. (Leah is a close friend of Susan's.)

To this, Susan associated the adolescent dream of intercourse with her father. She voiced feelings of competition to all women; hostility to her mother for her (Susan's) feeling that she has always lost out; a desire to get love from her father and to express hostility to her mother by winning his love. She felt there was a lot here she did not understand.

Susan was aware that she gets involved with men who are unobtainable or are interested in a girl friend of hers. Leah is a close friend of Susan's and Susan was tempted to involve herself with Morris.

Dream 7 / Session 53

I had this dream. I was moving into another apartment. It was something appalling to realize that I was renting an apartment, sight unseen, on the basic assumption that it could not be as bad as the present place. I walked in and saw all the plumbing in the middle of the apartment. This turned out O.K. because I had entered the wrong door. Then, from the correct vantage point, the place looked very nice. Then I was disturbed that I did not have enough furniture inside the apartment and had no money to buy more.

I was then visited by someone from the stock market, a securities broker. He was telling me of news of someone who was going to get a divorce, someone I did not know. I was feeling glad to hear of the news of the divorce, but this was a sweet kind of pleasure which I could not express openly. I felt guilty about my pleasure.

The visitor stretched out on a couch as if he owned it. I did not know him, and yet I stroked his testicles. I don't know why. It happened without any conversation and as if it was expected of me.

Susan felt the dream communicated the following themes: that she was entering into analysis "sight unseen" because nothing could be as miserable as her existence was then; that analysis was not as threatening as she experienced it initially. She saw the visitor as a friend of her husband's and expressed relief that she could recognize and express in her dream the hostility she feels toward Irwin and his girl friend and also that she could recognize her guilt over the expression of hostility. Seeing sex as a mode of relating to men by giving them pleasure, she at last, hesitantly, indicated "that maybe the visitor is you . . . that I'm bringing my typical way of relating into the analysis."

It occurred to me that the plumbing in the middle of the apartment referred to her inner problems. Looking at the apartment from another angle, with the plumbing out of sight, is her denial, her refusal to see. Her not having enough furniture may reflect a fear of her own inadequate resources.

It struck me again that the pleasure she derived from somebody else's divorce, and the guilt feelings her pleasure aroused, might refer to her relief when she herself got divorced.

As to "stroking his testicles," I assumed that I was the visitor and that she would try to please me by being a good patient.

Dream 8 / *Session 60*
I had a discussion with a man about investing in the stock market. I gave him all my money for this. Then I searched for a woman to clean my apartment. My next-door neighbor, a man, took over to find one. I came home and found my neighbor in my apartment, asleep.

The cleaning woman came in and started to act in a very disturbed manner. She wanted me to give her my sweater. I was afraid of her. She threw me on the floor. Then I pulled off my green sweater. At one point, as the cleaning woman paced, she straddled my body. As she was walking over my head, she said, "You're lucky I didn't piss all over you." But I did not ask her to return the key to my apartment or not to come again, because I was afraid.

Then I remembered that stocks were bad and they were about to go into a depression, and I wanted to make some arrangements. Oh yes, the woman had already taken another sweater while I was not there.

Ann, a policeman, and I were seated. The policeman said I should get the key back and not to worry about anything the woman stole because the government would reimburse me. Just then the madwoman walked in at that point and just sat down in a very relaxed manner. She had a small round case with a key. In her presence the policeman insisted that I give him the details about the sweaters. I told the policeman but I stuttered because I feared the madwoman. As I gave the description of the green sweater, the policeman asked the woman if she stole it. She casually said yes, that she intended to return the sweater. As she took out the sweater, she took out a gun, too, and aimed it at the policeman. She pulled the trigger but there was no ammunition. As the madwoman and the policeman wrestled, I woke up. I was in a cold sweat.

Susan felt the policeman was me and the analysis. She felt that she was herself and also the madwoman; that the madwoman reflected her childlike view of mother when crossed. The green sweater was given to her by Irwin as a present. The other sweater belonged to mother and Susan had forgotten to return it twice. The keys referred to the keys to mother's house which she had never returned. Ann was a friend of long standing who was maternal toward her.

Susan saw the dream as representing her fear of her mother's anger if she did not comply. "If my mother ever let go with anger, she was like a madwoman. . . . I was terrified of her all my childhood. She could jerk and be furious at the littlest thing." Susan indicated that the affect she experienced in the dream "is similar to the feelings I had as a child when my mother was full of rage. It's also the feeling I have now when I have to relate socially."

I was impressed by the intensity of rage and helplessness tied in with Susan's relationship with her mother, and I wondered whether Susan's fear of contact and her masochistic tendencies stem from this.

Regarding the crazy woman's way of relating: Is Susan afraid that she is crazy in the same way?

I was glad that the analysis was sufficiently supportive to allow Susan to look at these deep-seated childhood feelings. Does she experience the hostile, mad, unacceptable part of herself as wrestling with the analysis?

Dream 9 / Session 64

Susan: I had a dream while I was visiting home. I dreamed I was living with my girl friend. Two distant relatives on my mother's side, my aunt and cousin, visited. I always felt a discomfort with them as a child. I had the same discomfort in the dream. I was worried about how they would interact with other friends of mine due a little later, that the relatives might not accept them. After my friends arrived, I was panicked how things would go, what my relatives would think of me. I was afraid my friends would just not be acceptable to them. I woke up anxious.

Dr. C.: Any ideas on the dream?

Susan: It has something to do with meeting requirements and getting approval. Come to think of it, I had several vague dreams I can't remember about meeting requirements while home [in Boston].

Dr. C.: Meeting requirements and getting approval.

Susan: I had a peculiar feeling in the dream. A jumpy kind of feeling.

Dr. C.: Ever had this feeling before?

Susan: Whenever I went to visit this aunt and cousin, I

Susan's Eight Card Redrawing Test Protocol

The Eight Card Redrawing Test (8CRT) [1] is a projective technique based on a series of eight figure drawings.

The subject is given a pad of eight onionskins and told to "make a picture of a whole person." After he draws the figure on the bottom onionskin, the next transparent sheet of the pad is turned down over the first. The subject now sees his first drawing through the blank sheet before him and is told: "You may do anything you like with this figure of a person. You may add to it, take away from it, change it, or leave it alone. Only, again make a picture of a whole person." This procedure is repeated on the remaining six onionskins. Each time, a cardboard insert is placed under the last completed drawing, so that the subject sees only his most recent effort as a stimulus drawing.

The completed 8CRT protocol consists of the series of eight drawings which reflect the subject's self-concept and his pattern of defenses as environmental-interpersonal stimuli (the blank page) and intrapsychic pressures (the preceding stimulus drawing) interact. The total 8CRT protocol reflects the subject's approach to life situations and to himself.

I am presenting the drawings Susan made in the fifth week of her analysis and giving my impressions of them, based on extensive experience with the 8CRT and with projective techniques in general.

Drawing 1. Susan depicts a fantasy-dominated, ill-defined, chronically anxious woman. She is fearful that her fantasy life will spill over into her behavior despite her attempts at encapsulation. She experiences herself as incapable of coping with environmental-interpersonal impingements.

As I went through drawings 2 through 8, my overall impression was that Susan, when faced with interpersonal pressures, turns to these characteristic modes of coping: intellectual control, avoidance, pulling back from stimulation, narcissistic defenses expressed in posing for the world and playing a charming feminine role, negativism, and hiding what she experiences from herself and the world.

Drawing 2. Susan demonstrates her capable intellectual critical faculties, which can quickly modify the persona she shows the world into a more appropriate social form. The figure is better contained than the first, is less anxious, but has much more of a manikin quality. Susan is retreating from her own stimulus drawing (her intrapsychic processes) and must make herself empty in face and body. It is as if she experienced herself as nothing but a boundary line between an inner vacuum and the environment.

Drawing 3. Susan again avoids following through or elaborating on any inner process. She negatively and defensively turns from her own inner stimulation, presenting herself to the world in the role of charming, graceful, narcissistic feminity—avoidant, uncontactable. This represents a mode of functioning without giving herself away, without revealing to herself or to the world what she feels is her unacceptable inner self.

Drawing 4. Susan shows an ill-defined self-concept, still covered by a façade of sensuous, posing feminity, coupled with a helpless, dependent role. In actuality, without truly experiencing herself, Susan is withdrawing from environmental-interpersonal contact, is experiencing herself as smaller and the life space as more engulfing.

Drawing 5. Susan continues the role she has established for herself; she knows no other way of relating or experiencing herself. She cannot move, *not* because of rigidity (there are indications of considerable flexibility in the protocol), but because she does not know herself and fears this unknown self, so that all interaction becomes a struggle to maintain at least some persona. Ending this role-playing would arouse great anxiety. She would then have to face what she fears seeing: her inner, fluid, undifferentiated, amorphous self-concept.

Drawings 6, 7, and 8. Susan continues the same pattern of avoiding relatedness to self and to others. She has literally crawled into a corner and cannot move from there, cannot get out. She is terrified to know or show what she is feeling. She is caught and immobilized; she cannot break out of her isolation because she fears her inner self and any true relatedness to others which will expose how she really experiences herself.

Susan's defenses are strong. The immediate pullback from drawing 1 is quickly and effectively carried out. Susan avoids, denies, withdraws, and plays roles—but does not crumble.

The most important clinical impression the protocol left with me is that Susan cannot tolerate the anxiety around her self-concept. She withdraws from experiencing herself or truly relating to others. There is much less anxiety and much more narcissism and exhibitionism in drawings 5–8 than in drawings 1–4. This suggests to me that Susan avoids anxiety by being cut off from herself and from meaningful relatedness to others, by fleeing intimacy before it can be established, and by resorting to an unrelated feminine role-playing façade.

[1] For further information on the test, consult the monograph "A New Approach to Figure Drawing" by Leopold Caligor, Ph.D. (Springfield, Ill.: Charles C Thomas, 1957).

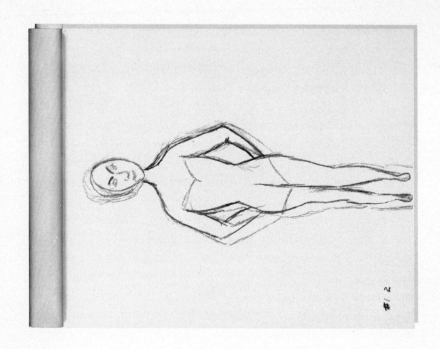

#2

#1

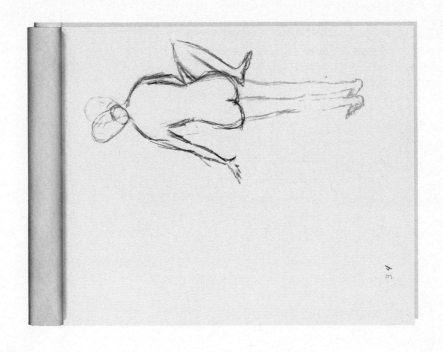

34

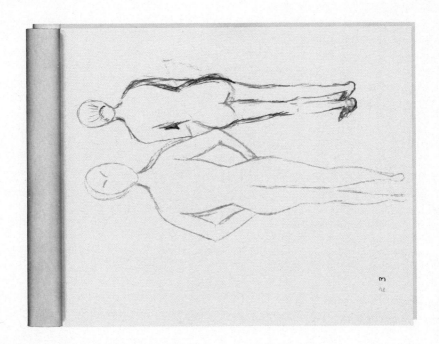

23

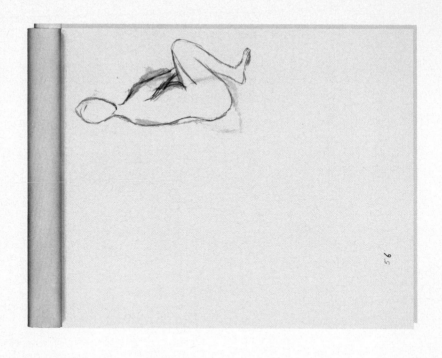

56

45

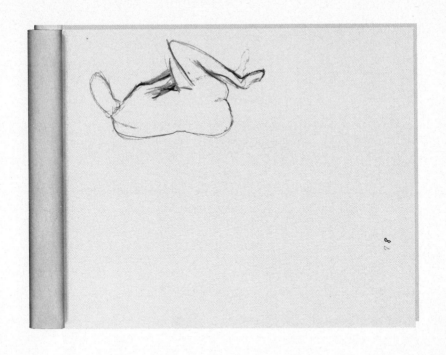

78

79

felt gauche, awkward. This feeling came back in the dream Friday night.

Dr. C.: Ever have these feelings anywhere else?

Susan: I have these same feelings in any new social setting where no one will talk to me or I feel I will not have anything to say. The same feelings with those relatives. (*Silence.*) During my childhood and adolescence I always felt inferior to these people. My parents, especially my mother, felt this way. I felt unliked by them, felt unwanted, a misfit. I really felt acutely unhappy in that setting. (*Silence.*) Today I feel similarly in a group and I try to fade into the wallpaper. (*Silence.*)

Dr. C.: When you think of the dream, does anything that happened that day come to mind?

Susan: (*Silence.*) Funny, I had this dream after my talk with my mother about the money for the clothes.[4] Now why did that come to mind? (*Silence.*) Last night in class I had these feelings and fears that I would be called upon to answer a question and would show up a social failure.

Dr. C.: How do you mean a social failure?

Susan: Not being able to make chit-chat, looking foolish to others, feeling ashamed of the impression I make. (*Silence.*)

Dr. C.: I wonder why this comes to mind?

Susan: (*Silence.*) We were talking about my mother and this popped up. (*Silence.*) You know, it's the same feeling in the dream, in childhood with my aunt and cousin, and now socially. I felt inferior socially with them, and now too. During my childhood I had the feeling of being ashamed of my parents, especially my mother. I saw them, especially her, as socially inferior, that others would judge me inferior like her. It's like in the dream when I was ashamed of my friends; I think they were parent substitutes. (*Silence.*) You have no

---

[4] Susan is referring to her setting up a situation in which her mother pleads for the opportunity to buy clothes for her—which her parents cannot afford. Susan has become aware of the implicit manipulation, hostility, and contempt.

idea of the shame I felt at the impression my mother made, talking, talking, no awareness what others were saying. It's a feeling that even now I have difficulty in accepting: my mother just never measured up in the eyes of my friends. I felt that I too would soon appear to be not as good as her. (*Silence.*) What comes to mind is the poor-paying jobs I would get, how resentful I would feel. Yet I always felt that soon my worthlessness would be discovered because I had nothing to offer. (*Silence.*) Until recently I've sidestepped any connection between how I feel about myself socially and any negative thoughts, no matter how fleeting, I felt toward my mother.

Dream 10 / *Session 67*

Susan: I wrote my mother a letter and returned the money she gave me for the clothes. I gave her some plausible reasons. (*Silence.*) I feel good about it; somehow, it's breaking a pattern with my mother. (*Silence.*) I wonder what gifts mean to me. (*Silence.*) I've been thinking about a trip to Europe.

Dr. C.: I wonder why you introduced this.

Susan: I guess I'm aware that going to Europe is an escape. This is typical of me. (*Silence.*) I had a dream last night. I was listening to the radio, to an old soap opera. Suddenly, at the end of the program, at a crucial point, the announcer said: the program will be set x years from now. I realized that the now children would be adults—a tremendous gap. I realized that this would be dishonest, an avoidance of the real problems. (*Silence.*) You know, I'm starting to realize that I do really care for Lois and Bob [friends of Susan's], that until now I've thought myself incapable of caring.

Dr. C.: How do you mean, incapable of caring?

Susan: Taking from Lois and Bob and giving nothing in return . . . taking gifts from my mother and giving nothing in return.

Dr. C.: Taking gifts from your mother and giving nothing in return.

Susan: Part of me wants the gifts for practical reasons: I need the money. Part of me does not want to take it because I give my mother nothing in return and I'm using her, though she [mother] does not see it that way. Part of me wants gifts from her for less clear reasons. (*Silence.*) I think of a necklace I got as a gift from my mother. (*Silence.*) Now, why do I say "from my mother"? My father worked overtime for the money . . . he picked the necklace carefully. Yet I feel the necklace came solely from my mother. It really is rather unaesthetic. Yet I wear it daily and it makes me feel good. I wouldn't change it for anything [*said slowly and sensitively*]. (*Silence.*) I'm beginning to think that maybe my father did love, maybe does care for me in his own way.

Dr. C.: That's a touching story about the necklace.

Susan: (*near tears*): (*Said very slowly.*) Yes. It's touching in its own way. In their own way, I suppose they care.

Dr. C.: Yes. (*Silence.*)

Susan: During most of my life, I could not stand to see others criticize them. I keep swinging to extremes from total coldness and no love for me to their really caring and giving. I guess neither one is right. (*Silence.*)

Dr. C.: Tell me more about gifts.

Susan: I felt that my mother gave them and that my father had nothing to do with it.

Dr. C.: How come you had this idea?

Susan: My mother helped me form this picture by coaching me to not mention my mother's extravagant spending on me, as my father would be angry. I felt my father did not want me to have these things. I'm becoming aware that I have distorted the picture and cut my father out of being giving or loving, that just my mother gave to me. Actually, I hated [*said with emphasis*] the clothes she bought for me. There were constant conflicts between us. She never approved of my independent purchases and nagged, nagged. She continued as long as possible to shop for me.

Dr. C.: How long?

Susan: Until past college years.

Dr. C.: You mean she had this power over you.

Susan: Nnnoo . . . Actually, by that time, I was so demoralized and afraid of doing the wrong thing, making the wrong purchase, that I feared any independent judgment. (*Silence.*)

Dr. C.: What do you make of your dream?

Susan: Maybe I'm saying that this (what we've talked about) is an old soap opera. I don't know . . . (*Silence.*)

Dr. C.: Could be. Maybe you're also saying that, to use your words in your dream, that you are being dishonest with yourself and have avoided looking at many real problems. Problems in the present.

Susan: (*Silence.*) Yes. Maybe you're the announcer. I do run away very easily.

Dream 11 / *Session 72*

Susan reported two dreams in the same night. She didn't awaken between them.

In the first, she was graying. In the second, she was relating to a married man. With reference to these two dreams, she described feeling that she was getting older and time was passing; and that she always picked on a man who was inaccessible to her. She tied this last in with the relationship between her mother, her father, and herself, in which she played down her mother, indirectly competed for her father's love, and always felt she had lost out. She believed she was making the same kind of mistake with men—and this reflected her relationship with her father. That is, she saw him as inaccessible and as representing the fact that she always lost out in competition with another woman for a man.

Susan characterized the men she had been involved with in the past as having little to give her other than sex. All had difficulties with women; all had severe personality problems; none had any future for her. She was aware that she saw them out of loneliness, a need for sex, and she realized that this did not just happen to her, that she played a part in setting up these relationships. "If the man is not for me, I knock myself out with a lot of anxiety in order to win him."

At the end Susan was beginning to have some anxious and hesitant awareness that she chose these limited men because of fear of closeness; that it was easier and less anxiety-provoking for her to feel lonely and to experience herself as an unattractive wallflower.

Dream 12 / Session 85

Susan: I had a dream last night. It involved a dog that jumped on me. He showed his teeth and I was not afraid of him.

Susan felt the dream reflected that perhaps she was less afraid of attack by others, less fearful perhaps of showing her own anger.

She went on to state that of late she was aware of feeling less afraid; that when someone extended himself to her, this did not mean he would necessarily attack her; that somehow she felt less vulnerable to attack.

Dream 13 / Session 109

Susan: I saw Morris [5] last night. And I'm becoming aware that sex is getting better, that I feel more. This is quite different from the first time Morris and I went to bed. (*Silence.*) I have often thought of that night and there is something frightening about it. (*Silence.*)

Dr. C.: In what way frightening?

Susan (*hesitantly*): I've often thought just what happened or how it happened and I can't remember any of the details. All I can recall is being in bed with Morris, I have no awareness of our getting undressed, or what was said or if anything was said, or how long we stayed in bed. I don't

[5] Morris is the husband of Leah, Susan's friend. Morris and Susan had started an affair four weeks before, which was still going on. During the analytic sessions since the start of the affair, Susan showed a wide range of reactions: (1) glee at having defeated Leah, no guilt, feeling euphoric, strong, victorious; (2) bursts of depression and diffuse anxiety. Not being able to think clearly or face the true intent of her actions or her own destructive self-image, Susan attempted to plead helplessness: she had no choice, she was at the mercy of her sexual needs.

recall any sensation other than pain. Pain and a feeling of victory, as if I strove for this and brought it off. Morris did not stay the whole night. The next morning I felt ashamed and even thought it was a dream, it had so little reality for me. During the intercourse, I kept worrying about the pain, of not being able to experience pleasure, of being frigid. Yet there was this intense feeling of victory; of surprise, pain, victory.

Dr. C.: Surprise, pain, victory. Anything come to mind?

Susan: (*Silence.*) (*Is embarrassed and squirms.*)

Dr. C.: Any thoughts?

Susan: I feel uncomfortable. For some reason I was thinking of that dream where my father has intercourse with me. I had these feelings there, too. (*Silence.*) You know, I remember more of that dream that I had forgotten. My father comes in and sees me necking with the boy. My father says nothing and stalks out. The boy then opens his fly and takes out his penis. My father comes back and sees this. My father gets furious and orders the boy out of the house. "So that is what you want," he said furiously. He made me have intercourse with him and I protested. But he exerted his authority. I remained dressed in the dream. He plunked me down in the chair on his lap and had me straddle him. I protested all the time. But I felt compelled to obey his command. Then I woke up while having intercourse in the dream, feeling miserable. But I had the same feelings of victory, pain, and surprise. (*Silence.*) It's the same thing with Morris and the dream: of my being the chosen one, the desired one, whether over Leah or my mother. (*Silence.*)

Dr. C.: What about the chair position?

Susan: I knew two people would lie down to have intercourse. The way he had me straddle him on the chair was the correct position for chair intercourse. I must have seen something somewhere. I must be blotting out something just as I did the first contact with Morris. (*Silence.*) Sitting up, straddling with my legs apart, has always been a favorite position. (*Silence.*) I used to have intercourse in a chair with Irwin, using that position, before we were married. (*Silence.*)

Dr. C.: When you think of that position, what comes to mind?

Susan: When I masturbate. When I masturbate, I sit on the toilet seat, because with orgasm, some urine is released. Letting go with an orgasm is like peeing all over the place for me. (*Silence.*) I recall the dream with my mother standing over me with her legs spread and saying, "You're lucky I don't pee all over you." (*Silence.*) I'm aware of going through life repressing a lot of hostility. (*Silence.*) Funny, I also think of when I found out about intercourse. When I asked my mother, I was seated on the toilet seat. I was shocked. I thought intercourse horrible and a punishment. As a child I always thought of sex as urination, slimy, terrible. (*Silence.*) I guess in some way I still feel this way. Otherwise, I would feel more pleasure, less pain. (*Silence.*)

Dr. C.: What do you make of the additional parts of the dream you remembered?

Susan: I brought back my father, as if to continue something with him.

Dr. C.: Any ideas why?

Susan: (*Silence.*) It's like continuing something with him to shut out the boy. (*Silence.*) Maybe I was afraid to get involved with boys, so I brought my father back. It's like the second-date situation. Maybe I'm afraid of getting involved.

Dr. C.: (*Hour is near end.*) Could be. And in the first telling of the dream, as with Morris the first night, you shut out how you had helped set up the situation. The parts you did recall involved things happening to you without your having an active part in them.

Susan: I never thought of that. (*Silence.*) It's true.

Dream 14 / *Session 114*

Susan: I had a dream last night. My apartment was very filthy. I was on the floor, nude. When I got up, there was about an inch of dirt—no, it was clean sawdust—clinging all over me. I was nude. Suddenly Morris was with me. Then we were dressed and walking along the street, then riding in a taxi. He put his hand on my breast. I felt disturbed. I moaned, "It's too soon; it's too soon; I'm not ready yet." I awoke feeling anxious.

Dr. C.: What do you make of the dream?

Susan: I've given it some thought. I see this as a conflict between the part of me that sees myself as filthy; the part that is Leah's friend. And the other part which wants sex and closeness with Morris. (*Silence.*)

Dr. C.: What do you make of his putting his hand on your breast, and your feeling it is too soon, you are not yet ready?

Susan: Maybe I'm saying that I'm not prepared for this and it is too soon. It's again a conflict between what ought to be and what I want to do . . . and being disturbed about having to make the choice. (*Silence.*) I have been toying with the possibility of entering a relationship without fear of closeness. [*Here Susan spoke of wanting closeness but not being able to attain it because she never experienced closeness with her father.*] (*Silence.*)

Dr. C.: What are you feeling?

Susan: I must admit I feel rather complacent right now. I have no feelings at all. Actually, I feel great and that all is O.K. I guess the analysis must be taking.

Dr. C.: Do you feel you understand your basic problems, that you've worked them through?

Susan: (*Facial expression drops its cheerful aspect.*) I felt a wave of anxiety when you asked me that. (*Silence.*) No. I'm aware I'm running away. That I'm not looking at the Leah issue, that the relationship with Morris has no future. Somewhere inside me I feel pretty lousy about Leah. But at this point I feel gratified and smug, like a satisfied child who does not want to look at what is going on.

Dr. C.: (*Silence.*) Like a satisfied child who does not want to look at what is going on.

Susan: Doctor, I'm anxious but relieved that you didn't let me pull that old stuff again. I'm pretty talented at kidding myself and so good that I can convince others. I want you to know this. I'm glad you do.[6]

[6] Susan terminated her affair with Morris after session 118, seven

Dream 15 / *Session 147*

Susan: I awoke at 5 a.m. yesterday. I had this imaginary conversation with David,[7] with a lot of hostility toward him. . . . Now I'm wondering if I didn't go through this [imaginary conversation] to show you I won't be like this always. Maybe this was an effort to please you. . . . I'll do what I want when I want to. I do have a right to tell you what I feel, to ask you anything [*all said with some rage and hurt*]. Then I fell asleep and had this dream.

David and I were having intercourse. I wanted intercourse with David in the chair facing him. I initiated and we had intercourse. I recall the adolescent dream of intercourse with my father. That had a feeling of punishment and of terror. This dream was less terrifying. Actually, it was pleasant and a relief. I see the dream ties in with my fantasies before I fell asleep. Maybe I'm saying that I want to initiate when I want to, to express what I feel without fear. This is what I want.

Dream 16 / *Session 153*

The flow of topics this time was as follows. With reference to dependence-independence, Susan described in detail how her mother would not let her be independent, make decisions for herself. However, to the world Susan appeared to be independent. Her mother would proudly comment about Susan at age nine: "Susan travels alone." Susan felt that this was a front to cover her inner feelings of dependence. On the surface, she looked independent and in revolt against her mother, yet she really felt bound and submitting. For example, her mother said to her that she would not like Susan to have intercourse until she was thirty, if she was not married before then. Susan thought, "Aha, I'll wait until I'm twenty-eight."

With reference to sex, Susan still projected considerably to

---

weeks after the start of the affair. She was able to work through her destructive way of relating to Leah, and her own destructive "animal-like" self-image.

[7] Susan met a young psychiatrist, David, shortly after the affair with Morris ended, and had been seeing him steadily for seven weeks.

her mother. Her mother painted a picture of sex as nonsensuous and painful. When Susan first had intercourse with Irwin at twenty-three, sex was painful; she felt no sensitivity in her breasts when they were touched. She described in detail how her mother made her feel that sex was an attack upon the woman by the man, something a woman must suffer. When Susan was eight, her mother said, "And now you know [about sex]. Now if anything happens to you, it will be your own fault." Susan evinced great rage toward her mother.

At that point Susan recalled the adolescent dream of intercourse with her father. She felt that more than the idea of sex was involved there. "Rather than sex, I wanted my mother out of the picture and my father to be with me on a loving basis, that somehow I did not have the closeness with my father and sex was my idea of having closeness with a man.

"All my life, until recently, I have gritted my teeth with sex and said, 'I *will* enjoy it.' I'll show you, Mother. But I never did enjoy it. Instead, I had orgasms and peeing mixed up. The revolt against my mother, but the submission; that even when I outwardly revolted against my mother's values, I clung to them internally."

Dream 17 / Session 154

Susan reported that she had two dreams that did not awaken her. These were:

I was wearing a necklace of a string of beads. I kept fingering them until it broke. It was a new string of beads. I felt upset. My friends were vaguely present. I don't know what it means.

Another night, I was dreaming about sexual intercourse. Several doctors were present. One of them was Ann's doctor. The experiment concerned me and my own family doctor. This doctor and his wife were asleep in one room. In the course of this experiment, this doctor and I were to have some sexual relations but through some mechanical device, since he did not physically leave his wife. I felt uneasy about doing wrong and being unfaithful to David. It was also important that my doctor find his sex with me satisfactory.

There was this mechanical gadget that went from me to the doctor, something like a cystoscope. The next morning, I saw the doctor come out of his bedroom in pajama tops and no bottoms. I noticed his penis was abnormally small. I did not feel disturbed when I awoke and remembered the dream.

With reference to the first dream, Susan had no ideas. She wanted to look at the second dream, so we set the first dream aside until some future date.

In the second dream, Susan saw the doctor and his wife as her mother and father or Morris and Leah. The cystoscope, she feels, is her way of saying that sex between David and her is mechanical and painful as a cystoscopy she had undergone had been painful. She saw the dream as her desire to compete and to not compete with another woman, rationalizing sex by connecting it with a scientific experiment.

I emphasized the following two aspects of the second dream: (a) She related by giving the other the gratification. She was underconcerned about her own gratification. She related, that is, through approval, through the need to please the other. (b) Perhaps the reference was to mechanical sex with her doctor, that is, me. She was communicating her fear of relating directly and therefore did it through a mechanical device. Also, was she trying to relate to me by pleasing, by being the cooperative patient?

Dream 18 / Session 155

Susan: I have a lot of physical symptoms tonight. I've made an appointment for a physical checkup tomorrow. But I feel it's psychogenic.

Dr. C.: What kind of physical symptoms do you have?

Susan: Along the urethral tract. Sex and urination are painful.

Dr. C.: What is the history of this urethral pain?

Susan: I had it the first time after Irwin and I broke up. The first night we decided to break it off, I committed adultery with someone in my office. (*Silence.*) Also, I had it while awaiting a letter from the graduate school where I applied. I was turned down. (*Silence*.) I somehow have always associated the urethral pain with the marriage ending. (*Silence*.) I think all this is related in some way to rejection. But bite back your feelings and don't show them.

Dr. C.: Bite back your feelings and don't show them.

Susan: You know, I've told you I have a bad teeth condition. My dentist tells me this is due to a form of tooth grinding all the time, and that this is most detrimental. I think of my mother's early advice: "Grit your teeth and hold your chin up." (*Silence*.)

Dr. C.: What are you trying to say?

Susan: There is much hostility I have to David that I have been trying to ignore. (*Silence*.) And yet he is so understanding. I do enjoy being with him. (*Silence*.) For some reason, the dream, the one with the beads, comes to mind. I think I'm saying that if I look carefully, if I finger the beads, the relationship will go up in smoke, maybe. That I haven't taken an honest look at what my feelings are. (*Silence*.) Maybe I'm afraid that if I look, I will tear the beads, the relationship apart.

Dream 19 / *Session 156*

Susan: I had this dream last night. Janet and I were in my mother's living room. Janet, is an old, good friend who acts maternally toward me. I felt that some conflict arose between what David wanted and Janet wanted. It had something to do with David and me going some place. But Janet already had reservations for her and me. I felt disturbed, torn inside. (*Silence*.) I see this as my concern about what others think, and not what I want. Letting the other take over for me. (*Silence*.)

The dream was discussed as a representation of her conflict, her desire to run away, to retreat from the problems posed by the relationship with David. She and I noted a fear of the new way of relating, which made adult demands for relatedness, adult femininity, and hence created much anxiety. She preferred the old, safe, familiar way of relating by being the dependent child in relation to mother, feeling and saying this was not what she wanted, yet unconsciously being pulled into it again and again.

Dream 20 / *Session 159*

Susan: I remember a dream I had last night. I remember biting into something and something came loose in the upper right part of my mouth. I asked my mother if I had false teeth in my mouth. She said no. Then I realized all my fillings had come loose and lumped together. I asked my mother if they were gold or silver fillings. My mother said silver. I thought, it will cost a lot because it will be replaced by gold. I felt no sensation, no feeling, no anxiety. The only feeling I had was relief when my mother told me that I did not have false teeth. (*Silence.*)

Dr. C.: Anything come to mind that happened yesterday?

Susan: Yes. I ate a salt-water taffy in the office and I lost half a filling when I bit into it. I went to see my dentist and he put more gold in my mouth. This happened a few weeks ago. Yesterday my teeth ached. (*Silence.*) And I think now of my dental trouble due to clenching my teeth. (*Silence.*) I have thought about the dream. I think it's related to the analytic work. That analysis is expensive. In the dream I knew I would do it and did not mind. Maybe I'm talking about hurrying along here and getting to a point where there's not so much to do. (*Silence.*) I had a feeling of hope because I still had my own teeth; that is, they were not false teeth. That though I need personality repairs, I am not hopeless, false. It's gratifying that now I feel I don't have to put on an act for anyone's benefit. There's a feeling of relief that silver, not gold, came loose, that some of the good work was sticking in me, and that I have to replace the bad aspects of my previous failures in analysis. A lot of very old silver fillings have been falling out and will have to be replaced by gold, my dentist says. (*Silence.*) Not worrying so much about going back but looking ahead, a feeling of optimism. Having said that, I come to a conclusion that not every dream is worth looking at. I have been dreaming a lot of late but have only been able to remember some of the dreams.

Dr. C.: As long as we have enough material to work with, to see what's going on inside.

Susan: (*Silence.*) And now nothing comes to mind at all. Now there's nothing more to talk about. You know, the work we did last hour has, I think, really made a change in my feelings. I feel that Karen is not going to be a problem if she calls tomorrow and I don't feel like a rat because I didn't go out to coffee with her. (*Silence.*)

Dr. C.: Any thoughts?

Susan: I was thinking about Ann. Something lovely has happened to her and Ann is happy. And I feel happy for Ann. I feel good *for* her, and not competitive. (*Silence.*) I met Leah. It felt good being able to tell her I love David but that he is still uncertain. (*Silence.*) The idea of not competing . . . that it's what I feel rather than what Leah thinks. (*Silence.*) Leah is a good friend. At times I feel unhappy about the betrayal with Morris. I feel warmly toward Leah and I do feel some regrets. This is not an overwhelming feeling, though, and I feel I should feel qualms at times . . . that I have not been a loyal friend. I feel my guilt or qualms are understandable but not necessarily neurotic. I have this coming. But it was not conscious maliciousness on my part.

Dr. C.: Your regrets, your guilt, are understandable.

Susan: (*Silence.*) For some reason I feel closeness does not threaten me any more. There's a lot I still don't understand. But I think the major hurdle is behind me. (*Silence.*) I feel I'm coming to a point where I ought to take all I know about myself and try to integrate it. Yet this does not seem crucial to me. Funny, in the last year I'm beginning to feel hope, not only for the present, but the future.

Dream 21 / Session 167

Susan reported the following dream fragment: "There was a man vaguely involved. Somehow, I had to take off my shoes, grit my teeth, and step into a foot bath, like at a swimming pool. The foot bath was full of snot, spit, slime."

Susan felt that the discussion the previous hour had set off this dream.[8] She mentioned that to her the dream reflected a need to get approval from Burt; after all, he dared her to perform fellatio, and this is what he wanted. The feeling afterward was unpleasant, but she could not admit that to him. It was important that Burt think her a good sport.

There was a silence, and then she went on with a number of questions to me, trying to get me to tell her what I wanted her to talk about. I pointed out to her the flow between topics and asked what she made of it. She was able to see in it a desire to please me, to see that she was doing the same thing she had done with Burt and in the dream. She also indicated that the discussion of Burt and fellatio during the last hour had made her anxious. She felt some discomfort with me, wondering how I would respond to it, and was seeking some reassurance or approval.

At the end of the hour she asked if I could change the time for the next appointment. When I told her I could not, she looked momentarily disappointed, then let it pass and said she would see me as scheduled.

Dream 22 / *Session 168*

Susan: Dr. Caligor, I've had one of the nicest weekends with David I've ever had. I don't know what is changing or in process. But I realize I'm not feeling shut out any more [with David]. Also, it's much better in bed. And today, at lunch, I went and bought a scarf for David. I wanted to do it and I did. It was a nice feeling. (*Silence.*) I had a dream before the weekend [the night of our last interview]. I don't remember too much except it involved a relationship with a man I met several times but did not particularly like. He was married in the dream, just as in reality. He and I were arranging appointments. I don't know what interest I had in him, but I felt flattered. He was aroused sexually and could not wait until the next appointment. Then it became apparent

[8] She is referring to her discussion of a sexual affair several years ago with Burt, an old boy friend, in which he dared her to perform fellatio.

that he was losing enthusiasm; and I knew that I would not see him because he would not keep his appointment. He was off with his wife. Basically, I did not care, but was concerned with a loss of face. I don't know if anyone knew of these appointments or not, but I really didn't care for him as a person. One reason the notion of the appointments gave me pleasure was because other women did not have men, and this indicated that I was very desirable. Actually, he and I planned the appointment, but he never came back. It was evident that the future appointments would have been of a sexual nature. (*Silence.*) It was not a disturbing dream. There was a mixed reaction in the dream. Of being stood up. Also, of feeling relief as much as any feeling, as he really isn't interested in me. (*Silence.*) And now I recall I wanted to talk about something else. Sunday night I had a real anxiety attack. It was while David and I were talking about child-birth. We got on to the question of anesthesia. I said I would not want to use anethetics because I would want to experience the birth of my child. At this point I experienced real anxiety—it didn't last very long. (*Silence.*) I felt I was anxious because I was saying to David, "I want to have children—your children." And at the same time I got a little scared of the idea. Perhaps this is a fear of being a woman, or a fear in connection with this particular relationship and what I want it to be and what it will be. (*Silence.*) I've been having these pregnancy fantasies. I see this as a manipulation of David—if I got pregnant, would he marry me? And I would not want to use this tactic to force a change, although I feel that is what I'm trying to do in the fantasy. In the fantasy I see myself as having an abortion, though I would hate that. (*Silence.*) Incidentally, since David, menstruation has been much more regular. (*Silence.*)

Dr. C.: How do you see the dream?

Susan: Somehow, the dream is apart from what I've been talking about. The dream has a feeling of history, is not related to my immediate concerns. I may be wrong, but time will tell. I thought of Morris when I awoke; not really liking the guy and feeling relieved that I had not won the competition with Leah. (*Silence.*) And now I think of the weekend with David and how warm and feeling-full. There is a change in me, in David, in the relationship. It's as though we are both able to satisfy each other more.

Dr. C.: When you think of broken appointments, what comes to mind?

Susan: Nothing in particular. The idea of the old second-date situation is another story. Part of you wants him to come back and he doesn't and you feel bad.

Dr. C.: I wonder if the broken appointments are tied in with my not giving you a different appointment time?

Susan: (*picking this up with enthusiasm*): It fits. I think this other person is you. Deep down, I'm saying I don't really like you. But I don't let myself go beyond these mixed feelings. I'm saying something more important than like or dislike of you. These appointments were to be of a sexual nature. I'm not aware of having any sexual designs on you. Maybe, but I really don't think so.

Dr. C.: Well, you express the need in the dream to be adored, desired.

Susan: This is so. Maybe I'm ambivalent . . . that I wanted the same things from you as I did from every man . . . adoration and being thought wonderful. But I felt relief in the dream, and I think I really do, that you do not relate to me this way, that you do not fall into the trap. Maybe this expressed the realization that what I want and need is more than being adored. Maybe I'm saying that I have mixed feelings—that I no longer think that what I want is only adoration. Also, this competition with other women is in here somewhere. (*Silence.*)

Dr. C.: Maybe the dream and the weekend are related. In both, maybe you're talking about a new way of relating—with me, with David—relating in a way more meaningful and gratifying than just please adore me, and aren't I wonderful, or submitting to the other person to win approval.

Susan: Yes. And basic here is that I no longer feel helpless.

I'm in this because I want to be in it. (*Silence.*) What's happening between David and me is new. It's never happened before. I've never felt this way before about anyone.

Dream 23 / *Session 171*

Susan, with considerable sensitivity and honesty, was able to verbalize experiencing closeness with David and then the anxiety that followed or accompanied it: that she felt open and vulnerable, that she could be hurt, that there was nothing she could do to defend herself when she cared. She felt closer to David, but also more threatened.

She continued to have pregnancy fantasies. There was a dream that did not awaken her, only part of which she vaguely recalled: "I was pregnant. Would it be a baby? Or was it some malignancy, a cancer, a tumor? I don't recall more. I was anxious, and continued to sleep." She saw the dream as representing that something was going on inside her and she did not know what.

She ended with: "In the beginning of the analysis I used only headwork. I had to understand and rationalize everything. I backed away from feelings and avoided closeness . . . played roles. Now [currently] I'm feeling something . . . the feelings are growing into the relationship with David. I don't understand it all, but that does not bother me."

Dream 24 / *Session 173*

Susan: Today I'm not feeling very well. It's hard to go back to last week. Thursday, when I came home, I had all kinds of feelings about giving up the third hour.[9] (*Silence.*) I had a dream Friday night. I had an abortion. I had conflicting feelings about getting it. The person who did the abortion also did an oophorectomy [removal of an ovary]. David had been at the operation and he did not like some of the things the surgeon did. When I came out of the operation, I was disturbed that the surgeon had done more than he was sup-

[9] During hour 172 Susan raised the question whether to cut down from three to two sessions a week. The decision was left open.

posed to. I think in that dream David wasn't David but you. It was the question of cutting back too soon, is it the right thing to do, am I going to make the analysis an abortive experience. Today I haven't got the doubts. I feel that cutting back from three to two times a week isn't really ending the analysis. (*Silence.*) (*Tearful and upset.*) The question of my graying hair came up at the end of last hour. I think I have a tendency to think of my hair in terms of time pressure—a perfect sign of the passing years. (*Silence.*) The surgeon applied the pressure to the abdomen to make things come out. He did not cut me open; he did everything vaginally. When he did apply the pressure to the abdomen, a lot of blood came spurting out. He wanted this; he thought it was the right thing to do. (*Silence.*) I guess, right now, my guts are engaging more of my attention than I expected. It was an effort to come and I guess I feel genuinely sickish. (*Silence.*) Assuming you are the surgeon and applying the pressure, it would mean you're taking out more than I would want you to.

Dr. C.: Do you feel I apply pressure in the analysis?

Susan: No. I really don't. I feel that last hour I felt quite the reverse, that I wanted more from you than I was getting, whether what I was proposing was the right thing to do. (*Silence.*) It may very well be that this pressure I was applying to myself, when I got home Thursday, was seen in the dream as pressure that maybe I put on you. Also, you are David in the dream, that you are not satisfied with what goes on. I know I was thinking of a whole host of things Thursday night, and I kept wondering to what extent they were neurotic problems or a lack of self-discipline. Today I'm not feeling the things I'm saying at all. I'm preoccupied with my physiological state, almost as though this voice isn't mine— detached. I know I'm avoiding. (*Silence.*) I had agreed to one operation, the abortion, but not the other, the oophorectomy. Maybe I was trying to say that I feel that you want me to go further than I want to go in the analytic work. Yet I have no idea what I may want to hold back.

Dr. C.: The surgeon took out too much.

Susan: Yes, he took out more than I had bargained for. Maybe I'm saying that about the analysis.

Dr. C.: Could be. Tell me.

Susan: I don't know what I'm holding back. I feel you want me to go further. I bargained for just so much. You must not make me feel I must go beyond that. (*Near tears.*) You remember several months ago I was talking of analysis as the removal of symptoms, of being able to function. Maybe I'm harking back to that in the dream. Of course, at that time I was trying to avoid looking at the nature of the relationship between David and me. But I think I've been taking an honest look. But there may be there is a feeling of being at cross purposes between the two of us. You give me the feeling you want me to do more than I'm prepared for. I think that would follow, feeling that so much had got under way in terms of basic change about the problem. I also feel that the remaining problems are not clearly defined in my mind. (*Silence.*) The feelings about the abortion were bad enough, but this additional operation made it much worse. (*Silence.*) (*Starts to cry.*) I think on Thursday night what bothered me was, are you doing the same thing in pulling out before you're ready to?

Dr. C.: That's a problem of long standing.

Susan: Yes. I don't know why I call this pulling out. Two times a week is not pulling out. I think that I was interpreting your attitude to say you're not ready to do this. Suddenly something else comes to mind in which I projected a judgment on to you. When I felt I wasn't getting from David, when I felt closed out and spoke to him, I felt you felt I should have pulled out. I know this isn't so, because a couple of sessions after that, I kept fantasizing about pulling out on David. Here, too, I projected all my feeling on to you—I just thought of that now—my feeling of you shouldn't pull out on David was also projected to you. (*Silence.*) You know, part of me wanted to pull out on David too soon. Now I don't want to. This week I had a reaction to David as never before. David said he was detached. When I think of what has been going on between David and me in the last few weeks, I *know* he is not detached. (*Silence.*)

Dr. C.: You feel you've put part of the problem on to me in the analysis. Do you think it would help for us to look at it?

Susan: I feel this is different from other times in cutting back. Before, I was on a pink cloud, but not now. (*Silence.*) I want to tell you how grateful I am that you haven't let me fool the two of us. In recent weeks, when I was riding my emotional seesaw and would come in here and see how I was torturing myself and have a dim notion why I had done this, I walked out feeling a shot in the arm. . . . How I have been able to tell you of my hostile feelings. Incidentally, I feel a lot more alive than when I came in here. Maybe because I'm being honest. You know, this feeling I had about David—that David is more involved with me than he thinks he is—is true, and *not* a pink cloud. It reflects an expression of confidence in what has gone on between us, and something *has* been going on between us. (*Silence.*) And there are parallels between you and me, and David and me . . . in that I can feel close to both of you . . . that with both of you I can be honest and look at myself more in the last three months than ever before. And I'm not as afraid of rejection from David and you. (*Silence.*) [*It is nearly time to end the session.*]

Dr. C.: Any other aspect of the dream come to mind?

Susan: You mean the dream about the sweater [where the washerwoman straddles Susan]?

Dr. C.: No. But why did this come to mind?

Susan: That dream was fraught with the fears of closeness. I remember cowering on the floor as this aggressive woman wreaked her vengeance on me. (*Silence.*) Sure, that woman was my mother, but also part of *me!*

Dr. C.: Could be!

Susan: (*Laughs.*) Well, I won't say what's happened to that hostile aggressive me, except it is a much less important part of me. I can't tell you why, but I feel that. I know I have a problem with closeness—with you and with David—

and that it's the same problem. (*Silence.*) You asked me what my goals were three months ago when I found myself without symptoms. Maybe I saw it as a challenge. But I'm glad I did. I've changed more in the last three months than I have in the last three years. (*Silence.*)

Dr. C.: Well, where do we go from here?

Susan: I'd like to try two times a week, if it's O.K. with you.

Dr. C.: Whichever you decide will be most meaningful and productive is O.K. with me.

Susan: I'd like to try two times a week, then.

Dr. C.: O.K. Then let's leave it at twice a week. But let's leave it as an open situation. If you should change your mind at some future date, we can discuss it further.

Dream 25 / Session 179

Susan: Dr. Caligor, when I was here on Friday, I mentioned my flirting. I was feeling near tears. On Saturday I talked to David about it and I cried. I don't know why. David and I talked. He mentioned I had been seductive when we first met. But I did not know that and was surprised to hear it. (*Silence.*) I see this seduction as manipulation and controlling through sex. . . . I really had no awareness of what I was doing and that this was how I related to David. (*Silence.*) I had a dream Monday morning. I took this job as a counselor but I did not want to take it. I was talked into it by my parents, who were counselors at the same camp. One of the things that influenced me was that a man—I think David, though I'm not sure—was a nature counselor at the camp. David, my mother and father worked at the boys' camp; I, in the girls' camp. In the dream I was looking for David and having a hard time finding my way. I was lost in a valley with steep sides and could not find him. I was in some kind of recreation room and I did not quite get to see David. But I'm not sure it was David, though he was meant to be. I was quite anxious. (*Silence.*) I think the dream is a fear of not reaching David. I think I want to reach him and not manipulate or push him, but to touch him. Yet in the dream I could not. I think my parents were encouraging. (*Silence.*) I think I can substitute you for my mother and father. This was a dream of return to a camp where I had been as an adolescent. (*Silence.*) I think I'm looking for a new way to relate and not being able to develop the kind of close relationship I want. But when I do get close, you [that is, the parents] did offer me encouragement. Not by taking over, but a feeling of faith: you can do it. (*Silence.*)

Dr. C.: What about the nature counselor?

Susan: I wondered who the nature counselor was that summer. I don't recall. (*Silence.*)

Dr. C.: Maybe you're talking about David and me.

Susan: (*Silence.*) Trying to find myself in a natural way.

Dr. C.: Trying to reach the nature counselor in the recreation room.

Susan: I think of the analysis . . . trying to recreate myself . . . trying to reach another person. (*Silence.*) If my parents were really my parents, it's the first time I can recall making them as genuine parents, well meaning—my mother not attacking me, my father not raping me.

Dr. C.: Could be you're beginning to see them through the eyes of an adult rather than the eyes of a child.

Susan: Yes. (*Silence.*)

Dr. C.: Any idea on being lost in the steep valley and not being able to find David?

Susan: I think of being hemmed in. Being closed in and not being able to move. In this last year I feel I was closed up from myself. In the last six months I have been trying to come into the world. (*Silence.*)

Dr. C.: Any other thoughts on the valley?

Susan: No. (*Silence.*) Now I think of a vagina. Maybe I'm saying that the valley is my vagina. That I want to reach David and relate in ways other than sexual. (*Long silence.*) You and David are the first times I have ever attempted to be honest with a man.

Dream 26 / *Session 182*

Susan: Dr. Caligor, I've been thinking. I'd like to continue changing [as a person] but I'm wondering about working one hour a week instead of two. I wonder if I cannot do it productively on a one-time-a-week basis. I know I raised this question when I cut down to twice a week. (*Silence.*) Right now I feel I'm not running away, not riding the pink cloud. (*Silence.*) What do you think?

Dr. C.: Let's talk about it.

Susan: Well, I feel much less anxious. It is very helpful to look at things with David. I feel I don't make an analyst out of David but he is helpful and it is nice to confide in him. I feel confident in raising this now, much more so than we talked about it when I switched to twice a week. . . . I think David does love me, that it is just a matter of time before he commits himself. (*Says all this with no overt anxiety and with some affectation.*) (*Silence.*) I had a dream the other night. It involved two diaphragms. One was in poor condition, the other a new one. I got them mixed up. It took place in my mother's house. Dr. Morgan [Susan's boss] was there. I was aware I had left both diaphragms out so that Dr. Morgan would see and not see them. David was the only man around. Dr. Morgan took me by surprise. He would have to infer a relationship between David and me. When he did see the diaphragms, I did not feel uncomfortable. Dr. Morgan picked up the poor diaphragm and said, "You're blushing." I said, "I'm not." He teased me and said, "Your face is as red as this shirt," and he pointed to his red shirt he was wearing. Then the ash fell from my cigarette and landed on his shirt-sleeve. It nearly burned a hole, it melted the fabric, which was synthetic. It melted the fabric but it did not burn through. I felt bad. The hole stood out in the white fabric.

Dr. C.: The fabric was white?

Susan: Did I say that? I meant red. It was red.

Dr. C.: Let's go on with the dream.

Susan: Then I was asleep with David. I had slept until five after ten and I had to be at work at nine. David also worked at my office [in the dream] but he was not concerned about my being late. I said, "You mean you can walk in and say you're late and need time for another cup of coffee?" And he said, "That's right." I awoke with a start. (*Silence.*) I have given this some thought. I think it's important to mention that my diaphragm is more than two years old. Although it is in perfect condition, I thought it might be defective. What if I should get pregnant. I would like that in some way. Then I thought, this is manipulative of David. So I bought a new diaphragm. (*Silence.*) I think getting the two diaphragms mixed up reflects two ways of relating to David: direct or manipulative like my mother. (*Silence.*) In the fantasy, I felt David would want me to get an abortion and I resented this. (*Silence.*)

Dr. C.: Anything happen the day or night of the dream that comes to mind?

Susan: I stayed over at David's. I knew I would be fifteen to twenty minutes late to work, as he drives me down. I felt uncomfortable at the idea of lateness. (*Silence.*)

Dr. C.: Any further thoughts on the dream?

Susan: I still have my doubts about the best way to operate in a relationship. That there are still questions about whether my mother's way of relating is right—the philosophy about how to get a man. I don't want to trick David.

Dr. C.: I wonder if there might not be more to this dream.

Susan: The diaphragms refer to two ways of relating to David. It could also refer to the analytic situation and a bad job and incomplete versus a more successful therapeutic situation. Tonight I spoke about whether I need continue coming two times. I wonder if I'm saying I have to be careful not to botch things up. (*Silence.*) In the dream this is the first time anyone teased me in a nonharmful way. I didn't feel there would be any hard feelings against me if he saw the diaphragms, and nothing happened when he did. (*Silence.*)

Dr. C.: I think I'm Dr. Morgan. I take you by surprise in the dream, yet you want to be discovered. You feel the doctor tweaks you—

Susan: But not hostilely.

Dr. C.: Dr. Morgan in effect says, "You're embarrassed about something"—

Susan: So I get angry at you and burn the sleeve. Anger . . . then I'm angry at David because he does not hurry up.

Dr. C.: As if I'm saying, "What gives in the relationship?" And you say, "nothing." And I say, "You're blushing." You deny this and feel anger. Perhaps you're saying that you are embarrassed that in the analysis there is some unconscious duplicity with me—the confusion of the diaphragms, the blushing and not blushing, the red fabric that turns to white. Yet you don't want me or yourself to fall for this—you want Dr. Morgan to see, the hole does not burn through the fabric. (*Silence.*) Of course, it is constructive for you to let us see how your neurotic difficulties in living express themselves and operate. But, in the process, let's not close the door on further constructive collaboration. What do you think?

Susan (*affirmatively*): Let's continue twice a week. (*Silence.*)

Dr. C.: Fine. We both realize that in the past you've tended to act impulsively, then be regretful. Let's slow this process down and take a look at it.

Susan: (*Heaves a big sigh, wears a broad grin.*) Swell.

Dream 27 / *Session 187*

The flow of topics was as follows:

Susan: You know, the bad feature of some of the things that happen to me when I'm disturbed is that I don't retain a picture of what happened, what I did, what really went on. Ordinarily, I have a remarkable memory. When I think of the talk David and I had Saturday night, I recall very little. Sometimes, when I'm worked up after a discussion, I can't remember five minutes afterwards.

Susan went on to explore her need to feel exploited by David, helpless. She realized that there was an improvement, that she had these irrational outbursts because "I know I get panicky at the closeness. . . . I know I've been cutting off feeling the last few weeks . . . that I'm getting ready for the kick in the teeth . . . David's rejection . . ." And she was aware that the improvement in the relationship made her feel this way.

After a silence, toward the end of the hour, Susan quite spontaneously went on.

Susan: I recall the dream of dyeing my hair two times and fearing that I might not be able to find my own hair color. I was saying I wanted to change, yet was very much afraid of what a change would be like. I had a need to hang on to all of my problems even though I was dissatisfied with the way I lived. Yet I was afraid that giving them up would be even worse. The feeling of being caught. (*Silence.*) I think my feeling now is that I don't feel trapped and helpless. I don't know all the answers yet. But I don't feel as trapped as I did. (*Smiles.*) It's funny, I think of dyeing the hair. At this point I looked into the mirror after my hair wash and I realized the speed with which the graying hairs are coming in; I raised the question about hiding the gray. I don't think I raised it seriously, though it did come to mind.

Dr. C.: How do you feel about your gray hair?

Susan: I'd just as soon not have them—it's time pressure. I do have some feeling about the age difference between David and me. Gray hair does make me look older, unfortunately. (*Silence.*) I don't worry about the gray hair, but I'd prefer not having them. Yet it's not that important enough to me to invest the time and money to cover them up.

Dream 28 / *Session 188*

Susan: The last time I was here, I was talking about the dream about my worry about getting gray after I knew I was going back into analysis. We talked about going gray. (*Pause.*) Last night I had another dream about going gray. I was pleased that instead of a few gray hairs there were several gray spots that were really right because it looked more attractive than several sporadic gray hairs. I felt good on awakening. It represents, I feel, a change. The first thought that came to mind is that I don't maybe have the need to avoid facing myself as I really am, and being more accepting of myself. It was while I was combing my hair that I remembered the dream. If gray or not gray, it doesn't seem to matter very much. I've taken off some of the pressure that comes about my age and looking my age. In the dream, the gray hair was becoming. (*Silence.*) I don't know why this change came about. Gray hair is a fact I recognized but didn't like. But this morning it seemed terribly unimportant. (*Silence.*) Funny, I remember when my mother began to get gray. She became gray pretty early. Eventually, she dyed her hair. My father and I kept telling her not to, that gray hair would become her.

Dr. C.: I wonder why this comes to mind now?

Susan: I was talking about accepting the facts and feeling a release of pressure. I'm saying that I'm more willing to accept change. Trying to disguise the gray hair would be denying the facts. Maybe I don't have to. (*Silence.*) It's very curious. When I began therapy in Albany, I began toying with the notion of dyeing my hair. The color that would have been appealing would have been in the red family and the hair was red in the dream before coming to see you. Also, my mother's hair dyed with a red tint. (*Silence.*) Well, this notion of external changes I've concentrated on for quite some time. External changes aren't so important now. I know in all honesty a lot of my attitude depends on David. He doesn't give a damn if my hair is gray or not, so it's safe for me to feel this way. He doesn't care about the age difference. . . . I know I have been having a rage reaction most of my life and have not been able to get my way directly. So I sit on the rage or express it deviously. (*Silence.*) I feel there is a very close relationship between the need to be rejected and the need to be exploited—they're both facets of the same problem. I used to walk about with a lot of resentment at my father because as a kid I wanted him to choose me in some way and he didn't do it. And I was mad—I was angry. I think I've been doing the same thing in relation to David. I wanted him to react in a specific way, and when he didn't, I reacted with anxiety. And then, as time went on and I began to feel safer and safer, when he didn't react as I wanted him to react, I was able to let myself go far enough to experience resentment and hostility. (*Silence.*) I don't like to think of myself as a spoiled brat. But I think that is a fact. But I'm not reacting with the same horror as a year ago when I discovered how narcissistic I was. Maybe it's not so horrifying because I don't have to be that way. A year ago I could have said something about being narcissistic: "You don't have to be that way." I would have changed on the surface and made myself behave differently. Somehow, I was worried about how it would look to others. With this spoiled-brat idea, I'm less concerned with how it looks to the world. The idea of being narcissistic and seeing it for myself was very uncomfortable. I had to hide it—like hiding the gray hair. I couldn't accept my narcissism. I just felt that no one must know—not even myself clearly. I didn't want to let myself know, though part of me knew. I was fighting awfully hard to keep it from coming into awareness, and most of the time I managed to fool myself. And this has been going on all my life; it's not a recent development. (*Silence.*) I think there were many occasions before the analysis, and in the first year of analysis, when I very sincerely felt that I would just as soon be dead as alive. I don't think I would ever have acted on any of these impulses. But when I had these feelings they were very real. (*Silence.*) I recall in October when I was free of symptoms —there was no anxiety. You don't know, you don't realize how that was a tremendous change for me, to be rid of intense anxiety, just to be without symptoms and to be able to feel a positive feeling about myself. I would never have dared hope for more. If you've never had it, you don't know what you're missing.

Dream 29 / *Session 195*

Susan: Dr. Caligor, you know, I'm cooking up something. Something's going on and I wonder what it is. When I left Friday, I felt particularly lighthearted. As if something had been found out and I'm glad. I felt a sense of relief. (*Si-*

lence.) I certainly have thought about Friday. I may be misinterpreting you completely. But one thing I just can't buy is a feeling of competitiveness in connection with your wife, in relation to you. I can buy a feeling of competitiveness, yes, but not in relation to you.[10] (*Silence.*)

Dr. C.: Could be. How do you see the fantasy you had?

Susan: Saturday night we spent with some friends of David's. They have a child. This mother has a conflict about staying home and not working. Sunday morning I don't remember what happened—I was feeling a little disturbed. And David and I were talking about the way I was feeling. It's true that every time that we spend time with people and there are children about, I start reacting. . . . (*Silence.*)

Dr. C.: How do you mean, react?

Susan: I start reacting to David. It's similar to a number of fantasies I've had with David. (*Silence.*) All right, I saw your child and I reacted somehow. I feel competitive here. I feel I have a right to have a child of my own. Until the relationship with David, I didn't start to have these feelings, to want a child. But does this necessarily mean I'm competing with every woman I meet? (*Silence.*) All right. It could very well be that I do have a competitive reaction to seeing your wife, but I don't think it's competitive for you. I may even be competing with you as well as her in this area. (*Silence.*) I had a dream Sunday night. (*Silence.*) There are three sections in the dream, one of which is hazy. I was visiting my parents, and David was there, too. There was something I was concerned about, money, but I'm not sure. And it had something to do with others evaluating what I was doing— like making a train on time.

Then the next section of the dream. I was in a store, there was a shoe counter. I was looking at shoes that were on sale, reduced, sports shoes, reduced from $5.90 to $3. Mr. Lambert, my office manager, was standing there, looking at me. I began to be concerned whether I was extravagant, would he

[10] After session 193, Susan met my wife and child in the elevator. She discussed this in regard to her problem of competing with women and her desire for a child.

see me as extravagant. I felt I didn't have the right to indulge myself. Mr. Lambert is a man who has had strong feelings against the project for which I was hired. I feel he has unfriendly feelings toward me. I also feel he may be anti-Semitic.

In the last section of the dream, I was in the office. I was rushed and David said he would like to help me. He didn't ask me what to do and did some computations for me. He knew we based this on a 10 per cent sample. He went about it scientifically and I felt that he was so sweet. But he had data originally a sample, so that instead of a 10 per cent sample, he ended up with a 1 per cent sample. I hated to tell him because he was so helpful. In trying to describe the feeling I had— like a little girl who helps mother by making muffins that do not taste good, yet everyone valiantly eats them. At one point David says, "You're keeping something from me!" That notion made me uncomfortable because I had been feeling so able to say anything to him. He also said, "Maybe you're hiding something from yourself." Then he said something that I found very disturbing. He said my conceptualization in the dream was of him as a child, not mature. Now I feel pretty sure that Mr. Lambert represented you. And yet, when he did appear in the dream, he did as usually—as a son of a bitch. The reaction I had to these notions left me very disturbed all day yesterday. But I do remember something earlier today. I've talked about changes I've felt in our relationship. I've often told him I wish he could express in words what he feels; it would make me feel good, that he would get pleasure out of making me feel good. (*Silence.*) And while I was telling you about this dream, I remember something about David's taking the sample of the sample. He tried to give me something, but it wasn't enough, because there was only one tenth of the people there should have been. (*Silence.*) The thing that hit me, and it ties in with the computing rates—to some extent, I do feel what goes on between David and me is an inadequate response to what I need. (*Silence.*) There's another thing about the dream. Running through all things is something quantitative. A shoe sale, reduced prices. And the train schedule. And the statistical calculation. I haven't really gone beyond feeling in the bit about the shoes that I was concerned about your evaluation of me as extravagant or not. Your evaluation of me was important. Also, running through this dream is a feeling of being a child myself. The feeling of being extravagant takes me back to Irwin. And my father has this attitude that as a child I was overindulged. (*Silence*.)

Dr. C.: What do you make of the dream?

Susan: In the first two parts, I was concerned about evaluation of me by authority figures. But in the last part I'm the authority figure, and there again I'm worried about someone else's evaluation of me. There was something maternal about my feelings to him at that point. I think that there is something that I have to tell David. There is something I am keeping from him. And I think that what it is is that there isn't an adequate response from him in the relationship. But there is something qualitatively different from the reactions in the past. I'm not aware of feeling resentful, rage because I'm not getting what I wanted. I guess I feel it doesn't have to be this way and this is something we can talk about. I don't feel hostility surging through me. But we'll see. I feel I can talk to him about it. And I won't have my head chopped off. (*Silence*.)

Dr. C.: You mentioned that in all three parts of the dream you're being evaluated.

Susan: Yes. It's much less obvious in the last session, but it's there, too.

Dr. C.: That's an interesting flow. You're being evaluated—

Susan: By my parents, by you, and by David. But I think that what I'm really saying is that I'm being evaluated by you and by him. Because my parents aren't evaluating me these days. But it's your evaluation that is much more important than theirs is.

Dr. C.: Well, you feel I'm Mr. Lambert. And you set the scene at a shoe counter.

Susan: (*Silence*.) (*Smiles*.) I take my shoes off here. I was looking at play shoes, new ones, not working shoes. I really don't think you are a son of a bitch, because you're not. But the office manager has to see everything. And what do you do? Don't you help me see things as they are, that I realize my potential? (*Silence.*) And maybe I'm pushing it too far. But there is actually something optimistic about the way David wants to help, and I don't want to make him feel I'm ungrateful. I think of the mother whose little girl wants to learn how to cook. She wants to encourage the little girl. It's like saying to David: "It may be inadequate now, but some day it can be something more." (*Silence.*)

You know, when I thought of that dream today, I wasn't as disturbed as I was yesterday. Part of the disturbance yesterday was that there was a lot going on and I didn't understand it at all. I feel I do today. (*Silence.*) Also, as you pointed out, I was at the shoe counter. I bought shoes last week. They fit in the store and they pinched afterward. Isn't that what we're trying to do here? My first goal was just to stop the shoe from pinching. When you were evaluating me at the shoe counter, you went far beyond getting a pair of shoes that just won't pinch. And that's what we're trying to do here, isn't it?

Dr. C.: Yes.

Susan: And if I'm honest with myself, of course I resent you. After all, in the past you've backed me into a corner. And though you have not of late, I feel you *know* and I can't kid myself. So though I feel some relief, I also feel resentment.

Dr. C.: Sure. (*Silence.*) You said you had a feeling of relief at the beginning of the hour.

Susan: Like a kid who has been found out and is glad. I walked out with a broad grin. But I still don't think that I have an impulse to try to take you away from your wife. I may be feeling competitive in relation to you, and to her. After all, I competed with my father, too. But I don't feel I feel competitive in relation to her because of you.

Dr. C.: Let's trust your feeling. You're the only one who

can tell. (*Silence.*) I guess my interpretation was wrong.

Susan: You really mean that?

Dr. C.: Yes.

Dream 30 / *Session 196*

Susan had been discussing her concern that I would think she was extravagant.

Dr. C.: What about the idea of my thinking you extravagant?

Susan: When I have these feelings, it's always in relation to my buying clothes. I see a conflict between a rational need and should, and at the same time feeling I don't have a right. (*Silence.*) Something comes to mind. When I talk about self-indulgence in this connection, I remember using the buying of clothes, or going to dinner or to a movie—I used it as solace. I felt I had a right to enjoy it this way. (*Silence.*) This was to compensate me for the real gaps in life. It's a using of things to be less unhappy. (*Silence.*)

Dr. C.: Let's see. Extravagance is an escape and you feel I disapprove of that—it makes you anxious.

Susan: In the dream, Mr. Lambert looks on disdainfully. Well, there is no denying that I've waged sporadic attempts to cut down on analysis, and you've not gone along. Oh, we've talked at various times how I would simulate health and escape. At these times I would think I want things and I have to pay for the analysis. And there is a conflict. (*Silence.*) In the last few seconds, when I haven't said anything, I've been sitting here and doing sums in relation to the money I owe you.[11] And I remember how uneasy I felt while I was, at the prospect of owing you money. And that came up at about the same time I was being manipulative in relation to my parents, and feeling guilty about their extravagant birthday gift to me. (*Silence.*) I start talking about extravagance as an escape and behaving like a child. One reason I have been so concerned about evaluations is because I feel I've had

[11] Susan owed me about $175, a credit privilege agreed upon. It was to be paid when she got her raise, which was just about due.

enough, I want to get away from you, from this situation. But at the same time I want to get away from it, not by running away. I want to leave because I've grown up and am not running away and am ready to leave. And I don't want to run away. So I've got to make sure I've put aside the childishness and to feel I can cope with life as an adult. And yet, while all this has been going on, I don't think I've been as irresponsible, as childish, etc., as I would have been a few years ago. (*Silence.*) I remember the dream I had Sunday night. I remember the last section, which can be interpreted in several ways. David and me, the experienced person and inexperienced person giving something that was inadequate. I could have been David. (*Silence.*)

Dr. C.: Tell me what you mean.

Susan: He wanted to help, he went about using a good sample; but it wasn't enough. And I've made a lot of progress and I see many changes. But if I do want to function as a mature person, maybe there just ain't enough yet. You remember the dream in which there was the maid who let me have it and terrified me. I saw that maid as my mother and me as helpless. Then I saw later, sure, my mother was the maid. But I'm also the maid. What I said last time was true. But this, too, has validity. But this is more directly related to an evaluation of *me*. (*Silence.*)

Dr. C.: Maybe you're saying that at some level, in your attempt to evaluate yourself, you're too concerned with what I think of you.

Susan: (*Silence.*) Yes. I should be able to set my own standards, but I can't. I'm still too concerned with what you, or the other, think. In the dream, I was buying what I wanted to buy [play shoes], but I felt you would disapprove and this made me anxious.[12]

Dream 31 / Session 205

Susan: Well, I went home and had a dream on Tuesday night. And I have a feeling the dream will confirm a lot of

[12] Susan paid her $175 arrears in the first two months after her raise came through, which was just at about this time.

the things said here on Tuesday. It's a weird dream, and a little frightening. I can't make anything of it, except to remember it. I've even had difficulty in forcing myself to do that. (*Silence.*) In the dream I was in Alaska, I was running away from some kind of danger, trouble. At one point I saw or was seen by two men who were doing manual labor. I heard their conversation but they did not know I was there. I knew they were desperate in some way. They were talking in a fairly calm way about their situation. Their manual labor—digging, I think—I don't really know what it was, but there were huge pipes on either side. I was frightened that they could kill me. I don't remember the details of their problem, but their killing me would help to solve it for them. I went on and found a woman in this relatively small community who was going to be joined later by her husband—a doctor. She was scouting to find some facilities for him; he was going to set up practice. I associate this woman with Ann, or a gym teacher I had in high school. I felt that if I joined forces with her I would be much safer. I don't think she was too happy about it. But we did form the alliance. (*Pause.*) Then the scene is in a restaurant. There was a large round table. This woman and I and others—men and women—were there. I said something about our cooperative effort; I somehow referred to this woman's and my relationship in terms of marriage. And as soon as I said it, it sounded as though she and I were in a homosexual relationship. I tried to say they must not misinterpret my words; I tried to retract the word marriage. But they kept looking at each other knowingly. I was disturbed. (*Pause.*) Then the scene changes. I was in a bathroom. I didn't have clothes on and was washing my body. This same woman came in and said, "Aha, I see someone is going to have a baby." I knew I was pregnant. I looked and saw that I was pregnant and realized it was visible to others for the first time. Also, that the pregnancy that was not visible when I had my clothes on was visible when I was nude. The dream was upsetting, very much so. (*Silence.*) I don't know what it means, but— except—I felt this was just a confirmation of something you said about the fantasy of my father dying, I leave David and go to my mother; and you said you leave the man and go to the woman. That crossed my mind. (*Silence.*) Last night when I went to bed I recalled my early situation with my mother. I was afraid of competing with her, taking something away from her. I began to think of this last night, if I wasn't terribly afraid of winning and having my father. (*Rubs eye.*) Gee, I've got something in my eye; are you good at this sort of thing?

Dr. C.: No.

Susan: (*Silence.*) Well, let's get back. I tried Tuesday to dismiss the situation by little jokes, that you and David are in the same league, that he's paying you to take this line. Then I spent time feeling neglected. (*Silence.*) The dream was upsetting. The following night I feared falling asleep because I might dream again. I feel the question you raised a long time ago, "Why are you afraid of closeness?" is answered in the dream. I felt the men could kill me, and where did I go for help but to a woman. When I awoke, I felt the two men were you and David. I do have the feeling that the threatening situation was a competitive one—I with them, in some way. And I think of those huge pipes; they were so large than an adult human being could fit into them. And they were piled up. And I think they were some kind of a sexual symbol. But I just can't seem to go beyond that, or I won't let myself. (*Silence.*) I do remember when you raised the question of "Why are you afraid of closeness?" I said I was afraid of being obliterated. That's what I'm saying in the dream, the same thing. (*Silence.*) I think this is the way I was speculating last night before I went to bed: I think I was more afraid of my father than of my mother. After all, I went through all these years erecting all kinds of barriers with my father; I erected the barriers for protection. (*Silence.*)

Dr. C.: When you think of those tubes, what comes to mind?

Susan: You can't possibly realize how *huge* they were. What came to mind just now was vaginal symbols. I said that a person would fit inside one of them. Sometimes when I think of going to bed with David I think of his coming inside me. (*Silence.*) And what happens when a baby is born? A child emerges from the passageway. And at the other end of the dream, there it was—I was pregnant. The only disturbing thing was that it was obvious to someone else. That's my mother—my mother was proud that when she was pregnant, it did not show for many, many months. I think she was a little embarrassed by being pregnant, and I think I was, too, in the dream. You know—I just thought of Frankenstein—I began to think of all the times my mother said, "Do not tell your father I bought you this." That he was the Franken-stein in some way. The fear that the person you create will assert and turn on you and destroy you, like Frankenstein. And that ties in with having children; the person who you create will destroy you. (*Silence.*) You know, this woman I turned to was not anxious to form this alliance. This is Mama. She had a husband who wasn't there, but she wasn't alone. This goes back to my childhood. There was an alliance between my mother and me—and she was around and he [father] was not. (*Silence.*)

Dr. C.: You feel that the two men are David and me.

Susan: You're out to get me.

Dr. C.: Yes, we're digging.

Susan: (*Silence.*) I just had a thought and said yes, you could both be digging my grave. This was related to the dream, though.

Dr. C.: Well, the two men share a problem.

Susan: Yes. And I interpreted that if they knew I heard them, they would kill me.

Dr. C.: Something in the dream that ties David and me together can destroy you.

Susan: Yes. (*Silence.*)

Dr. C.: Any ideas?

Susan: The first thing that comes to mind is that you can both find out what I'm really like.

Dr. C.: Tell me what you mean.

Susan: If you pull the covers off and what you see is not

very pretty, then everything will go smash. Because when you see what I'm really like, you are liable to spit on me. Before I go on, there's very little feeling here; yet these words are not coming from my brain. I feel this is true, but I'm not experiencing the same kind of despair I used to when I thought of people really finding out what I'm like. It's almost as if I'm of two minds about myself at this point: the parts of me I'm still afraid to explore. But then there are other parts of me that I don't reject because I'm really not so bad. (*Silence.*)

Dr. C.: When you think of Alaska, what comes to mind?

Susan: I think of the detection of the underground hydrogen-bomb blasts. (*Laughs.*) It's part of this whole question of detection. We were in a city in Alaska, I just knew we were in Alaska. (*Silence.*) It's the furthest away you can get and still be in the United States.

Dr. C.: If these two men dig and get at what's really going on underground—

Susan: I will be obliterated.

Dr. C.: Therefore, running away from being discovered.

Susan: Because it would mean my death. It was self-protection, running.

Dr. C.: That your being discovered would somehow be destructive of you. The fear of being discovered by a man.

Susan: Yes. Then turning to a woman for protection. Leaving a man to go to a woman. It's safer that way. (*Silence.*) I guess I am afraid of closeness with a man. (*Silence.*) When I think of being married to the woman, I thought, is this homosexual? But I really don't think that's it. (*Silence.*) In such a situation, you're not exposed to the same risks in a relationship because the woman doesn't want much from you as would a man. This woman didn't really want to team up with me. She wouldn't dig deep, she'd let me be. As close as you are to a woman, you don't give in the way that you have to to relate to a man.

Dr. C.: Yes. The two men, David and I are digging, getting to know you. You run away from the closeness with the men by involvement with the woman. And then the last part of the dream dealing with pregnancy. What's growing in there? Is it a child? Is it a Frankenstein?

Susan: Maybe I'm that baby. (*Silence.*) If I see myself, will it lead to my being destroyed? (*Silence.*) I know I'm afraid to look, to expose myself. (*Silence.*) In the dream, the two men were at the mouth of the tubes, waiting to see what would come out.

Dream 32 / *Session 206*

Susan: You know, I don't know what happened on Friday, but something did. And unless I try to dig in and find out, it will be a big mistake. Because I left feeling very different than when I came in. I felt annoyance with you, neglected by David. When I left, none of these feelings were there. Last weekend I felt for David feelings of intensity that I haven't felt for a few weeks. (*Silence.*) Certainly, what we were talking about caused this change. And yet I don't understand it at all. (*Silence.*) I had another dream Sunday night. I don't remember too much of it. I think it had the same feeling. The dream was about detection, X rays to be read. I don't remember much about it, except to say that what went on in the other dream was somehow repeated. (*Silence.*) I feel I have to understand what happened—up here [pointing to her head], but part of me is stalling.

Dr. C.: Yes.

Susan: And yet I know that the weekend with David was good because of that hour; yet I'm afraid, I stall. (*Silence.*) And my attitude toward you had changed during the session on Friday, too. (*Smiles.*) And now something also occurs to me. David is finishing his psychiatric residence. The faculty is making a dinner. My reaction is that I'm not too anxious to meet his department chairman, with whom David is quite confidential. (*Laughs.*) I have enough on my hands without bringing another detector into the picture. That comes up after we talk about stalling. (*Silence.*) I suddenly find myself very sleepy—I'm stalling. (*Silence.*) When I talk about being afraid of people finding out what I'm really like—this is something so old. This is a question that came up years ago. I used to have a dual feeling on my job in Albany: that if I wasn't careful, they would see how inadequate I was; and yet I walked around feeling exploited. I think that kind of feeling entered my relationships with my women friends—all of my relationships. I don't think it's that all-inclusive now. (*Silence.*)

Dr. C.: Last hour centered itself about a dream. How do you see the meaning of that dream?

Susan: (*Silence.*) It expressed a lot of fear in connection with having the real me emerge and be detected by the important men in my life. And I'm afraid that if it is detected, it just means the end of everything. I find it's much safer to avoid this and to center my activities on relationships with women because they don't demand as much of me. They don't demand of me what I'm not prepared to give them. They let me be. Well, it was men who were involved in what I remember of the X-ray dream.

Dr. C.: Yes. These two men were waiting near the tubes for a full-size person to emerge.

Susan: Yes. (*Silence.*) I feel different from Friday in one way. For some reason, I don't feel any longer that you and David are out to get me. That irrational belief just isn't there. And why should it go just because we talked about it on Friday?

Dr. C.: Any ideas?

Susan: No. (*Silence.*) I just had a couple of half-baked thoughts, to the effect that they wanted to dig and I didn't want to be detected. Maybe I am just projecting in the dream. And then I turned it off.

Dr. C.: I think you're saying something basic. In a sense, you're talking about a fear of facing yourself.

Susan: Yes. (*Silence.*) I don't know what I'm afraid of finding, but it could be that I'm afraid of that new me that might emerge. There was the question of pregnancy at the end of the dream. The only thing that bothered me about the pregnancy was its visibility, that it showed. Now I go back to the pipes at the beginning of the dream—and I associated that with the passageway the baby had to travel on its way into the world. (*Silence.*) Yet, what's so great about the old me—that I'm so afraid—it wasn't really worth hanging on to. I can't see why I'm afraid of avoiding a change. But I sure as hell do. And I came into analysis to get rid of the old part. (*Silence.*) All right, one of the things I saw on Friday was a fear of change. Maybe it wasn't articulated, but that's one of the things I saw there. But why should that make such a difference on Saturday? I was eager for David to arrive. I just couldn't wait. I wasn't afraid of him. And I didn't hold anything back—any passing ideas or passing emotional reactions. And every time I have tried to keep from experiencing these feelings, well, I just didn't try to hold anything back. (*Silence.*) And for some reason I think of something that happened a long time ago. David is one of the pickiest eaters I've ever come across. Some time in January, we visited someone and we were served chocolate cake for dessert. I noticed David ate it and said how good it was. I didn't say anything. And once I nearly bought one but asked David first. And he said he didn't like that kind of cake at all. And I asked if he would have eaten it if I had served him and he said no. (*Silence.*) I don't know why this came up—except that what I'm really talking of is honesty. He's always been honest. And that has made for trouble because there were times I wanted to hear specific things and he would not say them. (*Silence.*)

Dr. C.: Why do you bring this up now?

Susan: I don't know. But I feel it's related. I don't think I'm stalling. (*Silence.*) Maybe I'm saying that I do have a feeling or a recognition of something that is true and has been true all along—and that is, here is a person with whom I can be completely honest, that I don't have to be afraid, that I don't have to worry about detection, that he can accept me. And this weekend was a shared experience. I couldn't feel this way unless he did, too.

Dr. C.: So we're talking about detecting yourself and being honest with yourself.

Susan: Not only that. Also letting someone else see me. And that didn't seem to bother me this weekend. So I don't think we're just talking about seeing myself as I am facing myself. It's more complicated. It's coming face to face with myself and passing on that picture to someone else without distorting it. You don't have to impress someone with what a *nice* person you are; to do that, you have to do a certain amount of acting. (*Silence.*) And I just found myself thinking about Sunday night and Monday morning. I guess I realized that David did express the way he was feeling. Monday morning, before we got up out of bed, we had intercourse, on his initiative. This never happened on a workday before. To me, this seemed to be his telling me he felt pretty much the way I did. (*Silence.*) I think I have a beautiful relationship and maybe I'll be able to enjoy it fully. I could this weekend. (*Smiles.*) I think I told you that one thing David reacts to is my feelings of martyrdom. I have some free time and offered to do something for him—and I made a martyr's face. But I was kidding and he knew it. But there are other times when I do put on the hurt act. (*Silence.*)

Dr. C.: Why do you feel you were anxious at the end of the dream?

Susan: Here was something I couldn't hide much longer and would be detected soon. In a way, it was a dream of what people will think. This business about being seated around the table, the statement about marriage and being very anxious what they will think. The same is true of the anxiety associated with this pregnancy of mine. (*Silence.*)

Dr. C.: Why the anxiety?

Susan: A fear of what people will say, I will be detected. And I'm saying this this hour. I've been trying to do a certain amount of distorting to have a picture come through to David—and when I try, I get into trouble with him. I think we both feel the same way about this. I want him to be honest with me and am glad that he can. And I think that something I realized this weekend is that I don't have to eat the cake in his house either, that he doesn't want me to. We're better off when I don't; and the fact that I don't eat the cake means just that. He can take me as I am. (*Silence.*) Maybe, if I went home tonight and redreamed the dream, I don't think I would be anxious. (*Silence.*) There was this anxiety about the pregnancy, that it would show. I remember having the association of the monster that would turn on its maker. (*Silence.*) You know, I think of you asking a year and a half ago: "Why are you afraid of closeness?" It's really conformity. I needed my mother's love. If I wasn't what she wanted me to be, I could be destroyed. I think this applies in the relationship with David—to hold back the parts that were not very nice. That is, he too would push me away if I didn't conform. I feel this is my distortion. Because David doesn't want what my mother wanted. (*Silence.*) Maybe this is why I'm afraid of closeness. Because closeness means someone interferes with this game of presenting yourself. And if you can't do an editing job on yourself, it has to end in disaster. Yet I must be skirting something—because talking along these lines, when I think back, there was a lot of anxiety. (*Silence.*) The anxiety that I'd be destroyed; also, what would emerge from my pregnancy. (*Silence.*)

Dr. C.: The anxiety that you'd be destroyed, what would emerge.

Susan: It's like a part of me dying off. And there's as yet an unknown quantity to take its place.

Dream 33 / *Session 207*

Susan: You know, I haven't been doing any thinking about myself at all since I left here Tuesday night. I think at this point I've got to really exert pressure on myself if I'm to get any place—because I feel I'm fine, all is O.K.—and we've been through this before. I also feel that the fears I felt a few weeks ago about David do not exist any more. Then I'll get impatient with David a few weeks from now. (*Silence.*) It's the same old merry-go-round—the same one I've been on for years. The fact remains that I haven't answered why I'm afraid of closeness, if I am—because this fear I was talking about a week ago doesn't have reality for me any more. (*Silence.*) I think I said something to you the other night, of not looking forward to meeting David's department chairman. This is totally irrational, but it's there anyway. The fear is of, ah, his thinking in terms of my not being the right person for David. I know it's irrational, but the feeling is there anyway. I think it goes back to what I was talking about in the dream: the question of being found out, of somebody seeing the real me. And I think this is akin to the feelings I was talking about when I went to the party last June. (*Silence.*) You know, I just remembered a dream I had. I recalled it while coming here. The frames of my glasses, in the dream, were broken by someone else; I think a man, but I'm not sure. (*Silence.*) I think I'm talking of seeing myself, of seeing what's been there all along. (*Silence.*)

Dr. C.: Were the lenses broken, or just the frames?

Susan: Just the frames. I heard it crack. Incidentally, the glasses in the dream were a new pair I had bought on Saturday. (*Silence.*) I guess I'm afraid to go any further at this point; I'm afraid to dig in and have a look at myself. And I think that there have been a great many changes that have taken place since last June, but over the last few months I don't think much has been happening. There has been a recognition of what goes on between David and me. But in terms of basic changes and understanding, there's still an awful lot that's just not coming up because I'm not letting it. (*Silence.*)

Dr. C.: You feel the broken frames refer to a fear of taking a look.

Susan: I would think so. And I know when I don't want to take a look I walk around feeling as if I don't need to. (*Silence.*) And I was certainly successful in fooling myself. There were a good many points where I did not know why I was continuing coming here. I'm not saying that now. I have wasted a certain amount of time here and I've got to stop. And yet it's very hard to break through the shell of how I defend myself—by cutting off feeling. I just thought of something—of how I have been wearing my feet out shopping this week. I've been trying things on and been dissatisfied with what I see. I wonder if this isn't a reflection of some basic confusion—the way I see myself and want to see myself. Who are you? And I've noticed that nothing I found to try on looked really good the way I want to look. (*Silence.*) Last night when I spoke to David he told me we had received an invitation to a party. I look forward to going, but at the same time there's a little bit of apprehension about going to a party where I won't know anyone but David. I bring this up after being afraid to look. (*Silence.*)

Dr. C.: You have a new pair of glasses, you can use them to see something new, but they get broken.

Susan: But the lenses aren't broken. They're my eyes, because I can't see without them because my eyes are so bad. I think a man broke them, but I'm not sure.

Dr. C.: Well, as you say, you have your eyes.

Susan: It's a question of getting them to see. (*Silence.*) And now I don't want to use the glasses. In the last few seconds, thoughts have started to flit into mind—clothes and various places. What am I doing? Sure, it's wasting time—but in an interesting way. I'm excessively concerned at what's outside, what shows. I told you I'm uncomfortable about seeing David's department chairman; he might see inside. Last week I said you and David were out to get me. Every time I think of seeing inside me, I'm afraid what is to be seen is that I'm inadequate. And I know that comes from me. (*Silence.*)

Dr. C.: What would happen if you took a good honest look on the inside?

Susan: I don't know. I don't know. (*Silence.*) It's that what's inside is wholly bad, something that everyone would want to reject. But don't ask me why, because I don't know why I say that. (*Silence.*) I think that part of me is afraid that there's nothing inside of me; that's even worse than having something bad inside. And now I just feel stuck. And I think now I'm a little bit anxious. (*Silence.*) But a few seconds ago I said there's a fear of there being nothing inside. That's just another way of expressing myself as something you've heard often before a long time ago. And that is, the picture of myself as a nonentity. (*Silence.*) I know the reason why I didn't want people to get too close was they'd find it out. And there was no one there, the way I used to live, when I was afraid to express a differing opinion to someone I respected. (*Silence.*) I'm just not going any place. And I never do when I talk about a problem and am not really experiencing a problem. (*Silence.*)

Dr. C.: Well, supposing you just relax and let's see what thoughts, feelings, impressions, come up.

Susan: (*Silence.*) You know, I still think buried in me is the desire to be the belle of the ball, to have everyone turn around and look. And yet I'm afraid to be in that position. It's something that I recognize in myself for a long time and is represented to me by Gloria, in the first chapter of *Butter-field 8*. I remember I did literally want to have the clothes ripped off my back. There was always the desire to be wanted, to be admired. This just came to me when I was out shopping, looking for something very, very smart. Yet I'd be afraid of something too daring, too elaborate. (*Silence.*) You know, we're back to that question you asked me one and one half years ago. That cocktail party; the time I articulated a fear that someone would engage me. And that's what's up now. We're at that point again. And I think I've been chipping away, getting little pieces. I know I wanted to be admired at these gatherings. (*Silence.*)

Dr. C.: And yet you were afraid to be approached.

Susan: Yes. And if I was approached, I never let anyone come too close. (*Silence.*) I think it was a real knowledge that closeness was impossible, because what was inside was anything but admirable. (*Silence.*)

Dr. C.: When you think of someone getting close, what comes to your mind?

Susan: Right now, nothing; except that at the same time that I said that, I think of a major portion of last year, which has been pretty wonderful in terms of the developing closeness to David. (*Silence.*) If they get close, they won't see something admirable in me. You know, in that dream, I never let myself see. It was just fear of what might emerge. But not a hint of what was inside those cylinders or inside me in the last part of the dream. (*Long silence.*) I don't know if this is an attempt to evade the question or not, but when I was a little kid, I had to work very hard to get my mother's approval.

Oh, I had to control all sorts of things. I wonder if I always haven't walked around feeling that whatever is there inside has to be completely covered up because it ain't any good. (*Silence.*) I just found myself taking another direction, thinking about David and the way in which he is so unsure about what he wants from this relationship, and I on the other hand know what I want. And I can still manage to feel hurt because he doesn't. I was wondering if I don't put myself into a position of feeling exploited. After all, David does have a brutal schedule. And then I complain here of neglect.

Dr. C.: Yes. You've often accused him here of neglect, exploitation.

Susan: Well, I think that part of the reason that I have had the need to feel exploited and set things up that way is that I'm afraid of what's inside. At the same time, I want people to relate to me in an admiring way. (*Silence.*) It's easier to blame him and avoid taking a look at me. (*Silence.*) All right, the thing that I want to say is that I don't even know how to go about looking. And I can hear you in effect saying, "You poor helpless thing" [*said sarcastically*]. I guess that I do want you to do it for me in some way. Maybe that's why I haven't been getting anywhere tonight. (*Silence.*) I guess I think I'm playing a game with myself and I'm just plain stalemated.

Dr. C.: Or, to use the image of your dream, you get the frame broken—not by you, of course—but the lenses are O.K. But you can't use them.

Susan: You know, at the same time that I'm doing this, I can't help it. There's something struggling in me. (*Silence.*) I think in addition to the fear of looking, there is another fear: that I'm at the beginning of a bog-down period. I had one when I started to work with you, when I did a lot of stalling and there was not much in the way of movement.

Dreams 34 and 35 / Session 208

Susan: You know, I spent a lot of time just treading water here last time. I've been doing it here and outside. For the last week, I slept gingerly, took a long time to fall asleep. I felt

I was afraid of dreaming. (*Silence.*) I did have a few dreams about other people. Peculiar; not me, but other people. (*Silence.*) I had a dream Saturday night. This was, the narcotics squad of the Treasury Department was using Riker's Island. They were holding parties for narcotics addicts, to gradually wean them from drugs by gradual reduction. And the F.B.I. felt this was making their work more difficult, they were furious they were not told of the parties. (*Silence.*) I had this dream Saturday. Saturday was a mixed-up day. I went out shopping to buy a dress for a party David and I are going to. I bought a dress and showed it to David. He reacted, this dress was absolutely impossible. The dress was not returnable. I felt terrible, thrown-out money. Two friends reacted to the dress in the same way. I felt very bad and like hiding myself during the first act of the play—I wore the dress to the play. Then, during the second act, I threw back my shoulders, said inwardly, "Fuck you all," and stopped feeling ashamed of how I looked. (*Silence.*) During dinner, David and I discussed New Year's Day, when I flirted at that party. I felt like crawling into a hole, consumed with guilt. Later, after the theater, we discussed it again, and for some reason I didn't feel guilty. I'm sorry it [her flirting at the party] happened, but I could talk to David in a rational way without feeling I'm no good. (*Silence.*)

Dr. C.: What do you make of the dream?

Susan: I had a peculiar dream Sunday night; only this time the people were not strangers to me. It was about David. I remember that the blanket cover had been changed on his bed.[13] In the dream, David was some other kind of doctor. He had invented a machine that had a blanket cover on it; it was used to treat cancer, and it emitted rays of some sort. And these rays could penetrate to the primary sights of the cancer and get at them like no other technique could. There was this machine in use, and another one that he had developed that he was reluctant to use. I may have been in this, but I can't remember the part I played. But there was a certain amount of anxiety whether or not the newest ma-

[13] It had in fact been changed.

chine would be successful and when David would use it. As I talk now, I wonder if the anxiety about the new machine, the penetrating rays, could be that David is about to take a step that will bring him even closer. Before I go back to the first dream, I do recall saying to David that if I wore my new dress, he could be sure that everyone would turn around and look at us. He asked, why do you want that? And I knew part of me would feel uncomfortable. I don't like clothes that look dull; and yet I'm afraid of things that look too exciting. Like at the party a year and a half ago, when I was so afraid no one would talk to me and that someone would. And how surprised I was when this was raised in analysis. And how I wanted to crawl into the woodwork at the theater when people looked at me at the end of the first act. (*Silence.*) All this is related—like wanting people to see me and not being comfortable when they notice me. And I feel this is true with David. The more he notices me, the closer he draws, the more uncomfortable I get. (*Silence.*) Sure, if people look, then afterwards I can't live up to the initial impression I created. I guess I feel that what's best representing the inside me is a dull, drab, not too exciting exterior. Like my fear of meeting David's department chairman, that he, too, would have penetrating eyes and see I'm not right for David. (*Silence.*) But something happened on Saturday night when I said, "To hell with you," and threw my shoulders back. I just stopped crawling—but not like I would have ten years ago. I wasn't gritting my teeth. I stopped feeling bad about the wasting of money. I just stopped feeling guilty. I don't know why. (*Silence.*) And I also remember on Saturday I was dreading telling some of my friends about this, because I felt like such a fool. Yet I felt an obligation to tell people; part of the price you pay is to look foolish to atone for the guilt. But Sunday I felt I didn't have to tell anyone—just hang it in the back of my closet. But at that point, midway through the evening, I stopped beating myself over the dress, and also over the New Year's Day flirting. (*Silence.*) Maybe the narcotics division and the F.B.I. represent me, how I see myself. Because in the dream two different agencies are trying to handle the same problem. The F.B.I. feels it is sneaky of the narcotics division to start these parties without discussing them first. (*Silence.*) The conflict is narcotics, taking dope, running away from your problems—and that was after I had talked on Friday about where I would go and when I would get there.

Dr. C.: Yes. That was the night you told us the dream of the broken frames.

Susan: Yes. It's a continuation. (*Silence.*) Riker's Island. Isn't there a prison on Riker's Island? (*Silence.*)

Dr. C.: I think so. What do you make of this?

Susan: I feel there is a part of me imprisoned, that I don't want to see it. (*Silence.*) And when I think in terms of someone looking at me, noticing me, I think I'd like to be attractive, very interesting. And why is the only alternative to this impossible image someone who can't say anything, is dull, uninteresting? Two grades: one hundred or zero. (*Silence.*) This smacks of something I haven't talked about for some time. The fears of relating to my father and mother, the fear that in any competition with anyone I must lose. And I recall you asking the question if I was afraid I'd win. And that takes me back to the dream of the penetrating rays that cure the cancer, and the anxiety about finding out about the new machine. Because I know I need a close relationship with a man to get well—and I never had one. Then I met David. It's a new experience. And at the same time I'm afraid of getting too close. I never understood why I was afraid of winning with my mother. It was not just her wrath, but what would go on between my father and me—of what's going to happen to me. "Why are you afraid of being engaged?" Sure: I was afraid of being obliterated. It wasn't just that they'd find out that I didn't live up to the surface impression. (*Silence.*)

Dr. C.: Any ideas?

Susan: I just thought of something else—about David and the way I feel about him. And that I've never felt this way in my life. And yet, as time goes on, my feelings just seem to get more intense, deeper all the time. (*Silence.*)

Dr. C.: Let's see. There are two dreams. The first one deals with escape and tapering off.

Susan: Yes. Because I used to run away to escape from problems. I did use alcohol to numb the pain, to escape that way. I feel that people who take dope are operating in the same way. It's [the dream] about escape, about imprisonment, and about conflict how to handle a problem. There are two methods: track him down and root him out—or—tapering off gradually. (*Silence.*)

Dr. C.: And then the second dream.

Susan: Penetrating to the heart of the problem and rooting it out. And the use of the new machine carries with it a certain amount of anxiety, anxiety that the machine won't work— also anxiety that it will.

Dr. C.: This was the second machine David made.

Susan: It was an improvement over the first one, but un-tested. And that, I think, is related to what's going on be-tween us. (*Silence.*)

Dr. C.: Yes.

Susan: (*Silence.*) Well, it's been getting better and I think that what David said to me Saturday night was a pretty major change; the fact that he gives of himself to me and tells me what's going on inside him. (*Silence.*) And if my inter-pretation is correct, and if things do develop along the lines I expect them to, then things will be a lot closer than they have been between us.

Dr. C.: I wonder about those two machines.

Susan: They looked like electric blankets—electrical equip-ment of some sort in a blanket cover.

Dr. C.: It seems to me that you're talking about a more effective cure—to get to the heart of the problem.

Susan: To get to the heart of the problem and kill the malignant tissues that cause all the trouble. To get to the heart of the neurotic problem that seems inaccessible.

Dr. C.: When you talk of the improved machine, it could be you're referring to the analysis; to use it in a more pene-trating and meaningful way.

Susan: (*Silence.*) Well, you know, you may be right. Be-

cause one of the first things that came to mind when I got up
in the morning was that it sounded like the hallucinations I've
read some hospital patients have. But I guess I tend to think
of the relationship with David as developing between the two
of us [Susan and David] and as a result of what goes on
between David and me. But that's an oversimplification—
because we are both in analysis.

Susan sat up toward the end of session 215. "My feet started to
move. I could just as easily let the impulse die. I was anxious.
But I had to sit up and face you. [*Silence. Eyes filling with
tears.*] I guess I'm saying that I don't want to be alone any
more, I don't want to be alone any more." Susan decided to sit
up and took my silence as a tacit agreement.[14]

Dream 36   /   *Session 217*

Susan sat up for this hour. She looked directly at me, and
although she was still somewhat anxious, it was decidedly less
than during the previous session. The flow of topics and the
actual transcribed dream material went as follows:

She had had a perfectly fine day, though she started to
develop a headache on the way to the session. She felt that she
was not afraid of me at present, but of her problems which she
was learning to face with more and more honesty. Her feeling
sexually constricted still continued. She had told Ann that sex
was not too satisfactory at present, and somehow this had made
Susan feel better.

Susan: I had a dream Wednesday night, only part of which,
snatches, I remember. In the dream, I went to visit someone
who lived in an apartment house. There was a revolving
mechanism where there usually is a revolving door to the
building. This mechanism, which revolved constantly, was
like a huge revolving plate that had another turning mechanism on it; you had to contort to get on; like crawling
through tubes, as soldiers would in basic training. You had to
maneuver through to get into the building. I was afraid but

14 Susan sat up for sessions 216–263.

noticed others jumped on the gadget. So I jumped on, too.

I don't know if I knew the man I was visiting or not. In the apartment there was only one man there—an Indian I had never met before. He was very tall and heavy-set. I liked him. There were four of us in the apartment: the Indian, me, another woman, and another man. We were all going to an exposition or exhibit. It was like in Boston in that we took a streetcar.

I don't remember what happened at the exposition, but something happened to the Indian. He was killed, and I felt bad about it. I think there was a time interval between meeting the Indian and going to the exposition. And I think that I had some kind of relationship—not sexual—with him.

Then I'm at the exposition. There was some question of wanting to have sex with the Indian and being hesitant. In some way I injected myself with his semen, and after that, found out he was dead. I suddenly knew I was pregnant. And I wondered how I would feel about having his child now that he was dead.

There was a lapse of time.

Then I was in my apartment alone. The contrast between my apartment and the other was important. Then a woman visited me. She was very tall and had dark hair—no one I knew in reality, but in the dream I knew her. I think she was the fourth person in the apartment. I was surprised to see she was very pregnant. She seemed to have expanded in all ways physically since I last saw her. She said she could not stay long because Ben, some sort of person of authority, had planned for her to make a large dinner for eight or ten, despite the fact that she was pregnant. Ben was responsible for my going to the apartment in the first place.

Then I awoke and felt confused. (*Silence.*) I had another dream last night; I do not remember except that it was something competitive. When I got out of the exposition, I knew I was pregnant and was alone. Yet I wasn't terribly anxious. And I was startled when I saw this woman pregnant, because she was pregnant in my place.

This dream had another quality. I felt much better, more

at peace with myself yesterday than the day before. I felt very few physical pains yesterday. The pains have been there to some extent all week until yesterday. I feel there's something I don't want to see here—and so I developed the headache.

Susan then gave the following data, which was recorded in sequence.

What awakened her was her neighbor's radio. During lunch, she had talked with Nat Berman and Ben about an article she had read on pregnancy. Berman was her maiden name, also Ann's maiden name.

As to the huge, heavy-set man, Susan had seen a doorman at Ripley's "Believe It or Not" who was huge, about six feet ten; he was dressed in Oriental clothing.

Susan recalled going one time to buy ice cream for David; on the way, she realized she wanted it for herself. She mentioned her feeling that it was morally wrong to indulge herself, that she shrugged off responsibility on to others.

With reference to the mechanism and to crawling through the tubes, Susan associated this with failing gym and with how she felt on a bicycle and on ice skates. It also reminded her of sex motions. "Maybe I can let myself be seen."

She emphasized the fact that the dream started in her own apartment and that there was a difference between her apartment and the other apartment. The other apartment was more luxurious.

Ann's first husband was named Ben. Susan thought the woman in the dream was Ann. Ann, like Susan's mother, was very efficient. "Ann is short and yet I made her huge. So is my father short; so is my mother."

Susan interpreted the dream as follows. The big Indian and the big woman were her parents. She did not have a sexual relationship with the Indian, but she toyed with the idea. This reflected her preoccupation with how to relate to her father and with her adolescent dream at sixteen of having intercourse with him.

Susan felt that she was trying to kill off an old way of relating to her father and to men in general: she was relieved that her mother, and not she, was pregnant with the father's child. "It's like giving back my father in some way to my mother, disengaging myself from their lives. Maybe this is why I felt so good the last few days. It's like giving up seduction of the man and constant competing with the woman as ways of relating. And that's how I have related. And this is what I must change."

Dream 37 / *Session 219*

The session went as follows. Susan described a "mild fight" she and David had had. She felt that, despite the anxiety, she was able to see the total situation and hold her own. In retrospect, she saw how petty it all was; she felt she was developing a sense of humor.

At the same time, the relationship was becoming more meaningful and closer.

Susan: I had a dream Tuesday night after this [the "mild fight"] happened. I don't remember the dream, except for a part where my coat was ripped across the shoulder so that one quarter of my body was exposed to the cold. Someone told me about it, then I noticed it. The coat in the dream was similar to a coat I bought in 1946. The thought was: "Now I have to go out and buy a new coat." It wasn't anxiety but "Oh dear, now I have to buy another coat." (*Silence.*) Now I realize why I thought of this dream *now* . . . part of me was exposed, but it wasn't anxiety-producing. Of course, only a piece of me, about one quarter, was exposed. But it's a start. This time I don't have to wait for the rays of the machine to root out the cancer.

I suddenly think of the coat I bought when married to Irwin; it was a coat Irwin considered too expensive. The dream is an expression of the fact that I can take a look, am less threatened by exposure, of taking a line of action. Irwin was so upset by my buying the coat he threatened divorce because of my unilateral action.

Something else was exposed Tuesday night: that part of

me I'm ashamed of—I want what I want when I want it, *now*. David saw that, and he didn't turn away in disgust. (*Silence.*)

Something different comes to mind. Irwin and I had a lot of difficulty about money. David and I are going shopping today for some clothes for David, Irwin was well dressed; I encouraged him, so that he would not object to my paying a lot for clothes. But I felt that he did just not play fair, because he complained about my extravagance. I wanted Irwin to spend as a tool to get expensive clothes for myself. (*Silence.*) [15]

Dreams 38 and 39 / *Session 222*
During this hour, Susan sat up.

> *Susan: (Smiles.)* I'm beginning to feel I have a problem with closeness. I knew it all along, and I paid a certain amount of lip service in the past—it's no longer just an intellectual realization—it's a far different thing from reviewing everything logically.

Susan then stated that this was due to her talk with David. After the talk, David left to go to the university, and she had an acute attack of anxiety that she recognized as a fear that they *would* go on vacation together. Susan said that she and David were closer this weekend than ever before. But when he left, "I had the shakes and was ready to jump out of my skin." She described the tension in detail as very severe: she had felt extremely tense in her torso, was perspiring, and her heart was pounding.

Susan associated that kind of panic with the time Steven told her he was a homosexual. "Maybe I'm reacting to the same thing: you've got to come to grips with the problem." She defined the problem as "the way I relate to men and the fears of a close relationship."

[15] Because of Susan's desire to discuss material other than the dream, and because the dream came up rather late in the session, no further interpretation of it was attempted.

There was a certain amount of duty in my saying these words before, but it had no real meaning. I would always start with, "*If* I had a problem with closeness—" It hit home emotionally this weekend. I was busy trying to deny it (emotionally, in the past), but I can't now (*Silence.*) There's no question in my mind now about running away from the problem. I don't think now of taking flight; it just doesn't even cross my mind.

Susan told David this weekend how she felt about taking vacation together. She said each had to decide whether he or she wanted to resolve the problems in the relationship. She felt that "each of us turned to the other—in contrast to the previous weekend, where each withdrew from the other." In the past when she had experienced this kind of anxiety she had not recognized it and had pushed David back in some indirect way. This time, Susan said, knowing what was happening, she did not have to push him away and did not try to.

(*Silence.*) Yet the next day I did experience this extreme reaction [anxiety]. I knew then it was that I was making more and more of a commitment. I felt the walls closing in. (*Silence.*) I used to have a very similar reaction to you when I used to say: "You're backing me into a corner." This time, in spite of the anxiety, I behaved differently. I didn't push David away.

I think that talking about a fear of closeness is all very fine, but I never felt what was really happening until this weekend. Because I know I can find a few germs of truth and erect an elaborate superstructure. I can convince myself—I think that by this time David and I do know each other well enough to not be on guard, run away from each other. Actually, as exhausting as last week was, I'm glad it happened. It brought something out into the open. And I behaved like an adult: I didn't come running to papa [me].

Susan noted something new in the past month: she was more at ease socially, less anxious: "less fearful of being exposed."

I had a dream Saturday or Sunday night in which there was a line: "At your high tide, come to low tide." High Tide is a private sanatorium I had heard about from a patient who had been treated there. In the dream, I was talking to the person who runs High Tide; he was talking directly to me about some commitments he was making for doing research in working with patients for their benefit without enriching himself in any way. He said, "I can't just run this private hospital where everything is centered in just bringing the money in." In the dream, this had a very real quality.

I had another dream the other night. I was in the kitchen of an apartment I lived in, though it was not my present apartment. There were some high cupboards that were filthy and crawling with ants, maybe even a couple of roaches. I felt that the housekeeper was not keeping the place clean, was not doing her job. And I realized that I would have to do it myself. I did not relish the notion; and I felt terrible that I should be slob enough to have bugs. But I knew I would do it and clean it up. The bugs were there. I knew I would go away and leave them for a while, but come back and clean them up. In the dream I was not happy that the bugs were there. But I knew they were there and that I had to do a job to clean them up.

Susan felt that the first dream referred to me: "that you are interested in helping me above and beyond a fee."

Time was running short in the session. Susan smiled and said the second dream was obvious: no one could do it for her, she would have to clean up her own mess; and she felt some confidence.

I pointed out some additional meanings of the dreams: "At your high tide, come to low tide" represented Susan's awareness that when things went well she would then undo them. In the second dream, she was facing her need for a cleanup within herself, as symbolized by the kitchen, the filth, and the bugs. But she had not yet done the cleaning up, though she was heading in that direction. This, I felt, was where she was currently in the analysis.

Susan was pensive. She then said that "at your high point, come to low point" reminded her of her dream of fingering the pearls, tearing something apart. Again she referred to the problem she had with closeness, especially when things were going well. After a silence, she agreed that she was seeing the need to "clean up" but had not yet done the cleaning. She felt some confidence that she could, though.

Dreams 40 and 41 / *Session 224*
Susan began the hour with an account of David's reluctance to spend his vacation with her; her pressing for a greater commitment and a deeper involvement from him, and his response that he felt torn but could not commit himself. She expressed her fear that the relationship was ending and she wanted to know what her part in this had been.

> I know I still have a problem with closeness. I want and don't want this relationship to continue. I have never before experienced feeling in the way I have in the last year. But the closeness makes for intense anxiety; what comes to mind is the idea of me actually ice skating. I need to go to the rail to hang on because I get scared and anxious. (*Silence.*) I know I felt no anxiety when David started to pull out—maybe even relief. (*Silence.*) He may have started to run, but I helped him. It was I who first raised the question, "Do you want to pull out?"

Toward the end of session 224, Susan told two dreams. Of the first dream, she said: "I had a dream over the weekend which involved Irwin and his second wife. There was a lot of chasing about; but I'm not clear and I was terribly concerned about what they would think of me." All she could recall beyond that was that the wife was a blonde and that she (Susan) was anxious. About the second dream: "I had another dream. I realized my menstrual period had begun. Nothing else. I think that to me indicates that maybe I'm becoming a woman." As to the feeling tone of the dream, she said: "None. Just a recognition. Just a fact. I was not happy; I was not sad. I accepted it. Somehow, it was the acceptance of me as a woman."

When queried what she thought of the dreams, Susan had no ideas.

I pointed out to her that perhaps the two dreams were related. In the first dream she was expressing her fear of losing David, and this induced frantic anxiety. There was a strong need for approval, and a deep-felt doubt of her own worth if she didn't have the relationship to sustain her. The second dream involved acceptance of herself as a woman; she was alone, unfulfilled as a woman, and had apathetically deadened all feelings.

Susan said that my comments made her feel really anxious: "a wave of anxiety." When I asked why, she said this touched on her deep fear that she would be alone and unfulfilled as a woman.

David ended the relationship at about the time of interview 225. Susan was very upset, not only because of the loss of the relationship but because of the fear that she would remain alone. She indicated that she felt more ready for and capable of a relationship than ever before, but feared it might be too late. She described herself as feeling "like a hothouse flower, blooming in the desert all alone."

Dreams 42, 43, and 44 / *Session 228*
Susan reported feelings of diffuse anxiety, and diarrhea. She initially attempted various intellectual explanations.

Susan: But I, I don't know how productive it is for, to, to sit here and, and, to in a sense speculate about what may be bothering me. I don't know and I, I said to you the other night that I had been having some dreams and maybe I'll be able to, to get a better notion there than just sitting here and trying to, you know, what, what do you think of when, in connection with this anxiety and diarrhea.

Dr. C.: O.K.

Susan: The, the dream that, that I had that, that woke me up on Sunday night was about David. And I, I had been seeing him over a period of time and things looked hopeless for marriage. And I loved him but, but I felt that the situation would never come to fruition. And I married somebody else. I married Fred Lerner, that's the fellow who works under me. And although I married him in the dream, I just seemed to forget about it after it took place. I was seeing David again, and finally David and I decided to get married. And I don't know whether I asked him or well, I, I look at the notes I had made and I see that I have here that we finally got married at my suggestion and I didn't remember whether it was a direct suggestion or whether I had been trying to manipulate him into this move. And it was a ceremony that wasn't attended by anyone. It was performed by a judge, it was very quiet and it wasn't until after we were married that I remember that I was already married. And I was, I felt terrible and I felt very much afraid to tell David. And I, I decided and to have the name on the marriage certificate, the first marriage certificate, changed from Lerner to David's name, and David agreed, although—this is kind of cockeyed —although I still hadn't told him that I was married to Fred. And after we were married, right after we were married, no period of time, suddenly I had a child and I know it was David's child, but at that time the pressure of the two marriages began to build up and I think that I just felt like a rat caught in a trap, and, and I began to compare David and Fred. And there was just no comparison, none whatsoever, and one of the things that bothered me about being married to Fred was that he would always remain a relatively poorly paid worker and that living would be very difficult for us, and even though Fred was trying, Fred was trying very hard because apparently he had published a book. It was a humorous book describing his experiences in this country and describing humorously his life with me and with my parents. Apparently we were living with my parents, and, and I think that in the dream that it wasn't until, that I had been feeling that I could get away with this deception by just changing the names on the marriage certificates. But when I saw the book that had been published, I knew that, that the jig was up and I felt the pressure on me again and then I, I, I talked to everyone in the family about going along with me on the question of changing husbands and there was still a lot of fear of David's reaction and I didn't know what to tell him but I knew I must face him and I was afraid that he would leave me and at the same time I was afraid that he was the only man that I would ever love. And caught in that dilemma, I woke up. And I remember the first reaction that I had when waking up was that in the dream what I was expressing was a fear that I mustn't, that I was afraid of getting involved with someone who was much less satisfactory to me than David was and that I would have to be very careful about choosing someone and that I mustn't act too quickly. All right, that was what I thought of as soon as I woke up from the dream, but I don't think that that was what I was talking about in the dream.

Dr. C.: Have you any ideas on that?

Susan: No. I don't. But one thing bothers me very much. And I think it bothers me because it comes back to the phony values again. This business of being concerned because I would always have a difficult economic life with Fred. (*Silence.*) Incidentally, I, I, I'm a little anxious now that [*pause*], I became a little anxious when, when I went back to this, this question of the difficult economic life, and, you know, I have the feeling that dreams, that the dreams I have been having since then have been saying the same thing, and I, I don't know what that feeling is based on. At least I think the dreams that I had the next night were. . . . It was a very mixed-up business and I don't have the whole thing in focus, but at one point a person at the office was in the dream, a woman who is, well, I, I don't, she is a woman who had never married and not a very sensitive person and is very abrupt and I don't think she has terribly many human contacts in this world. She was in the dream and I, I think that I got the two of us mixed up. I think that I thought that I was she, and there was another point in the dream when somebody left the office, I guess quit her job, and it may have been Ann, and I tried to take over and I couldn't do the whole job and I, I felt, I felt very anxious. And then, and then there were, there were a lot of scenes involving David and his sister and I wanted something from him, and he really wanted to pull out and I was fighting desperately against that and, and there was an awful lot of conflict about what I should or shouldn't do. And then I was in another situation with both men and women and, and I had a, I was paired off with a man and he, he left me and then I was paired off with somebody else and he left, and people, people kept leaving and gee, I think I, a lot of them reminded me of guys that I had known at one point or another in my life, not necessarily guys who have really meant something to me, but they. . . . I had thought them attractive in, in the past. And I, all I know about the situation is, is that there was some question of danger and, and people kept chasing me and then leaving me, chasing me and then leaving me.

Both of these dreams that I had before my last session with you, and in addition to getting a good look at myself, I think it's very important that I get a very good look, as good as I can, at any rate, at the relationship between David and me and the way I feel about the relationship, and, because, I think I know how I feel but, I think that's what I was talking about in those dreams, the relationship between David and me and [*pause*] it's something that perhaps I've got to understand better than I do. (*Silence.*) You know, I remember telling you two years ago about the little superstitious habits of mine of trying to see patterns in situations, and when you, you know, after a certain period of time passes, I will meet someone or someone will come back. It's, I was thinking of that again this week and I think that I've been doing, I think, I know I've been doing some kind of that, some of that type of fantasying in relation to David. And I think that, that, that, that's a hangover from a need to feel helpless because, in effect, it takes things out of your hands. You know, a certain time has to pass or you carry a certain good luck charm or you go through the motions that you went through before a particular thing happened and then maybe it will happen again and it's, it's an attempt to sidestep the basic question, which is what did you do to bring things to this pass. And I think that another thing that I'm expressing in these dreams is a lot of mixed-up feeling about how much I can do and about and I, I mean in the relationship with David. Because when somebody left the office I tried to take over the whole job. And I know that when I was thrashing about so ridiculously last week, I was leaving David out of the equation, feeling that if I change that would be enough.

Dr. C.: Mmmmmm. Well, there are the ideas in the dream of feeling helpless, that you might not find as good a substitute as David and also—

Susan: No. Well, feeling that he would be the only man that I would ever love.

Dr. C.: All right.

Susan: Which is in the dream, the substitute that I chose . . . [*pause*]

Dr. C.: Was not as good.

Susan: Was not a substitute, let me put it that way.

Dr. C.: Yes, that's why I think that there is the fear of not finding someone who can take his place. And there are also the fears you verbalize of drifting from relationship to relationship. People chasing you, leaving you, chasing you, leaving you, but somehow not really contacting you or remaining with you permanently, getting involved with you. And these are some of the fears we have been talking about in the analysis.

Susan: (*Silence.*) We still have time. There was another dream I had the night after that with another. . . . (*Pause.*) Yeah. A report that we give to one of our clients every three months was completed on time, but nobody delivered it to them. And I called their office and I spoke to someone and I learned that a very important official was going to a meeting that night and I had the feeling that it was crucial that we get that report over to their office that day, and I was very disturbed over the fact that it hadn't been delivered. And I spoke to Dr. Morgan about it and I wanted to send someone over immediately with it. So he said no, you have to talk to Mr. K. about it, and I remember his saying that we have to be diplomatic and not tell Mr. Klein what to do but, you know, ask him what he thinks, and I was, in the dream I remember taking time out to appreciate my boss' operation, and it was decided to get a certain number of copies of the report over to their office and I was to take them over. And I hurried down to the neighborhood in which the union office was located, and I met a friend of mine—I, I think it was a woman and there was a, it was when I met her I realized I didn't have the report with me and there was a big sale going on in the store in which I saw my friend and they were offering tremendous bargains, particularly in books and records and I had a great urge to browse in the book section and I did and I was torn between a desire to buy a lot of the books and a worry about the money that I would be spending, a real fear of spending the money, and at the same time there was also a feeling of, even if I buy these books I may never get to read them. And I was, I wonder what happened after that. Oh, I was more, I was worrying again about going back to the office for the report. And also that same night there was a lot of driving back and forth to Boston and there were a lot of torn-up streets and here again there was a situation that I felt was dangerous. And right now it seems to me as if tearing around in Boston, this just chasing in a car in the torn-up streets for some reason makes me think of that business the night before, involving the men chasing me and leaving me, chasing me and leaving me. It's almost like a purposeless activity, purposeless activity. (*Silence.*) And I think that I was also warning myself that I can't think of myself as somebody who is omnipotent in terms of doing the whole job, doing everybody's job. And I think that when you get right down to it, a lot of the feeling that I have about the possible future of a relationship with David, there's no other word for it, but feelings of omnipotence on my part.

Dr. C.: Yes, in a way your head tells you one thing; logic tells you that there's a good probability that he's on the way out. But yet something within you just refuses to accept it, emotionally, and this is a feeling of omnipotence. I feel, though, that the dream says something much more basic than that, and I was wondering if you have any further thoughts on it.

Susan: Which dream?

Dr. C.: This last one.

Susan: About forgetting the report? (*Pause.*) Leaving it at the office. I have been leaving things behind, incidentally, this week. Did it with a raincoat, did it with a pair of gloves, didn't get the gloves back, forgot the raincoat. (*Silence.*)

Dr. C.: You see, in the dream there is the element of not getting the report to the proper person. Now I think you're referring to me and the analysis. In the dream you say to yourself you have to rush out and get the report to the proper person at once, that very day. But then another part of you says, "No, no, let's escape; let's not face the issue, let's go through the old business of avoiding the basic issues." Books, records have always been associated with escape, as you have told us very often in the past. And what I hear you saying is that there is a part of you that wants to pull away from facing the basic issues and facing the truth, the realities.

Susan: Isn't that what I've been saying all hour?

Dr. C.: Yes.[16]

Susan continued the session with a discussion of her denial of reality, her refusal to accept an ending with David. This was what the first dream was about: the need to accept David's leaving, and her inability to do it. In fantasy she looked for a way to hold David to her, such as having a baby.

Susan said that all week she had been torn between two patterns: facing reality or running away from it. She knew she became deeply anxious at the thought that the relationship with David was over. When she said "no, no," her anxiety disappeared; she then fantasized that they would resume the relationship.

She saw this "tug" and was afraid that she might slip back and begin to shut off her feelings again, to deny the facts, drift,

[16] At this point the machine ran out of tape.

and depend on fantasy for gratification. As anxiety provoking as the thought of being alone was, she was determined to face the facts and not slip back into the old pattern.

Dream 45 / Session 231

Susan: I had a dream on Saturday night, I dreamed about David. I dreamed I went to him several times to try to get him to resume our relationship, and he always said no. And after leaving him, I had to go home by myself, and it was very late. And it was a dangerous situation and I felt an incredible amount of anxiety in going home by myself. And in the next section of the dream I was with someone, attending some kind of committee or subcommittee meeting. And I was on this committee with someone else from my own particular group, and this other person may have been my mother, and I think I wasn't paying very good attention to what was being said, and I wasn't taking notes. And then at the end of the meeting we were going to have to report on the matters that were discussed to a much larger group, and I was told by this person who I think was my mother that I was going to have to make a report on this area where I was totally unprepared. I think I may have even missed part of the meeting when this was taken up, and I said "no, no," that I refused to do it. I was very anxious. And then suddenly I decided to try to get my notes together, to try to get some notes together so that I could make the report to the larger group. Suddenly I was a little less afraid than I had been. And despite the fact that I was less afraid, I remember waking up in the middle of the night in quite a state of anxiety. I don't remember if I woke up in between the two sections or at the end of the second section, but despite awakening in the midst of an acute attack of anxiety, I was getting ready to do what I was so afraid to do in that dream. And I guess I haven't even stopped to really think about those dreams, because it seemed to me that just on the surface of it, that there wasn't much masking going on. It almost seemed to be a continuation of just exactly what I have been grappling with during the day, and it just doesn't seem that anything is hidden.

Dr. C.: You feel the dream's obvious to you.

Susan: Yes.

Dr. C.: Well, what do you feel the dream is saying? Or rather, what you're saying in the dream.

Susan: Well, what I just, what I said to you, that's, it's very hard to give David up. But it's something that I've got to face, and he made me face it several times during that dream, because I went to him more than once and it did no good. But then, even though I was so afraid of being by myself, that even though I was so afraid of the notion of speaking up in a group—this is something that has always been productive of a great deal of anxiety in me—and even so, I was preparing to do what I had to do at the end of that dream instead of just refusing to make the report, which was my first impulse. And I think that, I know I've been trying to do what has to be done in here, and trying to do what I really should have been doing two years ago, namely, do what has to be done.

Dr. C.: I go along with that. [*Susan talked again of missing David.*] But getting back to the dream itself, maybe you're also saying where you are in the analysis; where you are with yourself with this problem. That is, you don't want to pay attention to what is being said; you don't want to take notes; you don't want to face the reality of what you have been telling us in the analysis. There is the reality that David is not on the horizon at present.

Susan: That's very true. He is not on the horizon at present. And I think, all right, sometimes you talk statistically. And I think statistically the probability is certainly that he will not be on the horizon. I think there is also a more than remote chance that I will hear from him again.

Dr. C.: O.K., let's assume this is the case. But is that the message of your dream?

Susan: No, of course not.

Dr. C.: Well, what is the message of your dream, as you hear it?

Susan: The message of my dream is that, that I've got to do what has to be done, and that I've got to face reality, and that I can't have things the way I want them, just because I want them. But at the end of that dream, even though, incidentally, I don't know if it's that I wasn't paying attention or that I wasn't present when whatever subject it was was discussed, but at the end of that dream I was preparing to report.

Dr. C.: Yes, but you never gave it, you awoke, and you felt terribly anxious.

Susan: I don't know if it was at that point or after the business with David.

Dr. C.: O.K., the fact remains that in the dream there are two elements involved. One is, you go to David and try to resume the relationship and he says no, and then there's the switch in which you're being asked for a report, and you say you're not paying attention to what is being said, you didn't take notes. And perhaps this is your way of saying you—

Susan: I have a feeling that this area was not my responsibility.

Dr. C.: O.K., that you haven't organized the facts for yourself; that you haven't faced yourself with the facts.

Susan: I think I've been facing myself with a lot of facts. I take exception to that.

Dr. C.: Well, maybe both sides of the coin are appropriate here; that you are in the process of trying to realistically assess the situation, to realistically observe yourself in it. And yet, at the same time, there are the old parts which say: I refuse to take *no* for an answer. Now both are going on simultaneously.

Susan: But you know, this is progress for me. In the past I would have said: "I don't care." I wouldn't have let myself care. (*Pause.*)

Dr. C.: Susan, when you think of the word "committee," what comes to mind?

Susan: Well, the first thing that comes to mind right now is: committee for a sane, nuclear policy. Various groups have been organized in New York. Of course, I also must confess

—I had another marginal notion, of this travel committee, this subcommittee that was set up at the office on which they placed me, and it, I told you I went to one meeting and, ah, I didn't have problems about going to the meeting. Ordinarily, I would. . . . [*Susan expressed some resentment toward David, and then considerable resentment and anger toward her mother.*]

Dr. C.: We had seen each other Thursday, and we talked about commitment here. And at the risk of being way out in left field, I wonder if the term committee and commitment might not have something in common here. You talk about David and his saying no, and then there's a switch and suddenly we are with your mother.

Susan: (*Silence.*) Yeah.

Dr. C.: Now I think you're trying to tell us something in this dream.

Susan: And you don't think it's all this obvious as I thought it was.

Dr. C.: No, I don't. (*Silence.*) Granted the idea of committee and commitment, to commit, is something I dragged in, not you. I just raise that as a possibility. But the structure of the dreams start off with David, his saying no, your being alone and incredibly anxious.

Susan: It was dangerous.

Dr. C.: It was dangerous. And then you drag in your mother. I wonder what you're trying to say here.

Susan: I don't think she's dangerous to me any more. (*Silence.*) I thought I had a choice in that dream of refusing to do what she said I had to do, or doing it. At first I refused, and then I proceeded to, as I put it, to do what had to be done. (*Silence.*) Because I realized that I could, I realized that I could. And at the point in the dream when I was facing the prospect of reporting to a large group—this, incidentally, is the situation that I've told you so many times, is one that has been filled with irrational terror for me—I was able to face the prospect without terror. Of course, this belies my words if I woke up terribly anxious. I just don't remember it this way.

Dr. C.: Now, it's interesting in the dream you start off trying to resume a relationship with David, the man, and David says no. And then you're alone, you're incredibly anxious, and then you drag in your mother.

Susan: (*Silence.*) I said here on Thursday something that comes to mind now. I think that she's been a very important factor in my inability to make a relationship with my father, and later to make a relationship with people, not just men, people. To make an honest relationship, to be myself. But in the dream I found that I could, even though what she said to me filled me with anxiety at first. I found that I could, and set about organizing things, because it was as though someone consciously built up distrust of people. I think that she did it unconsciously, but I remember all of the warnings: "You can't, you shouldn't tell people too much." . . .

Dr. C.: You start off wanting closeness with a man, you don't get it and you feel anxious, alone, and you turn to the woman, as a result. But look at how you relate. You don't pay attention to what is said, you don't take cognizance.

Susan: Look, I'm not sure that I was there when this business is, is, is happening. Let me remind you of that again. Because there was a feeling in the dream that what I was being asked to do was not my responsibility. It was not an area of my responsibility. And I think that when I told you about the dream at first, I was unsure about whether or not I had been there or whether or not I had been inattentive. That's true, isn't it?

Dr. C.: You see, maybe you experience the analysis as bringing some pressure, in a sense as agreeing with you when you say that you have to face the facts. And characteristically, this has been just the opposite of how you've operated all your life. You've never faced the facts.

Susan: But I am facing them.

Dr. C.: And now you are starting to face them and there's a lot of anxiety about this.

Susan: I know, but I'm facing them anyway, and it's not a paralyzing kind of anxiety. When I say that, I mean it doesn't make me want to pull away from people the way it used to. Not at all. (*Silence.*) I don't want to be isolated from people now. . . .

[*Susan again expressed considerable resentment toward her mother for the way her mother taught her to relate.*] Being afraid of them [the other persons], feeling that if you reveal yourself you're in trouble, and feeling that the thing you must do in your relationships to people is to placate them, please them, otherwise there's no hope of your getting anything at all that you want. So, you see, this very strong person who knows all of the answers has infinite powers, and the only way of exercising any control at all over this woman is to placate her, to give her what she wants.

Dr. C.: You start off with David, wanting to relate to the man, and somehow the man is not available, he says no. And then you're thrown into a relationship with a woman where there's no real relating.

Susan: This is not an all-female group, incidentally, this committee. Yeah.

Dr. C.: Well, where you are really not relating, though you're going through the motions, in a sense. You're together. I think this is terribly important.

Susan: (*Silence.*) It is terribly important. You know, I don't feel really related to her [mother]. And if something happened to her and I heard about it, something terrible, and I reacted by crying, I think I'd come here next time and say to you that I was surprised when I found myself crying. I feel totally unrelated to my mother, and I don't know if that's neurotic or not. I mean, you've never met my mother. She's not an ogre, I grant you that, but I just don't feel that there's anything there, in any positive way. And yet I turn from a rejection. In this dream there is a rejection and I turn to her. That's, you know, that's something else that may be cockeyed, but you remember I've always had a need to feel rejected. And yet, during this whole period, during this whole month, one thing that I have not felt is rejected by David. That may be a refusal to face reality, but I don't think he rejected me personally. And I think that that was what I meant when I said to you that I don't feel inadequate as a person in all of this. Maybe I should feel rejected, maybe that's reality, but as a matter of fact, I don't.

Dr. C.: Well, in your dream, when you have to, you find that you organize your material.

Susan: Listen, I've, I've just been organizing everything in an astonishing way lately, not just in the dreams. I've been doing things that have to be done, instead of just letting them slop around and hang over my head. I think I've become a lot more efficient.

Dr. C.: And maybe a lot less helpless.

Susan: I feel, I don't feel helpless. I feel a lot stronger now than I did a month ago, a lot stronger, and I think you can see it.

Dream 46 / *Session 232*

Susan: You know, Dr. Caligor, I've been living in a state of anxiety for a good bit of yesterday and most of today, and I have the feeling that I've been this way for a long, long time. It, it doesn't interfere with my functioning. By that I mean I'm getting a lot of things done that do need to be done. But it's there; it's very much there, and I, I, I don't know, maybe it's not at all surprising. I want to, to pull something out.[17] I checked this when I got home the other day. When I told you about the dream that I was talking about on Tuesday, this committee meeting where I was the representative together with somebody else and then I, I thought that other person may have been my mother. After our meeting, our summary must be presented to a larger group. I'm told that I must report on a subject on which I know very little. I have missed a meeting when it was discussed. It wasn't that I, I was there and not paying attention. It's that I wasn't at the meeting when they took it up, and, and then what I, I explained here at the time that I, I wrote it down, that I indicate refusal to give the report, I want to

---

[17] Susan was referring to her notes on the dream we had been discussing during the previous hour. She had not had the notes with her then.

duck the job. But after some thought I decide to do it, though this is not in response to arguments of others.

Dr. C.: I see.

Susan: And I think, I think it, it's to me. At any rate, it throws a different complexion.

Dr. C.: Well, I agree with you there. How would you see it?

Susan: Because I don't see it as trying to hide from reality, which, and trying to avoid facing the facts, which is the picture that I do get when we talked about my not taking notes and my not paying attention, which is something we discussed. And even though this is a difficult job, because I don't have the background that I need, I do decide to do it, and it's not a response to the urgings of other people. And I guess, I think that that's what I'm trying to do here.

Dr. C.: Hmmmmmm.

Susan: But of course I know that I'm really my own worst enemy when it comes to doing it. And I also noticed that I, I had a dream on Sunday when I got back that, that I don't think I mentioned to you. In the dream I was going up to the White Mountains, where I spent last weekend with Lois and Bob, and I was talking and thinking about my birthday and, and what day of the week it fell on in 1950 and the day of the week it falls on this year, and I was trying to find some kind of pattern, you know, portents of the future. And in the dream a real feeling of, and at the same time, that I was carrying on like this, I felt very ashamed, of even thinking along these lines of superstition, but I was doing it anyway. And somehow at the end of the dream I had a feeling of optimism about this year, and it was, it was, some of it was based on patterns I had picked out. But the rest of the feeling of optimism was based on the way I was functioning. Most of this dream was not action. I was talking to somebody, and I felt a change take place.

But even while I talk about changes taking place, I feel that [*silence*] anything but change is taking place now, I feel as if I'm at this point very much in danger of slipping back, because I, I still think about David entirely too much, and I, I've been missing him very much, and I'm perfectly well aware that this is, you know, like asking for the moon and you can't get it so you're unhappy about it. And I do feel that it's crucial that I cut it out and get on with the job at hand. And yet, during the last month, something has been happening to my relationships with people. The people that I've known for a long time. A lot of the time I'm anxious. There's a mild anxiety. I feel butterflies in my stomach. It's not prickling, it's almost like a heightened sense of excitement, but I don't seem to be afraid of people and I can talk to them, not in any self-conscious way. (*Silence.*)

Dr. C.: You know, the dream you had Sunday, you just mentioned before, the idea of looking for a pattern in the birth dates; it's as though you're looking for some kind of meaningful pattern.

Susan: Yeah, but I've done that for years, and I, I remember the first time I told you about it, and I really felt embarrassed because I know how silly it is. You know, I still do it? I still do it. And, and I don't look upon it as trying to find a meaningful relation. I, I look upon it in another way. I think that it's trying to deny your own responsibility for what happens to you, and when you say the time is right, it's a way of avoiding saying something. [*Tape unclear.*] (*Silence.*) I think it's a very neurotic thing to do, and I, except that in that dream I know that the reason that I felt better at the end had something to do with functioning better. It wasn't just that the patterns were there.

Dream 47 / *Session 233*

Susan: This dream I had Sunday was not too clear, but it involved going to a wedding. I think I may have been invited by David, and I was, I went to the wedding with June Brandt, a friend of mine from college. And June, I think, also has problems with closeness. But she did get married a year and a half ago, and she's going to have a baby any—well, next month. And, but she wasn't pregnant and she was a guest at the wedding and I was sitting at her table and I saw

David when I came in. I don't remember what his relationship to the bride was, but I wanted to be sitting at the same table that he was, and I wasn't, and I felt, I guess, disappointed, a little anxious. And then when the ceremony began, and this was a very peculiar ceremony, and after the first exchange of words the bride turned and tore out of the room. She really ran as, quickly enough to win a race. And I thought I had to go after her to tell her something, how lovely she looked, and how much I admired something that she had done. And I came back into the room where the ceremony, after dashing off and telling her that, I came back into the room that the ceremony was being held in and it was dark and I couldn't find June. And I was pulled down, apparently we were seated at the tables. Somebody reached up and pulled me down into the seat, and it wasn't June. It was not someone I knew, it was a man. And I felt terribly anxious. I think I felt that I had made some kind of blunder in dashing off after the bride, and I started to say no, no, no, I have to get back, I have to get back to the table where I'm seated, and I, I just felt that I was in a desperate situation. (*Silence.*) And then I woke up. (*Silence.*)

   Dr. C.: Any idea on this? (*Silence.*)

   Susan: Last week I had a dream in which I kept going to David and wanting to resume our relationship, and I think that there's the same, the same thing running through here. And I think that [*silence*], well, I think that I was the bride who ran away. (*Silence.*) Although this was part of the ritual in, in the dream, there was nothing unusual about her running off like this. I was the one who ran away. And when you run away [*silence*], then you can't go back again to where you were. (*Silence.*) I think that I am still wrestling with the problem of giving up David, because you really can't go back to where you were.

   Dr. C.: By the way, Susan, when you think of this dream, does anything come to mind that happened—

   Susan: Yesterday? Well, ah, the first thing that comes to mind seems to be totally unrelated. [*Talks of plans to go on a week's vacation with Ann.*] And I don't know why I started to think about that when you mentioned that dream, except that I run out and I want to come back to June and I don't, and I feel frightened. This is a question of leaving the woman for the man instead of continuing to leave the man for the woman.

Dr. C.: Yes, and you say in the dream that you're anxious about the no closeness with David, you're not seated at the same table. And yet the bride runs away in the dream. You feel this is you, running away from closeness, and how you are in a situation when a man does approach you and does get close to you. And perhaps this is your idea of closeness; he pulls you down, he makes you sit down.

Susan: Well, I thought of something else in connection with that. That the party where I met David, I went over and said something to him and he reached up for my arm and pulled me down. It was virtually the same gesture.

Dr. C.: I see. Well, that's very interesting because it does involve closeness with a man in that case, and you're anxious about this. And you're saying, I have to get back to June's table. I have to get back to the woman.

Susan: Yes, that's what I said, but I also think that David was related in that need to get back. He had seated me there, you know.

Dr. C.: Nevertheless, it is the basic problem of closeness, closeness with a man, what to do with it. [*Susan then went on to talk of vacation plans. She was pleased that she was moving out toward people.*]

Dr. C.: In the dream there is the theme that has come up so often: the idea of being trapped by a man, of being close to a man causing anxiety, and wanting to get back to a woman.

Susan: Yes, but it wasn't just to be with June in this dream. It also had something to do with the fact that I, David knew I was there.

Dr. C.: Um-hummmm.

Susan: I wanted him to be able to find me, and I was afraid he wouldn't be able to find me, and that was part of the tremendous anxiety that I felt. And I think that I also made the, saying something about something that I said a couple of weeks ago, when I married someone, and then David was there, and he and I decided that we wanted to get married. And I think that this is another way of saying that. And I think that part of me, the part that keeps hearing "So long for now" [18] is saying: Wait. And there's a real conflict. I mean the conflict between loneliness and closeness is not the only one that's going on inside me. And I know, I keep telling myself it's over and you've got to live that way, but I don't fully believe it. And I, I think that the first thing I've got to do is to get to the point of believing that. So that I can stop just riding the merry-go-round; except that when I was on this date with Ed the other night, I was honest with him and I was direct. And I told him just exactly what was going on in me and I wasn't playing games. This kind of behavior would have been impossible two years ago. Despite all of these changes that I spent time talking to you about, I still feel basically there's no real change, because of this feeling of being trapped, and because of the fact that at the end of the evening he said, "Don't run away, Susan," and I didn't fall asleep for so many hours.

Dr. C.: How would you define the basic problem?

Susan: This feeling of being, of having the walls close in at the prospect of a close relationship with a man. That's the basic problem.[19]

Dreams 48 and 49 / *Section 236*

Susan: You know, I have been having a number of dreams in the last week, and most of the time I just can't remember what they were, except that I do know the night before last a very important part of this, of the dream that I did have, was an effort on my part to have someone else stop using euphemisms, and I was, I was struggling against this other person to call a spade a spade. But I didn't remember anything else

[18] These were David's last words to Susan during their last telephone conversation, to which Susan clung in the hope of a resumption of relations.

[19] Due to unforeseen circumstances, I had to cancel the next appointment. Arrangements for a substitute hour were made by phone.

about the dream. And I, sometimes if I really wake myself up and put the light on and force myself with a pencil in my hand, I can manage, but very often when I go though something like that, I find that I have finished sleeping for the night when I have finally recalled snatches and pieces, and I guess I wonder how important it is to remember every single fantasy you have . . . in bed at night. Isn't it all bound to come out one way or another, sooner or later?

Dr. C.: Do you feel it will?

Susan: Yeah, I do, and I also feel I, I'm also aware of the fact that since June I've had a sleeping problem and I haven't turned to pills and I don't plan to turn to pills. But I, it was after I had gone through this performance of, you know, forcing myself to get up and turn the light on and take a pencil and paper in hand. I realized I was cooked, I couldn't get back to sleep. And I decided that this was a little silly, and I just wonder if it's worth it because even when I got the pencil and paper out, I didn't do such a hot job. But I did get it, I did get a piece of it down.

Dr. C.: Is this the same dream you're referring to, the one about the euphemisms?

Susan: No, no, that's all I could remember about that. This was Saturday. I don't know if it means Friday night or Saturday night. But in this dream two animals, one belonging to me and one belonging to somebody else—the other person might have been my boss, the other animal owner—were being kept at my parents' house. My dog or cat, I don't know which, was smaller than the other, and it, it cost less to provide for somebody to tend to the removal of, of the feces of these animals. And one reason that it cost less was because I guess I must have had a cat. Because in the dream my animal could use a pan and Kitty Litter. And at one point I was having a discussion, it may have been my mother, on the cost of providing this service. And also involved was the cost of taking the bus three times a day to go back and forth between my parents' home and the school or office where I had to be. And I, I had a feeling that, that I was extravagant, that I was spending too much time on the animal and on the carfare. And I think that my parents might have been helping me. And part of this feeling of extravagance on my part also had to do with playing cards and, and with cosmetics. It must have, I guess maybe I was spending money gambling and devoting a lot of, too much money to appearance. And I, I had the feeling that I could do all the things that were involved more cheaply and I felt guilty because my parents were helping me and they shouldn't be. And I, I was talking to my boss about making some kind of a change and he told me to write to a friend. He, as a matter of fact, was setting off to visit this friend. He was going to give a lecture at a college and while he was giving this lecture he was going to stay with this friend, who had a non-academic, an administrative position at the college. And I don't remember his last name, but his first name was Jet, the friend who was the administrator. And my boss felt that Jet, or whatever his name was, could help me by giving me information about a possibility of changing my situation. And what I have down here is a scholarship, that may have been part of it, I don't know. (*Silence*.) But the worry about the money and three times a week and paying somebody to take the feces away. (*Laughing*.) It's pretty obvious, isn't it?

Dr. C.: Well, I think you can add these things together pretty obviously.

Susan: And of course, mine was smaller than the other person's, my animal. And the cost of care was cheaper and I wonder if I wasn't looking at two situations, David's and mine. You know, my boss' first name is David. That didn't occur to me until now, although this thought of, you know, of one being cheaper than the other, and this business of three times a week was [*silence*], was something that I thought of in connection with David before I realized that Morgan's first name is David. There is a feeling of extravagance in the dream, and I have to change my situation. And I think it's what I'm trying to do, not, I think that I'm trying to look at the situation for what it is and not just worry about changing the color of my hair. This business about changing the color of my hair, of course, is mine now. That wasn't involved in the dream. It was a question of spending money on cosmetics, that is, external, superficial changes, and [*silence*] I do feel that there does have to be a change and it's easier to care for my animal than it is to care for the other animal. Maybe in effect what I'm saying is that I'm recognizing that David and I are on different time tracks. And I know, I remember when I was talking to Ann one Sunday, I did say that the way I felt, that it didn't matter too much whether David did call me or didn't call me. I thought the result would be the same. Because he ran away, and I can't imagine anything happening during that period of six weeks when he wanted to escape that would make him more able to give me what I need, what I want. And I guess I'm feeling more of a sense of confidence in what I do want. The things that I want in the relationship are very different than the things I wanted a year ago. I don't want to be great, I don't want to be overpowered. Also, I don't think that it's necessary for me to get a slavish devotion from a man. I don't think that's what I want. I don't want a relationship that just revolves around me. I think that a year ago the test of, the test of how a man thought about you, was whether or not he would do everything you wanted. I don't know to what extent I would admit this. I think it was true. It really, it left no room for anyone else but me. I don't think that's true any more either.

Dr. C.: Well, what do you think of this dream?

Susan: I just told you. I told you about a feeling that I'm beginning to accept at a deeper level, than merely at an intellectual level, that David and I are on different time tracks. (*Silence.*) I wonder if also involved in that dream was a weighing on my part of you, and David's analyst. My animal was smaller than his. And my animal, it costs less. (*Silence.*) And I think that that's something that was involved there. (*Silence.*)

Dr. C.: The idea of paying someone to take away the feces, the bus fare three time a day—

Susan: Yeah.

Dr. C.: The idea of spending too much on the animals—
Susan: No.
Dr. C.: On the carfare.
Susan: There was also cosmetics involved when I was thinking about spending too much. It wasn't just this, it was a way of life and it involved, involved in this feeling about too much money being spent on cosmetics and playing cards, gambling. (*Silence.*)

Dr. C.: When you think of the name Jet, does anything come to mind?

Susan: An airplane, a jet pilot. Of course, on second thought, I think of black, but the first thought was a pilot. (*Silence.*) In the dream I remember taking, making note of the name, and saying to my boss, "Is this Jet, whom I heard you talk about?" And he said, "Yes, this is Jet," and [*silence*] of course, running away is involved in this dream, too. (*Silence.*)

Dr. C.: Tell me what you mean.

Susan: I want to change my situation, and as soon as I spoke of Jet and pilot, I thought of my boss going to the college to give a lecture, and possibly his friend, who was going to help me by giving me information about a scholarship, maybe a job, going to another city, flying to another city. (*Silence.*) Well, all right, that's one way of effecting a change, but as I was writing these notes [*laughs*], I remember the story that has come up from time to time in here about what my mother told me about the last time I ever had an accident with bowels, at any rate, when she rubbed my nose in my feces and after that I think I used the toilet every time. And I, in the dream I feel that my parents are helping me and they shouldn't and I want to get away from the situation with them. And I want to, I had a feeling that I could do everything that was involved in my life more economically, and I wanted to change my situation. All right, I want to change my situation now, and from one point of view, you might say that I want to live more economically. I'm not talking about money now. I'm talking about wanting to stop throwing my life away, and I'm talking about wanting to realize the potential that I do have. And escape doesn't have to be running away to another city to get a fresh start. It can be leaving the past behind, and it can be something that's positive and not just a flight from reality. (*Silence.*)

Dr. C.: Yes. In the dream you talk of the cost of paying someone to take away the feces; the setting is in your mother's home.

Susan: Their summer place, their summer place, incidentally.

Dr. C.: Their summer place. And maybe you're talking about the price you have to pay to get someone to clean up your mess in life. (*Silence.*)

Susan: I don't feel that somebody is cleaning up the mess for me. Even though there is, I'm very clearly paying someone to take care of the animal; there is another feeling, that I'm not participating. Of course, what I found myself going back to just a moment ago was the feeling that my animal is smaller and [*silence*] the comparison. Mine is not as good. You know, I think that within the last month or so, I have begun to have some feeling that, about the importance of analytic work being done by somebody who is an M.D., and I think that that is involved in this dream.

Dr. C.: Tell me what you mean.

Susan: Well, I think that I have, from time to time, when over the last six weeks or so, ah, the question has come up in which I felt that you were using a euphemism, and I think I said that one of the first things that people who come here have got to learn is that they're sick. And I think that a doctor goes into medicine and gets experience before he goes into psychiatry in helping sick people get well, and I don't think a psychologist does.

Dr. C.: Do you think that's what you're referring to when you talk of euphemism in the first dream?

Susan: The second dream; the euphemism dream came after this.

Dr. C.: After this.

Susan: Yes, I think it may very well have been, although in the second dream, the, the setting was not here. I think it was more a work situation for me, but I think that that's what I was talking about. (*Silence.*) And yet, at the same time that I had these feelings I am perfectly well aware of what has happened in the two years that I have been working with you. And I'm perfectly aware of the extent to which change has taken place in comparison with the extent to which change has taken place in my work with people who went into medicine to help sick people to get well. I know that, ah, I hadn't really thought about this until the last six weeks or so, but since then, I remember once when you used the expression "It will be interesting to find out."

Dr. C.: That's right. You took very strong exception to that.

Susan: I burst into tears, I think. Because it sounded like intellectual exercise. (*Silence.*) And I think that while these individual experiences have come up, and I have expressed myself at the time that they have come up, that I've never put my feelings together, and expressed them as a whole as I did tonight.

Dr. C.: No, you didn't. That's so. Well, the whole question of pathology and how it can be treated is a long and complicated one which I don't think would be appropriate to discuss now.

Susan: No, and there are no two schools who agree on it either.

Dr. C.: And there are no two schools that agree on it. But I do think it's constructive that you've come to a point where you can verbalize your doubts. Perhaps some day in our work together you'll help clarify the picture of those areas where you feel the analysis wasn't as productive as it could have been; those areas where you still feel there's work to be done, where you feel that you can most productively use the time. I do feel that in the dream of the two animals you are talking about the analysis, and in some context, you and me. Not only in the euphemism dream, but the idea of the price one has to pay for analysis. And I'm not merely talking in terms of money, although that evidently is a factor in the dream as I hear it.

Susan: That's a factor in reality, too. (*Laughs.*)

Dr. C.: That's a reality factor. Of course it is. And the idea that you could do all these things involved for yourself more cheaply. I'm not quite clear what you're trying to communicate.

Susan: Not for myself, no, but that I could do everything more economically.

Dr. C.: More economically.

Susan: Less extravagantly. I could be less wasteful.

Dr. C.: And then you're talking to your boss about making some kind of change, and the idea of his writing a friend, named Jet—you know, something quick. It makes one wonder what this is all about, what you're trying to basically communicate here.

Susan: (*Laughs.*) Well, what I thought of just now when you said something quick: "Gimme a needle, or gimme a pill." (*Laughs.*) About time. And there's quite a difference between traveling by jet plane and traveling by bus. (*Silence.*) I was just thinking that since the last time I saw you, I have really become quite a cry-baby. You know, I think you're looking at the only [*laughs*] person in New York City who went to see Peyton Place and cried. And I didn't cry because of any artistic triumph that Hollywood brought off, because it wasn't terribly good. But I cried when the young girl who was on trial for murdering her stepfather was acquitted. Her stepfather, incidentally, raped her earlier in life [*laughs*] and she had had to have an abortion, and she didn't want this experience but he overpowered her. And there was another point, a scene between two people in which the man announces he wants to make a commitment, that he wants for the woman to make a commitment to him, too. And she says, "I can't." I cried during that scene, too, and I felt pretty ridiculous during the whole thing. And then last night I finished a book that I had begun a short time ago, and I, I could hardly read the last few pages because the tears were streaming down my face, and I, I wasn't ashamed of myself here, though.

Dr. C.: Well, why do you think all this is taking place?

Susan: I think that I have never been, my feelings have never been as close to the surface as they are now. They're very close, and I think that that's a good thing. I think I'm much bigger now. (*Silence.*) And I guess that, that does it. I feel that that does it. And I have nothing else to say. I don't know what time we began, but I feel it's over for tonight.

Dr. C.: Well, we have run out of time.

Susan: O.K., see you Thursday. Good night.

Dr. C.: Good night, Susan.

Dream 50 / *Session 237*
Susan had decided to discontinue seeing a man who was interested in her but whom she found uninteresting as a person.

Susan: You know, I think there was a time, I know there was a time when just someone being interested in me was a source of satisfaction for me. That isn't true any more. I think it's a sign that I have a much better appreciation of myself that I didn't have a year ago. Just some man being interested in me is not a source of satisfaction. The satisfaction comes from what goes on between that other person and me. I don't consider it flattering just because somebody shows some interest. (*Silence.*) I'm saying something else, too. I'm saying that I don't need to make every man I come into contact with. (*Silence.*) In addition to an awful lot of experiencing acute loneliness. (*Pause.*)

I had a dream on Tuesday night. I remember the last, I remember the end, the last sequence. And I don't remember much that occurred before that, except that I was with a man. And he and I were walking together, there were other people involved, people to whom there was some social obligation, and we were all going to a public place. And there, although we had to be with these people, we didn't care for them particularly. And we were walking slowly into a large room, public room in a hotel, must have been a restaurant, and two of the people we knew sat down at a table for four. And I think that this particular couple was a couple we liked less than some of the other people in this large group. And I said, "I guess we have to sit down with them." He said, "I guess we do," implying that I shouldn't even have mentioned this in a doubtful way. And I associated him with David, and with some of the social situations that we were in with people who were not particularly compatible. Particularly, the people we went to Williamsburg with, and they had a party in May that was a perfectly terrible party. I think I mentioned it here. And we both wanted to leave as early as possible, because we both reacted to the party in the same way. And ah, we waited a decent interval, we weren't the first to go, we were about the third couple to go. But the hostess said, "Oh, I wish you'd stay for coffee." But we couldn't. David had the feeling that we should have stayed. And I thought of that when I remember this very dim business about the other couple. But the last sequence was much more vivid. I don't know if we were still in the public room, or if we were in a smaller room; the new handbag that I had just acquired as a gift was on the table. And my mother picked it up, she wanted to see it, she wanted to look at it. And she was handling it very roughly, and I was afraid of what would happen to the bag as a result of this rough handling, and I asked her to put it down and she didn't. And I began to get indignant. It was my handbag. I began to get very angry, and the way in which I said "Put it down" began to change. From a request, it got more and more angry and more and more heated. And finally I picked up her handbag and said, "Put it down, or I'm going to do something to your bag, and something destructive." And I was standing in a doorway or near a door jamb and I heard a loud clank, and I realized I had taken my mother's bag and banged it against the door jamb. This infuriated her and she threw my bag down on the floor. And then the man was standing and looking on. I think that he may have tried to say something to my mother that was very ineffectual. It was really as though he was looking on passively. And I think that's when I woke up in this rage at my mother. And mixed with the rage at my mother for what she was doing to my possession was a feeling of a great deal of discomfort that I had behaved so childishly to deliberately destroy something, just because it's hers. The first thing that comes to mind now, and maybe it did dimly right after the dream, what really comes to mind with full force now is the dream of the sweater and the maid. There's just one difference; this time I wasn't terrified of her, I was angry at her. And this time I fought back. I fought back the wrong way. I was as ineffectual as the man, in effect, because I just destroyed something of hers, and that didn't stop her from destroying me. Because I think that my handbag, my possession, is me. I didn't stop her, I only destroyed something of hers.

Dr. C.: When you think of this dream, did anything happen the day or night of it that comes to mind?

Susan: I was here. That was Tuesday night. No. Nothing.

Dr. C.: Do you feel you were angry Tuesday night, or expressing any anger?

Susan: No. You mean in here, with you?

Dr. C.: Well, were you feeling any anger?

Susan: No, I don't think I am angry at you. I don't think I was in the dream. I think that I was, I think that I still am angry at my mother and I don't think I behave very well in relation to my mother. Now I remember, I wrote my parents a letter on Tuesday night. It was a, there was nothing notable about the letter, but as I pointed out when I spoke to them on Friday night, I hadn't told them where I'd be the next week and I think it's appropriate that they should know. But remembering back to that telephone call on Friday night, I spoke to my father first and he asked me how I was and I told him that I was feeling a lot better. When my mother asked me how I was, I didn't answer her in the same way and I think that I, I think that I was noncommittal and she said something about, well, you were feeling unhappy a while ago. But I, I didn't want to tell her that I'm feeling a lot better. And it was childish, it didn't accomplish anything, except that maybe it made her feel a little bad; I don't think that that's what I should be out to accomplish in my relationship with my mother, and yet I think that that's the effect of what I do, and I think I do it in this childish way because actually I want to punish her. I don't feel the fury now, but the fact that it comes out of me in little ways means that there must be an awful lot of it. I guess I feel that the lessons I learned from her, some of them really deliberate instruction, have made a lot of trouble for me and I'm angry with her because of that, and because she's still so sure that she's right. But all right, I'm angry at her. She did what she did and that's past and I shouldn't be continuing to carry a grudge around, but apparently I am.

Dr. C.: When you think of a new handbag, what comes to mind?

Susan: (*Silence.*) I got a new handbag, two of them; gifts from her. She bought one for herself and one for me. Then she decided to give me both. This happened at the time, at the time I married Irwin. (*Silence.*) And I thought that I should not take the one that she wanted to give me, the one that had been intended for her, but I took it anyway. (*Silence.*) I took it anyway, and I find myself remembering the time when I was a little girl, I think I was in the cellar, and a table, a living-room table was in the cellar, too. And I had some object in my hand and I can remember scratching things in the table—in effect, doodling on the table with a sharp metal object, just marring it. And I remember there were times when I, quote, absent-mindedly, end quote, went through the same kind of performance on the telephone table. I wasn't aware of doing it while I was doing it, but it was done, and I think it was something that was directed at my mother.

Dr. C.: Well, there is a very interesting flow in the dream. The idea of walking with another person and other people in a public place, and the idea of conformity, doing what you really don't want to do. "I guess we have to sit with them" —that kind of thing.

Susan: Yes.

Dr. C.: And then the second part of the dream is very

vivid, involving all this rage, rage which gets out of hand. That is, you find yourself—

Susan: When you say "rage that gets out of hand," just then I remembered my father's taking my books in the living room and throwing them to the floor in a fury, and yet I didn't think of that at all in connection with the dream. That didn't come to mind until you said "rage that gets out of hand," because I think that my fury is only directed to her.

Dr. C.: Well—

Susan: She was always the one that made me conform in many ways.

Dr. C.: Be that as it may, I wonder if the dream might not involve us. As you say, you did have this dream the night you came here.

Susan: Yes, but remember in that letter that I wrote to my parents when that telephone conversation with them came to mind, it—

Dr. C.: Yes. You see, you're talking of a new handbag. I don't know why a new handbag, but at any rate, the feeling that the other person, in this case your mother, is picking it up and looking at it and handling it in a rough way.

Susan: Yes, she was damaging it.

Dr. C.: Yes, damaging it and you were afraid for the bag.

Susan: Yes.

Dr. C.: Now, as I recall that last hour, that was the one where—

Susan: I reported another dream.

Dr. C.: Mmmm-hummmm. You mentioned, for example, one of the things you recall you brought in was my use of the phrase "it will be interesting," and that you burst into tears, etc., etc. The feeling tone of that hour as far as I recall had a snippy quality. There was a, you know, you said, "Let's call a spade a spade" in that euphemism dream, that kind of thing.

Susan: Yeah.

Dr. C.: But the feeling tone that I get is I wonder if you're not saying that maybe in some way you experience me as handling you or some of your problems or your sensitivities with a bit of roughness at times and that this is irritating to you.

Susan: I don't think that I ever experienced roughness. There have been times, and only recently, when I experienced a quality of noninvolvement almost, that has bothered me, and I've told you whenever that has come up. (*Silence.*) But I don't think that it enrages me. I think it has been, I think that I've reacted in a way that could be best described as disappointed. (*Silence.*)

Dr. C.: You asked your mother in the dream to do something, and she doesn't, and you say—

Susan: But she's harming.

Dr. C.: Yes. In effect, you say I'm going to strike back.

Susan: Yes. (*Silence.*) I'm not just lying on the floor in terror. (*Silence.*) I guess I, you, you said that you experienced Tuesday as an hour in which there was a snippy quality. I don't think I felt snippy when I was talking to you about my negative reactions. (*Silence.*)

Dr. C.: Well, that was a feeling you somehow communicated to me. I'm not talking of the content of what you said as much as of the feeling tone that accompanied it. Which is all right. I think that for anyone who has felt as helpless as you have felt in relating to people, why, I would expect there to be a lot of rage. I think the thought in the dream goes along that line, that you're walking with the other person, you have to conform to what the other wants, to what the others want. And then comes the vivid scene where there's rage, conformity and then the rage and the desire to assert yourself because you feel provoked. (*Silence.*)

Susan: But when I assert myself, I do it in a childish way. I don't grapple with the problems directly, I do it very indirectly. I said a little while ago that this represents quite a change, that I don't lie on the floor and cower, but I don't grapple with them directly either. (*Silence.*) I don't assert myself. (*Silence.*)

Dr. C.: No, you don't assert yourself. And when you do, it is because you feel pushed and threatened, and you do it in an explosive, destructive way.

Susan: I don't start explosively.

Dr. C.: You build up to it, though.

Susan: Yes, because she ignores me.

Dr. C.: Because she ignores you.

Susan: And goes on.

Dr. C.: Isn't this what you've been saying in a sense I've been doing? You say I've been unrelated to you, and you're disappointed.

Susan: No. Maybe we're both right. (*Laughs.*)

Dr. C.: Could very well be.

Susan: (*Silence.*) I don't know, I don't remember if I used the word "unrelated" a little while ago or not. I mean I don't remember the exact word I used, but I know there's been a letdown, a feeling of being let down when you ask a question that you're trying, you're probably just trying to go through some summing-up process, but you ask a question that doesn't need to be asked, because I've been answering it for about fifteen or twenty minutes. And you know the old joke, "who listens?"

Dr. C.: Yes. You feel let down, and understandably so, though my intent might be quite other than just asking a meaningless question. But what is important is that you're able to experience the letdown feeling and to verbalize it.

Susan: Well, yes, and as I remember, I verbalized it at the time.

Dr. C.: Yes. Now this feeling—

Susan: But I don't think it leads to rage.

Dr. C.: Well, the feeling that I may not be related to you is interesting. I don't like to use that word, since it seems to be such an emotionally laden one for you.

Susan: Well, it's, it's an intellectual, it's in the intellectual area, really.

Dr. C.: O.K., the fact remains that the idea of my not being emotionally related to you is something you tell us; and in the dream your mother isn't related to you. I think that having her or anyone—

Susan: Or David.

Dr. C.: Or David, not being emotionally related to you,

must be frustrating and perpetually a rage-provoking situation. And if you experience the rage in the dream, and if you experience the rage with me in reality, why, that is understandable—

Susan: Isn't that the essence of loneliness?

Dr. C.: Tell me what you mean.

Susan: Being with someone who isn't related to you is just the same as being alone, is being lonely and lost, and not tied to someone.

Dr. C.: That's right. If you recall, you mentioned having waves of this feeling coming here.

Susan: I had it last night, too, and during the day today. (*Silence.*) Maybe I am talking about what goes on here, too. (*Silence.*)

Dr. C.: In a sense you've made the complete cycle to where you started the hour: with loneliness. But the symbol of the new handbag which is a gift from your mother, maybe you're talking of something new.

Susan: A new personality—

Dr. C.: Something new within yourself anyway, the feeling tone of being vulnerable and wanting it—

Susan: Because it's so easily damaged.

Dr. C.: It's so easily damaged and wanting it to be treated preciously.

Susan: Not preciously. I don't want it to be overprotected, but I guess I want it to be handled with the respect that it deserves.

Dr. C.: Well, by preciously, I mean just that.

Susan: All right.

Dr. C.: Handled with care.

Susan: Yes.

Dr. C.: Handled with relatedness.

Susan: All right, but handled with relatedness is not, all right, you see, when you talk about precious care, I immediately react by thinking of more care than is appropriate. Because I don't think that asking for relatedness is inappropriate. (*Silence.*) And I don't think you do either. (*Silence.*)

And I wonder why you just nodded your head [*laughs*] in this way.

Dr. C.: In the dream, when the other person isn't related to you, you, as a defensive act, become destructive. (*Silence.*)

Susan: Yes. Of course, immediately I wonder, do I do that in real life, too. Did I do that to David. I don't know how much relatedness I wanted from him until relatively recently.

Dr. C.: Well—

Susan: But did I do that to him. I don't know.

Dr. C.: Maybe you'll tell us some day. But I recall Steven, for example, and the lack of relatedness and how that relationship ended: by your taking him to bed in order to hurt him. (*Silence.*)

Dream 51 / *Session 238*

There was a break of one week because Susan was on vacation.

Susan: I had another dream Sunday night. This was after I got back, the first night's sleep I had in my own bed. A man, and possibly the father of a friend of mine, I wasn't sure, who was an employee of the market where I shop for food spoke to me in the dream about my mother. I don't remember what he spoke to me about, but she was in difficulty. It was either nonpayment of a bill or possibly theft, and I realized that my mother needed psychiatric help. And I began to do something, to take some kind of action, to straighten out the difficulty. And then I got a call on the phone from Janet, a gal who was my closest friend when I was in college. And she called to tell me that her father wanted to speak with me. And I had a feeling that it was related to this difficulty of my mother's. And she was anxious to end the conversation and hang up, but I insisted on talking to her anyway. And I began to tell her about what I had discovered, and to, to also to tell her that I didn't have to talk to her father about it. And then I go to the store where my mother has the difficulty and I continue to, along these lines of talking to the people who were involved with the difficulty there and to try to straighten things out. Then I was with my mother and she and I were shopping together and I was feeling that I was extravagant and that she shouldn't be helping me by buying me things. But I was easing my conscience by stressing the, by thinking of the fact that we were visiting sales, and we were getting good buys and things were really much cheaper than they might have been. Then I, apparently I wasn't with my mother any more, I met Claire, another former friend, and I, I was talking to her about my own troubles, my mother's troubles, and I do this despite Claire's attempt to snub me. And then I found myself with Steven, and I found myself with Steven, and here too there was some connection with my mother's difficulty. And he wants me to have a drink with him, he wants to take me to dinner, a wonderful sea-food restaurant he knows, and he mentioned a name that I, I had never heard of, and I felt that it probably wouldn't be such a good place after all. And, but there was a feeling that I, that I should go, and I don't remember whether Claire was still there or not. I may even have invited her to join us. I don't know. But then I was, I don't know what happened at that point, but I do remember next there was a telephone call from a policeman who wanted to know—apparently my mother has had difficulties like this in the past—he wanted to know if my mother has had any further trouble. And I told him of the situation, pointing out that I am taking steps to resolve this problem. I think that there was some question about whether to go into this with him or not. But as soon as he established the fact that he was the policeman, that he did know about her past difficulties, then I went into it with him. And as I was looking at all these pieces, I began to wonder what I really was saying. But I do know that a little while ago I had the feeling that this was a continuation of the same thing and that I wasn't walking all around the barn this time, in some way. And I'm sure that I'm the person with the problems, and I think I'm also the person trying to straighten them out.

Dr. C.: Umm-hummm.

Susan: And I think that you're the policeman. But, you know, I wonder too, there's been something that's recurring in my dreams, this feeling of being extravagant and of shopping at sales and really not spending much money. There was something in the last dream about cosmetics. I don't remember it, but I assume that you have notes. No, it was in the dream about the cats. There was a question of feeling I had bought some cosmetics or done something along the lines of making yourself more attractive and I had been feeling extravagant about it and I see somebody is in trouble for nonpayment of bills. I, I bought a couple of dresses in the last few weeks at a sale and I think that part of me felt that I shouldn't be buying them because I really didn't have the money. And yet I did genuinely feel that I needed them. But I think that that's part of the feeling of extravagance that, that has been bothering me, because here in this last dream I dream about nonpayment of the food bill and I'm aware of the fact that each month it seems that I give you your check a little bit later in the month and, and this time I was going to ask you. . . . I was not even going to ask you, I was going to tell you I was planning to pay you after Labor Day for the summer, July and August. And I don't think that this is the same thing as the kind of feeling of obligation that I was talking about at the time when I was busily engaged in running up a back bill that I knew was going to remain until I got back to two hours a week. (*Silence.*)

Dr. C.: Well, there's a very repetitive element in the dream.

Susan: I keep shooting off my mouth to everyone, and people don't want to hear, two women don't want to hear.

Dr. C.: Two women don't want to hear, Janet and Claire, and you want to tell them.

Susan: But I, I tell the men too, but the men don't want to cut me off. Just the women do. This is quite a change, isn't it. It's always the other way around. It's always the women I've been turning to. In my dreams, too. Of course, it's also, I've been thinking of that Alaskan business, when I turned to a woman for protection. As soon as I said it's never the women who want to cut me off, I was going to say that's not true because I remember a dream I had a long time ago involving a sweater and my mother.

Dr. C.: Well, why go back that far? Why not go back to the dream before this one, and this dream too?

Susan: I don't remember the dream before this one. Oh, sure, well, there I lashed out at my mother indirectly.

Dr. C.: Because you felt that there was no adequate cognizance of—

Susan: Me.

Dr. C.: This new part of you that was evolving.

Susan: Yes.

Dr. C.: And there was the question of, "If you don't relate to me, I'll be destructive." Now in this dream—

Susan: But in this current dream I think what I see is [*laughs*] that in effect I say is, "You don't want to relate to me; I'll relate to you anyway." At least to the point of getting this into the open. I'm not going to pretend.

Dr. C.: But the basic problem here is of relating, relating and the other person hearing, wanting to hear—

Susan: And not wanting to—

Dr. C.: And not wanting to hear. And I think the feeling is right when you say you're talking about yourself through your mother, the image of your mother in the dream. (*Silence.*)

Susan: I may even be talking about myself through Janet and Claire, too, because they were two cockeyed relationships that I had a long time ago. (*Silence.*)

Dr. C.: In this dream, the man listened, the man, anyway Steven listened. The women want to shut you off, but you continue anyway. But you don't give the feeling of any real relatedness here.

Susan: With the women?

Dr. C.: With the women.

Susan: There was with Claire.

Dr. C.: With Claire.

Susan: There was with her. I don't think there was with Janet.

Dr. C.: In the dream—

Susan: I'm talking about in the dream. I'm not talking about reality, because in reality there wasn't with Claire. Let's say that we spent a good amount of time together a long time ago. It wasn't a time when we were really in contact. I think that we probably indulged in coordinated activity. Do you know what I mean?

Dr. C.: Um-humm. You know, throughout the analysis you've been pointing out that your mother doesn't really know how to relate. She doesn't know how to relate to other people. She's irritating to other people, and that she's irritating to you.

Susan: To my father—

Dr. C.: To your father, but that she doesn't know how to relate to you and there has been a lot of anger at this inability to relate to you. There has been the invitation to become confidential, and then, as you put it, the hand comes down, the curtain is drawn and that's it. Maybe it's no accident that in the dream you talk about your problem of relating, through the image of your mother or through the image even of Janet and Claire, relating to the woman. The woman has the difficulty in relating. And I think you're right, you're talking about yourself. Maybe in the relationship with your mother, you formed certain ideas of what relating was supposed to be like and this is part of your difficulty in living today.

Susan: Well, I think that there had been a number of occasions in here when I have realized that a great many aspects of my mother's method of relating to people, of seeing people, of using people, were rejected by me, but just rejected intellectually.

Dr. C.: That's right.

Susan: They were a part of me anyway. (*Silence.*) I don't think that that's as true as it used to be.

Dr. C.: Well, this raised the question of how you relate to the policeman in this dream, or to put it more concretely, how you relate to me, how you see this relationship.

Susan: Oh, gee, I don't know how I see it. I know I feel

very differently in the relationship with you and I'm not conscious of anything in the relationship that makes me uncomfortable. You know, ever since I've been coming here, I've been honest, but there was a time when I had to force myself.

Dr. C.: Ummm-hummm.

Susan: I don't have to force myself now. And I don't think that that's just the passage of time. I don't think it's just that I feel that I know you better, because actually I don't. I, I know you through the fact that we are both looking at me.

Dr. C.: Right.

Susan: And I don't think that that's just the passage of time in operation. I don't think that I feel more comfortable in the relationship because you've changed. I think it has to be because I've changed. That's a safe thing to say, isn't it?

Dream 51 / *Session 239*
Discussion of dream 51 continued:

Dr. C.: I have been giving the dream you mentioned last hour some thought. As you recall, you brought it up in the later part of the hour, and we really didn't get a good chance to look at it. We were talking of relatedness.

Susan: Yeah.

Dr. C.: I think it would be important for us to get a good look at it at this point. The dream involves a man who really feeds, he's a storekeeper if you recall, and he's not getting paid by your mother, who you felt was part of you. This was your association. And then that your mother needs help.

Susan: Yeah.

Dr. C.: I feel you're trying to communicate something about yourself and how you relate. And just at that point in the dream there's a switch, and then you bring in Janet and you try to tell Janet what you've discovered, but Janet doesn't want to hear. And I think you're talking about the you-me. I think the man who does the feeding is me.

Susan: He's a father figure. He was Janet's father.

Dr. C.: He was Janet's father, and then—

Susan: And I, I think that in many ways the relationship that I did have with Janet many years ago was a mother, she was a mother figure.

Dr. C.: So you have the man who feeds, he's not getting paid by your mother, and then your mother needs psychiatric help.

Susan: Yeah. (*Laughs.*) Well, this is true of course, but I don't think I was concerned about that in the dream.

Dr. C.: Well, I think you're talking about the fee, the analytic fee, and—

Susan: Well, I, I had that thought the other day.

Dr. C.: Yes, you did, but didn't spell it out, really. And that you're relating with this old part of yourself. And you're saying at the same time that this part which somehow you learned with Mama is the sick part that needs help and—

Susan: You lost me.

Dr. C.: Well, let me—

Susan: Say it again.

Dr. C.: I feel that there is a man who feeds who is not getting paid by Mama in the dream—that part of you, and that he tells you your mother needs psychiatric help.

Susan: Well, no, he doesn't tell me that. He points out this difficulty.

Dr. C.: Yes, he points out this difficulty.

Susan: And I decide.

Dr. C.: You decide.

Susan: I realize that she needs help.

Dr. C.: O.K. I think you're talking about us, how you relate to me, and that part of you needs help. And then you introduce Janet and you want to tell Janet what you've discovered, but Janet doesn't want to hear. I feel, as you pointed out, that Janet is part of you, that you're trying to communicate, the healthy part is. But the old part, the sick part, doesn't want to hear. And then you switch again and this time you're in a store and you're shopping with your mother and there's the extravagance.

Susan: Well, she is buying something for me—

Dr. C.: She is buying something for you. And I think that you're communicating something very basic here. She is buying something for you; there is the man who feeds you who is not getting paid; there is Janet, there is also Claire, who are supposed to lend you their ears; there is Steven, who offers to take you out, to feed you literally, if you recall, to take you to a sea-food restaurant. And I think you're talking about a way of relating which is old and typical in the past. And you finally tell a policeman and he listens and you're able to discuss this with him. And as you told us, you think this is me and the analysis. And what I hear is a struggle going on within you.

Susan: These people who appear in the dream are for the most part people who figured in the past and people with whom I did not have, I think, a healthy relationship. And they are also people with whom I never really tried to communicate. And in the dream I try [*silence*], whether they want me to or not.

Dr. C.: Um-humm.

Susan: And the dream did not take place in the past, and I, I have the feeling a lot of this snubbing that was going on was because these are relationships that have ended, and these were people who were talking to me because they had to for some reason. But I wanted to go beyond that.

Dr. C.: Yes, but do you notice what you do in the dream, which is typical of what you do in real life. Granted you finally end up communicating with the policeman. I don't think this needs any interpretation, I think it's obvious. You start off talking about a man who feeds and is not getting paid—

Susan: Yeah.

Dr. C.: And then you switch and you keep hovering back and forth with this problem and you don't attack it directly, you present it symbolically from three or four different vantage points, the points of view of Janet, Claire, Steven, the man who feeds. But all of it adds up to a way of relating.

Susan: Do you mean of taking?

Dr. C.: Of taking, of being given, would be a better way

of putting it; that you relate in a way where you are the passive one, you are the receptive one.

Susan: But that certainly wasn't true in the dream in terms of Janet, in terms of Claire. I wasn't passive.

Dr. C.: You were trying to relate to them.

Susan: I wasn't passive.

Dr. C.: That's true, I'd go along with that. (*Silence.*) But there is the emphasis on being given food—

Susan: Or taking—

Dr. C.: Or taking—

Susan: Without paying.

Dr. C.: Of taking without paying.

Susan: Which is different from being given nourishment.

Dr. C.: And what I hear in all this is there are two parts of you, one part which says, "I feel safe enough and comfortable enough in the analysis to start taking a good honest look"; and the other part which says every time you say to yourself, "Let's see how I relate," sort of pushes it into the background, because I think you are communicating how you have related to a considerable extent in the past.

Susan: And yet taking was always a very uncomfortable situation for me. I felt obligated. I guess I felt that taking [*silence*], that a responsibility went along with taking, that I didn't want to assume this responsibility. (*Silence.*)

Dr. C.: In the dream the women really do not want to hear. You can't communicate, relate to them that way, but you do get things from your mother. She relates by giving, and this is the pattern of the overindulgent mother who gives material things but does not really know how to relate to her child.

Susan: That's right.

Dr. C.: And what I hear you saying is that you learned this in the relatedness to your mother and now this is a problem for you, that you have used this mode of relating generally in life. You may be uncomfortable with being given, but the fact remains that you have been given a lot. And throughout the analysis there has been an emphasis on receiving. You have emphasized, always, of course, the discomfort you would have when your mother would give to you or your father would when they couldn't afford it, but it was important that you be given and it was important that you be able to take it, in some way. Well, the point is, it was important for you to be indulged in this way, for whatever psychological meaning it had to you.

Susan: Actually, I haven't been taking things from them—

Dr. C.: No, not since that suit incident.

Susan: All right, that was at the very beginning.

Dr. C.: Um-hum, yes, but we're talking of a pattern of relating.

Susan: And, incidentally, what you say about relating by giving material things is another pattern of mine.

Dr. C.: That's the other side of the same coin.

Susan: Yes. And it, it's been true of me ever since I've been working, with time out during the period that I was married. But aside from that, it has been true. I've given presents when I couldn't afford to, the same way my mother did with me. (*Silence.*)

Dr. C.: You see, in the symbol of the dream, it's like saying if you cannot get relatedness, you can get material things, tangible things, in a way as a form of substitute.

Susan: Well, that's the way I started out, certainly. But I don't think that satisfies me.

Dr. C.: No, I don't think so.

Susan: I go beyond that. I know it doesn't satisfy me.

Dr. C.: Yet you find that—

Susan: That's just not important to me.

Dr. C.: You find you end up talking to the policeman and he listens. This is the struggle throughout, trying to get to some kind of meaningful communication, and I think that what you're doing is giving us a historic development here. You start off with an image of me as a feeder, the overindulgent mother who knows no limits to her giving, and you end up with a policeman who is somewhat more of a rational authority, to whom you can talk.

Susan: I quarrel with one point. I don't know if you were tracing the development or if you meant to say the feeder, the overindulgent mother who knows no limits, because the first person in the dream—

Dr. C.: How do you mean?

Susan: This has got to stop. This difficulty has got to stop.

Dr. C.: Yes. (*Silence.*)

Susan: I think that the timing of the dream is interesting too, incidentally, because I had that dream right after I came back from that vacation last week, where I saw so much and was reminded so much of the way I used to be in relating to people. And it seemed that after such a week [of empty, meaningless contact] it would only be natural to take a look and, in fact, resummarize what happened along the line. And also, I knew that when I was coming back, it was one week, and then a break, and then a new year begins. I've never really recovered from my schooldays and I always feel the beginning of the year is September and never in January.

Dr. C.: You say you were frustrated over the weekend because of the lack of relatedness and that you came home and had this dream the first night back. The gist of it is the problem of relatedness, and what happens when you don't experience true relatedness for whatever reason, that you then—

Susan: I try to force it.

Dr. C.: You have to force it—

Susan: In the dream.

Dr. C.: And relate through the old means of being indulged, being fed, being given, and also indulging yourself. After all, the clothes, if you recall—

Susan: Well, I don't know to what extent it was an indulgence, but—

Dr. C.: I think it was. I think it was a lollipop, just as being fed would be a lollipop, being given.

Susan: Are you talking about the reality situation?

Dr. C.: Well, the old reality, the idea being that if you cannot get—

Susan: Or are you talking about the clothes that I bought that I told you about recently?

Dr. C.: I am talking about the dream.

Susan: Oh, the dream.

Dr. C.: Yes, where you could not get relatedness in reality, you come back and have a dream the first night home involving the being given, the being fed, and relating in the old way.

Susan: Not wholly—

Dr. C.: Partially. And it ends up with you relating to the policeman, and you're trying to—

Susan: But also relating to Claire by the time this ended.

Dr. C.: Well, then, do you notice the continuum here? The man is doing the feeding, then Janet, with whom there really wasn't too much relatedness, then your mother and you shopping, then Claire, as I recall—no, then Steven was introduced, and then Claire—

Susan: No, Claire came first.

Dr. C.: Claire came first.

Susan: And then with him.

Dr. C.: With him. There seems to be this continuum of trying to relate increasingly, but the gist of the dream, the starting point, is something that may be constructive for us to look at. The starting point is a man who feeds you, or who does the feeding, and is not getting paid. And then you're anxious at the idea of being extravagant. And then you also come in and make a statement: "I was, I planned to pay you for July and August in September. I was going to mention it to you and then I thought maybe I won't mention it to you." You said something along that line.

Susan: I said, I thought, maybe I won't mention it to you?

Dr. C.: That's right, if I heard it correctly.

Susan: I don't remember that.

Dr. C.: I remember I took notice of that, unless my recall fails. But the idea was that this wasn't something that we were going to discuss.

Susan: How can we discuss it?

Dr. C.: This was something you were sort of going to

announce. It wasn't a question of would it be O.K. with you *if*, etc., etc., etc., but, "I have decided that . . ."

Susan's withholding payment of her analytic bill was discussed. She was aware that this was a way to express resentment, and there was accompanying anxiety and guilt.

Susan usually paid all her bills promptly. Owing money, for her, meant being beholden emotionally; there was someone capable of making emotional claims on her. She thought she might be saying that she felt safer, more open to emotional interaction with me.

Susan asked if she could postpone payment until after the summer as it would be difficult for her to manage now. I was agreeable, once the analytic issues had been clarified.

> *Dr. C.:* Well, I think this dream is, in a sense, a very good stopping point, because it focuses the problems very sharply, doesn't it?
>
> *Susan:* Indeed it does.
>
> *Dr. C.:* The overall of it is that you start off with a man who is a feeder, and somehow the overindulgent mother who knows no limits to her giving. This is the feeling tone of being fed, etc., etc., and this goes through the dream to a considerable extent. But you end up with a person who is a policeman. Now, I don't know what your associations to a policeman are—
>
> *Susan:* They're very nice.
>
> *Dr. C.:* But as you describe the policeman in the dream—
>
> *Susan:* He called up, he was checking, you see, there had been some difficulty before and he was checking on it.
>
> *Dr. C.:* Yes.
>
> *Susan:* So he wasn't a very, well, he wasn't the image of a policeman that a lot of mothers used to use when I was a little girl when they were disciplining their children.
>
> *Dr. C.:* Put it this way: a rational kind of authority. And maybe these are two parts of yourself in terms of how you relate. (*Silence.*) Maybe this is where you are right now in

the analysis: trying to build up some kind of relating that does not involve being overindulged, given to, a child, or the person who in turn can only give, but a person who can interact with a rational authority, and talk and work something through, which was where the dream ended.

Susan: Yeah, very good timing. (*Laughs.*)

Dr. C.: I think so. We can trust your unconscious, evidently. (*Laughs.*)

Susan: Well, at times, I can, anyway—

Dream 52 / *Session 244*

Susan: I had a dream Wednesday, it's the first dream in a long time that I have remembered. And I woke up because of the dream. I wasn't feeling very anxious at the time. In the dream I was talking on the phone with Florence Bernstein. There had been some kind of a misunderstanding, I don't know if it was between Florence and her husband, Marvin, or possibly between Florence and me. But the effect of this call was to help and iron out this misunderstanding, and it seemed to be successful from that point of view. She and I made a date to have lunch, and it involved considerable planning and negotiating on her part, and I was thinking of a place to eat on my way to meet her, and I was very worried about money; and now the first time being worried about money and thinking of a place to go, for the first time I realized that a lot of the problem that I've been talking about in here for the past weeks is—I don't know where I'm going; and I'm also worried about money. I'm also worried about the fact that I put so much time, not money, into it—so much time in the past, been wasted, frittered away, and I still don't know where I'm going. But before I left, I left with a suitcase. I was carrying a small train case, but before I left to go and meet Florence, I remember looking at a pair of shoes that were in very bad condition. They were comfortable shoes, but they'd gotten banged up because I had fallen, and I had hurt my feet when I fell. And I remember the way I looked in the dream, I had a slight mark on my nose, and I had some Mercurochrome on it or some medication on it.

And at one point in the dream I realized that I must have broken the skin on my face when I fell also. But I was looking for the place to eat, and because after I left Florence I was going away on a weekend trip with a man; and at one point Ann was with me and she looked in this case and she pointed out that I had to be very thorough and remember everything that I would need. But I had not packed my diaphragm and I remember her going down the list, you care about A.,B.,C. I, I don't remember all the items now, except the last item on the list was you care about, as she pointed to the deodorant, she said something like you care about not smelling but you don't care about having a baby as a result of this and there was no time. For some reason, I could not go home and get the diaphragm and I was worried about how to get another without a prescription and then I remembered the druggist in my neighborhood who would give me one. I thought about my friend Ellen, who got a diaphragm from him by just asking for it when she was having an affair with a guy with whom she worked. She was married at the time. I don't know why I brought that up, either in the dream or after I woke up. It doesn't make any difference. Why should I think about her having an extramarital affair? What does that mean to me now? That was Wednesday night. I had thought about sending a [Jewish] New Year card to David on Wednesday night before I went to bed. I had this dream. I woke up. I wasn't anxious when I woke up and for some reason I seemed willing to let it drop and I wasn't going to do it, but then I did stop in and do it. I bought the card on the way to work. (*Silence.*) I'm anxious now. I've been anxious since I started to talk about this really not very important event. If it's not very important in terms of reality, but it certainly is important in terms of what's going on inside me. I was very disgusted with myself at one point this afternoon when I had to take some material up to my boss's office and Burton, whom I've mentioned here before, was in there with him. I felt very uncomfortable at seeing him, and the fact that I felt uncomfortable worried me, because it just seemed to be a reversion. I remember talking to you about, oh, a year and a half ago, about my reaction to his coming into the office one afternoon and my feeling very tense and very anxious, but during, I, I don't see him very often but when I have during the last six months or so, I haven't reacted with anxiety. But today I did and that's why I thought of it as a falling backward.

Dr. C.: When you think of this dream, does anything else come to mind other than the New Year's card to David?

Susan: Well, the New Year's card to David preceded the dream. I mean I was thinking about it before I went to sleep.

Dr. C.: Um-humm.

Susan: This feeling of not knowing where I'm going that I mentioned. (*Silence.*) The fall, the fall makes me think of the weekend I was in Stamford, Labor Day weekend. I fell there and I, I, I, I did think of that experience when I woke up. I don't know what relation that had to anything, except that a fall seems to fit in with reverting to the old me, which I feel is what I'm doing and have been doing for the last three weeks. Not completely, not completely, but I have been doing it and I've got to stop and maybe when I say I don't know how, it's another reversion, a reversion to feeling helpless, but I don't think I do feel helpless. I just feel, I, I need to find some way of [*silence*] feeling, getting myself to the point of feeling alive again, feeling, you know, when you talk about getting interested in something, it's the same thing as talking about committing yourself to something. Isn't it? Making a commitment. (*Silence.*)

Dr. C.: Have you any ideas on the diaphragm being omitted?

Susan: The first one that comes to mind is really very literary and I don't think it has anything to do with what I was talking about in the dream.

Dr. C.: What was it, anyway?

Susan: Well, I was thinking of the diaphragm as a method of blocking off life. (*Silence.*) And I think that one reason that I thought of that now was so that I could say, see . . . (*Silence.*) I haven't reverted completely. I don't want it, I forgot it, I don't want to shut myself off from life, but I'm not too sure from the basis of the way I've been living, just looking at it.

Dr. C.: Do you feel you've forced that association?

Susan: It does.

Dr. C.: Or did it come spontaneously?

Susan: Well, it came spontaneously but it sounds awfully forced to me [*silence*] and I think it could have come spontaneously [*silence*] because I could be making an effort to fool myself, you know.

Dr. C.: Could be. (*Silence.*)

Susan: You know, I just thought of, for some reason, of my great fear during most of my relationship with Irwin, that he was going to dominate me and that I would be nothing but what he wanted me to be, and I thought of that in relation with what I said earlier about problems that I would really have to work on if the relationship with David had gone in the direction that I wanted it to go, and I, I think that this is true of my whole life. I want it to be free and at the same time I'm scared to death. (*Silence.*) I felt helpless about being free. (*Silence.*) I just wish I could come to grips with this awful lethargy that, well I could say, I was about to say, that has come over me, and that too puts it in very passive terms. I have nothing to do with it. (*Silence.*) It came over me. (*Silence.*)

Dr. C.: Well, it seems to me, all this hour you've been talking about the same thing in various forms.

Susan: I have?

Dr. C.: In the dream you're worried about a place to eat and money. Again the security is outside of you. How you will be fed, will you have enough—

Susan: Money—

Dr. C.: Money—

Susan: To take care of feeding myself.

Dr. C.: To take care of feeding yourself. (*Silence.*)

Susan: Well, is it a question of security being outside me or am I worrying about whether or not I have the capacity?

Dr. C.: Well, I think you've answered your own question, haven't you?

Susan: Well, I think it's the latter.

Dr. C.: I'd go along with that. Now, you mention the fear of reverting to the old you, and—

Susan: I think I've been doing it, I mean, it's not just a fear.

Dr. C.: O.K., and also the problems that you feel you still have, and as you tell them I don't get the feeling of problems, but a general problem. You told us you feel too passive, too dependent, fearful of self-assertion.

Susan: It's the same thing.

Dr. C.: How to break through your isolation.

Susan: Is that the same thing?

Dr. C.: A loss of enthusiasm, and developing interests on your own, and I wonder if you're not talking of a basic feeling tone of helplessness. (*Silence.*)

Susan: I bet that's what it is. (*Silence.*)

Dr. C.: A feeling that you can't survive on your own; that you can't extend yourself into life; that you will have to be fed and taken care of emotionally if you are to survive as a person.

Susan: I just see myself in a hole, all alone. In effect, living like a pig, because you're all alone in a hole. When I say all alone like a pig, it's when you're all alone in a hole everything has to center about you. (*Silence.*) And, I think that to carry this further, there's a feeling that I don't know how to break out, therefore, if you don't know how to break out, you won't break out. That's why I've been feeling so discouraged. You know, this feeling of not knowing how to break out, so you can't break out.

Dr. C.: It seems to me that you're feeling this passivity, this helplessness in its full dosage, but at the same time you're awfully mad, Susan. Maybe you'll be able to pull yourself out of the hole.

Susan: You know, it hasn't made me cry until now, here tonight. I've just been feeling terribly frustrated and at war with myself.

Dr. C.: You see, I think you're saying that you doubt your ability to grow, your ability to emerge. Should there be a diaphragm; should this growth be stopped; shouldn't it be stopped; where am I in all this; can I feed myself; will I have enough money to feed myself; do I have the inner capacities? (*Silence.*) And all of this is your basic feeling tone about yourself, in a nutshell. (*Silence.*)

Susan: That's right—

Dream 53   /   *Session 249*

Susan: You know, it's very strange. It doesn't seem as long this week between sessions as it did last week.[20] I, I think that, that I had a very strange feeling last week about the whole business [of having only one session a week]. But not, not this week. I think that I left here on Friday feeling very dubious about this business. But I don't feel dubious any more.

[*Susan went on to say that she had had to make an extemporaneous presentation before a group; that she had felt the old panic but had quickly recovered and had done quite well.*]

Susan: Isn't it funny, as I talked about this I thought of a dream that I had at some point during the week. And I cannot remember much about the dream, except that at one point I fell down the steps. But it, it, I didn't go bump, bump, bump all the way down. I fell so that I had the experience of falling through the air. But I landed on my two feet. And they smarted a bit. But I did land on my own two feet.

There's another thing I've stopped doing in the last two weeks. I've stopped having longing feelings for David. For some reason, I accept that situation, you know, the ending. I find that I can still think of him very fondly, and I can still think of him in terms of wishing that things hadn't turned out the way that they had. And, but I'm not longing for him the way that I have been until very recently, very recently. And this statement is also made from the middle of the Sahara [referring to her being without a man].

I don't know where all this confidence [about being capa-

[20] In session 248, Susan decided to cut down the sessions to one a week.

ble of a stable relationship] comes from. I think I do know how now, in a way that I didn't a very short time ago. But I haven't proved it in any way.

And at this point it sounds as though what I'm saying is this: "I need an external agent to make me keep my nose to the grindstone." And that's child-, that's childish. In effect, I'm saying, "I can't do it without help. I need someone to make me work through to answers of this sort." And once a week isn't enough. (*Silence.*) And yet, at the same time that I'm saying these things, I have a feeling of confidence in myself that is not in accord with those words. Because I think that what I feel now is an ability to cope with what comes along. I know that I can.

Dr. C.: That is, you may be scared, and you may find yourself, or feel yourself falling through the air at times.

Susan: But even in my dream I landed on my feet.

Dr. C.: And it hurt a little, but you landed on your feet. They smarted.

Susan: I don't know if that was true at the time or if I added that afterwards, you know, in looking back, about how they smarted. I think I was a little surprised.

Dr. C.: Well, maybe you're beginning to feel, on the basis of how you are relating to people, that you are getting some kind of firm footing.

Susan: It's possible. (*Silence.*) It's possible.

Dr. C.: Well, I guess we'll stop here. Do you think you'll be able to survive until next week, or do you want a session in between?

Susan: I think I'll manage. Besides I, ah [*laughs*], I won't have time next week.

Dr. C.: (*Laughs.*)

Susan: O.K. I'll see you next Friday. Good night.

Dr. C.: Good night, Susan.

Dreams 54 and 55 / *Session 250*

For six weeks, Susan had been doing volunteer work with emotionally disturbed children. She had been notified that her income-tax return was to be audited.

She reported having a bout of anxiety the day before.

Susan: I had a dream last night. And I had a dream earlier
this week, too. They're the first dreams I've had in an
awfully long time. I remembered one aspect of this dream
when I was talking just now; about the anxiety attack not
being related to, ah, the federal government. And what I
remembered is, is so, it's something that I thought of in
connection with this dream. What I, I was remembering, just
now I was remembering the kind of fantasies I experienced
back in 1945, when I had an impacted wisdom tooth taken
out, and the dentist used gas. And I remember the, ah, as I
was going under, I felt that I was on the corner waiting to
take the streetcar to work. And, oh, I had a very, very long
trip to make, and after a long ride by El I went downstairs
and waited for the streetcar, and in the, as I was going under,
I was on the corner, and the streetcar approached, and pulled
back, and it approached, and it was pulled back. And I hadn't
thought of that for years and years until this morning some
time after, after the dream when, ah, it came to mind in
connection with one sequence. There, as, as I remember it,
the, ah, in the beginning I was, ah, one of a group. And it
was a social occasion, and oh, we were talking, drinks were
being served. There was a radio or a record player in operation; and a man came to take either the radio or the record
player because of nonpayment of the installments that were
due. And, ah, this wasn't a very happy situation. Nobody
was really distressed; it seemed like a very, very familiar
situation. And I, I'm not sure whether I actually participated
in this, in the dream, or whether this was a movie I saw as a
spectator. And because there was some talk in the dream at
one point about my having seen a particular movie, it was a, a
short picture that was not a feature attraction, but there was
some talk about my having seen a specific picture about four
times. Next I was involved with my boss and a man. A man
who wasn't particularly attractive, but somebody else referred to him as someone who had won a certain amount of
fame by acting. And I think he was acting in the movies. And

it was he, I think it was he, gave me some kind of a viewer, some device that I looked through. And this was a device that had the effect of making the moon seem to come closer and then to recede. And, as I was looking through this viewer, I began to have a very queasy feeling, at, ah, at seeing the moon come closer and then recede. It was the kind of thing I think people experience when they're seasick. And I attributed this to a recent change of glasses. I was having trouble with my eyes. And I thought that that's why this was happening. This man, I think his name was Scotch, or very much like that, was going to England with my boss. They were just going for the day, on business. They were going to discuss a research project with someone in England. And there was much talk about this remarkable jet age when it did become practical to go to England and return on the same day. And, before they left, there was some business about getting into a car. There were four people, no, there were five people. There was a woman in the back seat, and my boss was driving, and there was the man who was going to England with them. I was getting in the car, and there was another man who was getting in the car. And my boss started to drive before we were all inside. I got into the back seat, and I remember calling to the other man to hurry and jump in because the car was moving. And apparently while this difficulty with the car was taking place, I was confused and I, at, at my boss driving off before all of the passengers were in. At that time I didn't know he was off to England. Somehow, when I learned his destination, it made me feel better, perhaps because I could, ah, understand why he was in a hurry. And in the next sequence, I was entering my parents' home, and they had just come back from the country, apparently they had had some difficulty in getting transportation. On my way in, I dropped some wrappings, either candy wrappings or cigarette wrappings, on the lawn. And I felt guilty when I went inside and I saw that my father carried his trash in the house, and he commented on my carelessness, my sloppiness. And I felt very guilty about it, and I didn't know whether to go out and pick it up from the lawn or not. That was last night. And of course, this, it was only much later that I remembered what it felt like going under when, the one and only time that I've been given gas as an anesthetic. And I also thought of the relationship with David, which seemed very much like that. This coming closer, going back, coming closer, going back.

Dr. C.: Um-hum.

Susan: On both of our parts. But it was strange that I thought of the gas experience again tonight while I was talking about being anxious last night, on my way to the school [for emotionally disturbed children]. (*Silence.*) And I had a dream Tuesday night, too. At, in the early part of the dream I was with a man. And I think it's either a man that I know, or a man that I did know. Maybe it was David, I'm not sure, and I was very surprised to find myself with him. And at the same time that I was surprised I was pleased that he was interested in me. And I went to visit Leah. Sara and another friend of hers, Mildred, were there. And, I hadn't seen either one of these people for a long time, and I was embarrassed when I saw them, and I didn't know what to say to them. And I didn't exclaim about "Oh, it's been such a long time since I've seen you." I sat down and, and was very calmly asking Mildred questions about herself, and what had been happening to her family. Ah, I say Mildred, because at this point Sara went out of the room. And this was a very uncomfortable situation for me. I think that, ah, I felt embarrassed primarily because of Sara, a gal I used to see from time to time, and then I dropped her. I dropped her pretty consciously and pretty deliberately. I didn't want to hurt her feelings, but she's a very aggressive female, and I didn't enjoy her, and I just stopped seeing her. And the embarrassment that I was feeling in the dream was not apparent, but I felt uncomfortable inside. That was Tuesday night. And then this other dream that I told you about last night. (*Silence.*) I don't know what I'm trying to say in these dreams. I guess I'm interested that I went right into the second one, in talking, a, a, after bringing up this question of my anxiety, yesterday. Of course, this business of having them, having the man from the finance company come to reclaim the radio, or the phonograph record, I think ties in very neatly with the, ah, little note I got yesterday from internal revenue. But I think the fact that I place myself in the role of spectator, that I don't feel directly, too directly involved in this, is an indication that it's really not much of a problem for me. And the problem is my relationships with people, and distance versus closeness.

Dr. C.: Approach and pull back.

Susan: Rather than, yeah, rather than any realistic concerns about money.

Dr. C.: What was this bit about having seen a picture, a specific picture about four times?

Susan: Well, you know, I, I think that if I wasn't sure that I was present, a member of this group, or whether it was something, ah, that I had seen on film, is an indication of how removed I felt from this situation. Because, gee, when they take, when they reclaim something that belongs to a friend, you're, ah, not as involved as you would be if they were reclaiming something of yours, I would imagine. But you're even less involved if you see it in a theater. I, I mean you're much more of a spectator, in that situation.

Dr. C.: Well—

Susan: And I think that that, that that's my method of saying, "Now look, this ain't it, kid."

Dr. C.: Well, what is?

Susan: The coming closer and pulling back.

Dr. C.: Yes, the moon bit.

Susan: Yeah.

Dr. C.: I think we agree that the person who gave you the device to view through was pretty obvious, referring to me, the analysis.

Susan: Well, I was thinking of the relationship with David.

Dr. C.: Well, I respect—

Susan: Ah, of course, David didn't give me that device, I grant you that. You think you were the man named Scotch?

Dr. C.: Well, I expect you're feeling that it was.

Susan: Why would I call you Scotch?

Dr. C.: I don't know, but the idea of someone giving you a viewing device with which you can see the moon, and you can make the moon come closer and recede, I think is one of the problems you've been talking about here in the analysis.

Susan: But Scotch is something that you take when you want to make things recede really, isn't it?

Dr. C.: Well, do you feel that's so?

Susan: Well, I know it helps when I have insomnia. I've used it that way. Not for a while now, but right through the summer, right up until recently, when I decided that I was building a ritual in connection with falling asleep, and I just stopped. (*Silence.*) But it made me sick. It literally made me sick in my stomach.

Dr. C.: What made you sick?

Susan: This experience of watching it come closer and go back. Have you looked through a porthole? At the horizon tilting up and then straightening? A lot of people react to that, and that's the sa-, I, I mean they react to it physically. It's the same kind of reaction I had on looking at the moon through this device. (*Pause.*) Well, you know, if you watch something come closer, go back, at one point along the line you're getting a distorted view, aren't you? I don't think that, I guess what I'm saying is, why is the man who gave me the device you. Because this is a device that distorts. And I've used liquor to try, at various points, to try to help me maintain distorted views, to help deaden pain, etc. This is going back to the name Scotch again. I, I don't think I'm talking about the analytic situation.

Dr. C.: You feel you're talking about David.

Susan: No, I don't say I'm talking about David; I said that I thought of the situation with David. And this business of advance and retreat, advance and retreat is something that I know I would find uncomfortable. And I think that if I were in a relationship with David now, and there was a lot of this going on, I wouldn't just stay in this relationship indefinitely, with this advance retreat, advance retreat, advance retreat. I don't think that I would keep doing that either. And I know I did, at one point. (*Silence.*) I do remember, when I was feeling anxious last night I was thinking about the party that we're going to have next Tuesday for the children at the school. And I was, from time to time during the last few days I've been thinking of this experience with a certain amount of apprehension. I don't think that I'll make anyone miserable. But in many ways I've led a very sheltered life, and I don't, I think aside from my friend Sylvia, who had a couple of, ah, of acute phases of TB during the period that I've known her, I've never known anybody who has been in a hospital for years and years, chronically ill, and who may just stay in a hospital for years and years and years. And I guess I feel uneasy about whether or not I can really do anything to make these children feel better, for a time.

Dr. C.: It is interesting that you thought of approach and pull back, the moon come closer, then recede through this viewing device. Now this man named Scotch, and you think you're referring to liquor there.

Susan: Well, it's the first thing I thought of.

Dr. C.: And he's going to England for one day.

Susan: Well, it's mainly my boss who's going. I mean, my boss is the prime mover there.

Dr. C.: And they're talking about this remarkable jet age.

Susan: Yes. Well, to think of going to England for the day. (*Silence.*) (*Laughs.*) What I think of now, after you made this remark about this remarkable jet age, is look at me after, depending on who you want to include, but the way I look at it, after about four and a half years of therapy, here I am. This is not what I would call a remarkable burst of speed. (*Laughs.*) I just thought of Sara. She just got married. Sara is my age and has been divorced. She married a foreigner, I'm not sure, I think an Englishman, who is thirty-four. From all accounts, this is a sick guy. Maybe I'm saying something about myself. I was thinking that perhaps, perhaps I feel more relaxed in general about the question of possibly finding someone some day; I don't have any firm convictions I will. I don't have any firm convictions that I won't. But if it happens that will be fine. And if it doesn't, well, then it won't. But these days, I've, ah, I don't seem to have time to sit down and brood about it. I'm not aware of doing so awfully much, but there just have been a lot of things to do lately. And I, and I, I, I don't think I'm as self-absorbed as I was through most of the summer, and through most of September. And at this point I'm beginning to get a little anxious. Maybe I was, when I was looking through the viewer, and responded by, and I responded with, with a feeling of queasiness. Maybe I was expressing a little apprehension about what I'm going to be able to do in the future, in terms of relating to people.

Dr. C.: Um-humm. You know, you've described this anxious feeling with closeness at various times. If you recall.

Susan: I've also described it in connection with loneliness.

Dr. C.: Yes.

Susan: As you may recall. (*Laughs.*)

Dr. C.: Yes. Now the idea of approaching, and pulling back, being given a mechanism to view through, and you see the moon come closer and then recede. And you attribute this perhaps to a recent change of glasses.

Susan: Yeah. Well, I, yes, that's what I attribute it to in the dream. And it still makes a certain amount of sense to me. And I think that this is my own personal physical reaction. I don't know how prevalent it is. But I know that when I try to read on a bus, when I overstrain my eyes in one way or another, I very often get a queasy feeling in my stomach. And I can remember back when I have had changes in prescription, for my glasses, ah, I have had a little difficulty at some time, or when my eyes have changed rapidly, I've had a little difficulty. It's also affected me in the stomach.

Dr. C.: Well, could be.

Susan: And that's why I did that.

Dr. C.: But I wonder if there isn't a symbolic meaning to the idea of the changing of the glasses.

Susan: Well, I thought of something else, too.

Dr. C.: Yes.

Susan: I thought of something else. Ah, in the last year I have bought two new pairs of glasses. There was no change in prescription. Ah, I bought them because I liked the way the frames looked. I thought they were attractive. And that's why I bought them. And I don't think that I was using the glasses to talk about seeing more clearly. I think I was using the glasses in terms of my changing view about, well, forms of healthy self-indulgence. (*Silence.*)

Dr. C.: When you think of the moon coming closer, what comes to mind?

Susan: Oh, yes, this reminds me of, of something else that occurred to me a few minutes ago. Well, when you think of the moon, I, I, I, a minute ago I thought of, you know, crying for the moon, wanting the moon, and I think that maybe when I thought of that, I was thinking in terms of wanting a certain kind of life which I may or may not get.

Dr. C.: Reaching for the moon.

Susan: Yeah.

Dr. C.: And you hope perhaps that through the analysis it will come closer. But there is the fear, you see—

Susan: Well, I don't know, you see, I have the feeling that if I were meeting a man now, the course—a man who was not all whacked up, let us say, oh, I don't say healthy and well-adjusted, but not totally whacked up. I think that the course of a relationship would move along very different lines from the course of my relationship with David. I think that, I don't feel that I hope to be able to do this through what analysis is going to do for me. I feel ready now.

Dr. C.: Good.

Susan: I don't think I, I, you know, I think that I, I, here's a situation where I don't think I need more analysis; I need the other person.

Dr. C.: You need a little bit of living experience.

Susan: Well, all right, that's one way of putting it.

Dr. C.: What about this "one day" bit?

Susan: Well, I know what—

Dr. C.: He's Scotch, his name is Scotch.

Susan: I, I, I know what this "one day bit" means now. Once a week—

Dr. C.: Of course.

Susan: And you've been waiting for me to say this for a long time, haven't you?

Dr. C.: Well, I've been waiting for you to pull it together in your own time, in your own way, yes. This man's name is Scotch.

Susan: Ummmm yes, and Scotch means something else to me now. It's not just alcohol. (*Laughs.*)

Dr. C.: No.

Susan: It's also being stingy.

Dr. C.: Yes. Now maybe, I wonder if at some level you're not saying that I'm being stingy in giving you one hour a week. That in some way you feel this is a form of stinginess—

Susan: [*Again mentions the moving car.*]

Dr. C. (with reference to the moving car): But the point is this: the darned thing started to move before you were really in it.

Susan: Yeah.

Dr. C.: And you were worried.

Susan: Yeah, particularly the other person, completely outside of the car when it started to move, the man, the other man. In other words, I'm not ready to be cut back to one a week yet is what part of me still feels. I have qualms about it. But at the same time it's eminently practical to go to England for a day. In the world we live in now, in my dream at any rate. But in the world of my dream, things were so fast that it was practical. All right, maybe what I'm expressing is a conflict in feeling about what can be done in a day—

Dr. C.: In the flow of your dream you talk about seeing a specific picture four times, and I think you're talking about the times in the analysis when you've looked at this problem of approaching and pulling back. The fact remains this is a basic issue. Hopefully, with living experience you're going to do away with it and give yourself the proof you need. But I think there's something more going on. I think you're talking about approaching and pulling back in terms of the analysis itself, and where you stand with it. The entire analytic procedure, this question of cutting back to one time a week, is that enough, your confusion, will the car leave with you not quite in it, will you be separated from the man—

Susan: It was leaving. There was no question, it was leaving. Was he going to be able to get aboard?

Dr. C.: Ummm. What do you make of that?

Susan: That's funny. The first thing I thought of right now was David, and I don't understand it. (*Silence.*) I don't understand it. Because I think I said to you last week that I have stopped thinking of him in, in any, in the longing, yearning way I had been thinking of him. And I think I really accept the ending there. But if you talk about will he be able to get on board, and he is the first person who comes to my mind, am I in effect saying that it isn't over for me yet? I don't think so. I really don't.

Dr. C.: You see, I think you're talking of me in the analysis.

Susan: What, you getting on board?

Dr. C.: And the idea of the separation of some kind. I think that at this point you're very concerned with the idea of the analysis, where you are in it, where you're going with it. What is this analytic relationship all about.

Susan: But what does this have to do with your getting on board?

Dr. C.: I think that you're saying in some form that you're a little scared, that maybe you can't make it alone. Or you're concerned about giving something up here.

[*Referring to Susan's littering her father's lawn in the dream:*] You see, you litter his lawn, you drop candy wrappers on his lawn, and you feel guilty because he mentioned this to you. He carried his own trash. And I wonder if you're not saying that in some way you feel a little uncomfortable, perhaps a little guilty, for many of the indirect ways you have used in the past to express hostility to him, or to assert yourself in relation to him.

Susan: When you talked about guilt in connection with the indirect expression of hostility, my first thought was: that's the only way I could express it at all. The only way that was permitted was to express it indirectly.

[*Here Susan and I discussed her possible resentment toward me:* "a not particularly attractive man who won some fame as an actor." *Susan expressed her resentment that she was having only one session a week. She knew rationally that I was not depriving her, that she was giving up the extra time herself voluntarily. Yet she felt deprived and resented me for it. I tried to show her that she had a right to feel resentment and even deprivation.*]

Susan: (*Laughs.*) But I'll, I'll tell you what. Before you made these comments about getting even with my father, I was just going to walk off and leave this empty cigarette package.

Dr. C.: Oh, you were. (*Laughs.*)

Susan: (*Laughs.*) However . . . (*Gets up and throws the cigarette package into the wastepaper basket.*)

Dr. C.: Well, I see your dream has not been in vain.

Susan: (*Laughs.*) O.K. I'll see you next week.

The dream about Sara was not discussed because we were short of time. It was useful to note, however, that Susan described Sara in the dream as "a very aggressive female, and I didn't enjoy her; and I just stopped seeing her. And the embarrassment that I was feeling in the dream was not apparent, but I was uncomfortable inside." This was probably how Susan saw herself.

Dream 56 / *Session 251*

Susan saw her parents that weekend at a family gathering in Boston. Susan was aware of how much hostility she still felt toward her mother; she still had a need to punish her mother. A tape recording was made of the speeches at dinner and was later played back. Susan reported feeling anxious at hearing her voice.

Susan: Anyway, I did remember Monday's dream. And I'm not sure about the sequence, but as closely as I could remember it, there was one sequence relatively early when I was upstairs in a house. I don't know whose house. And I think I wasn't well, but I needed something downstairs which I couldn't get and which David agreed to get for me. And he went downstairs and he didn't come back. And after a while I went downstairs and I saw him enjoying himself with a group of people. And as I came down the steps, somebody was pouring a drink for him and I realized that he had forgotten all about me. And that's . . . the next thing that I remember, I was a member of a group. I was with my mother and two sisters who were fairly young. And we were going to stay with someone, a friend, ah, I think possibly the friends were Eve and Lester, very old friends of the family, while my father was out of town. I, I guess this was late afternoon, and I knew I had a date with Donald in the evening. He was due to return from a trip that day. And as I was in the group, I was talking to Carl. Carl is someone who works in the office. He's a filing clerk. I was talking to him about a play that was being produced by a group that he and I were associated with. I am not sure if this was at the office or not. And the female lead in the play was ill; and Carl suggested Leona, another gal who works in our office, as a substitute. And he pointed out that she could pretend to be married to the male lead and live with him a while before the show to get publicity. Ah, now both Carl and Leona are Negroes, and I, ah, I thought this was a difficult situation. And I said to Carl: "Gee, in the eyes of the public, ah, pretending su-, such a marriage would be, ah, considered almost as bad as marrying a Jew." And as soon as I said what I did say, I got very embarrassed, and Carl reacted, and I, I felt that I had blundered; that I had, ah, in effect made some statements to him that indicated anti-Negro feeling on my part that just wasn't there. I was, I was planning to have dinner with someone who was in this group before meeting Donald. And as we were all sitting there, my little sister began to entertain the group. Oh, she was a little girl, possibly about three or four. And she was singing and using standard grestures, and I was surprised at the performance because obviously someone had been coaching her, she didn't pick this kind of thing up herself. I didn't know she could sing. And, ah, the fact that she used the typical gestures to punctuate the popular ballad that she was singing bothered me. Of course, that's what I was talking about earlier in the hour in terms of my own reaction to the way I sounded on the tape recorder. At that point Donald appeared. He was dressed very sloppily, and he was with a friend, or his brother, who was also dressed in a very slovenly fashion, and they were both unshaven. Donald has come to pick me up, and I was very annoyed. Ah, we had said nothing about dinner and I didn't want to go with him yet. I, I, I wasn't ready. I didn't say so directly. Yeah, I did say that we had said nothing about dinner. But I didn't say, I don't, that I didn't want to go with him. But I expressed my annoyance by withdrawal, and I was cool and distant. And I had the feeling that he had absolutely no consideration, that he didn't care what I want. And he was talking, he began to talk to my mother and to others about me. They turned from me and this made me furious, though I did not say anything. And I was very annoyed that he was drawing them into the situation. That, at this point, something also came up, come, comes to my mind that my cousin had mentioned about how she felt about me, when we were little. She didn't like me at all, because I was so good. Apparently, I was always held up as a model. She said that whenever I did go over to visit, her mother would tell her: "Now, Susan is going to be there this afternoon," just as if, you know, "The goddess is coming, and she has such good manners, and I want you to watch your manners," and, and so on. You know, I was well-mannered, sweet-tempered, bright, and so on. I probably stayed very clean. I was a pretty docile, obedient child, and I think had particular appeal for adults, only I think that when my aunt worried so about the manners of her daughter when I was there, it was just a question of my mother and my aunt competing with each other. And I think that's probably what was involved much more than the relationship of my cousin and me, because, after all, if I was so wonderful in the eyes of all of these adults, it could only mean one thing. It could mean, and, and I think that my mother enjoyed these reactions; and I think that she enjoyed them because she felt that this was a reflection of her good mothering, and her good bringing up of me. And I think that she probably still sees me as something of an extension of herself. I, I, I don't know, maybe most parents do. But I, I, I thought of this in connection with the dream. Of course, this bit about the performing child was Susan.

Dr. C.: Um-hummm.

Susan: And you see, I don't remember the other sister, but I must have been the other sister, too. She wasn't in the limelight as the little one was. You know, this dream opened with me in a relationship with David. And when I went downstairs, when he didn't come back and I went downstairs, and I realized that he had forgotten all about getting me whatever he had said he would get me, I don't think, I might have felt a little resentment, but this was not a crushing experience in the dream. I think about David in a very different way now than I did a month ago. I, I think that there have been times when, ah, during the last month, when I have felt a certain amount of resentment upon recalling certain incidents. And I think that I've begun to look at the relationship in much less ideal terms than I had been thinking of it at the time when I was still grieving. And I begin to feel that I have lost less than I felt I had lost a month ago.

Dr. C.: Well, that shows up in the dream, doesn't it? You come downstairs; David forgot about you; but you become part of the group.

Susan: All right, he forgot. No. No, it wasn't the same group.

Dr. C.: Oh, it was a different group, there was a switch there?

Susan: There was, that's a different sequence.

Dr. C.: I see.

Susan: And I, I don't know what kind of a bridge there was. This is just all that I could recall, right after I woke up. I think that this group of which David was a part was probably a group of contemporaries. The other group I was in was a mixed group. I, I, I was an adult, but I was going with my mother to stay with friends while my father was away, while he was out of town. In effect, I was a little girl in terms of being with the children, the two sisters. And I was also a grownup little girl in this section of the dream. I, I, I don't understand this business that involved Carl and Leona. But when, when Carl raised the question of a pseudo-mixed marriage, I made this remark about, as far as the public was concerned, this would almost be as bad as marrying a Jew. I, I felt terribly embarrassed; and I don't understand what was involved here. I don't think I'm talking about my own feelings about being a Jew. I don't think I have a problem here. (*Silence.*) But I, I, I don't understand what is going on here at all. But, oh, that little girl. This is about a play, and about pretending to be something that you're not for some reason. And the little girl who sang was play-acting and was very much the picture of me when I was a little girl and I was phony most of the time, most of the time. Tried to give people what they would approve, and, ah, almost deliberately. (*Silence.*) And yet, when I heard myself on tape, that's the way I sounded today. I don't know if I sounded any different from the way I normally would, last Sunday, because of the certain strain that's there when I am some place with my parents. I told you about that recent visit to Boston when I spent the afternoon with a young man I met through my aunt who, ah, called for me at my parents' home, and I was very anxious while we were in the house. (*Silence.*) I've spent this whole hour, it seems, being concerned about being myself. And I think I'm afraid of not being myself, even when I'm not aware of it. Because this dream was Monday night, and the tape-recorder bit was, was on Sunday, and it's almost this, this kid singing, and the way that she was singing, like somebody who trained to go on the Horn & Hardart Children's Hour, was me as I was, and possibly as I'm afraid I still am.

Dr. C.: There was also the bit with Carl and Leona, about an adult play, the lead, or substituting—

Susan: Substituting Leona for the lead.

Dr. C.: For the lead.

Susan: And having her, having this, having the two leads try to get publicity by pretending to be married. Of course, that takes me back to something else that is typical of me. I think that it typifies my relationship with Steven where you have a pretend relationship because you have somebody who will take you to certain places where it's more comfortable to go with an escort. And I think that there have been times when I wanted a permanent relationship with a man, possibly for reasons of status more than anything else. That and there's, there's, well, there's certainly nothing could be phonier than that. And this is a phony situation: "We'll get publicity for the play by having them do this." And then I say, "You'll get bad publicity."

Dr. C.: When you think of marrying a Jew, what comes to mind?

Susan: When you think of marrying a Jew?

Dr. C.: Umm-humm, the phrase.

Susan: Nothing.

Dr. C.: I wonder why it showed up in your dream.

Susan: Well, it, it showed up in my dream. You know, I think that maybe it show-, it showed something else up in my dream. I said to Carl, "Almost as bad as marrying a Jew." But in our society that's not true. The situation is reversed. It's considered much more socially acceptable, in many circles, to marry a Jew than it is to marry a Negro. And I wonder, and, and I turned it around, and I wonder if there's not another aspect of phoniness on my part that is being turned up here. When, well, I won't, I was thinking of, I guess you could call me a "bleeding heart" a few years ago. I don't think I am now. But I think that I really appreciated people, in the abstract. It was easy to get worked up for, on behalf of specific causes, much easier, than it was to relate to a specific person. And I think that there was something that wasn't really me that went into all of the feeling that got marshaled into these causes. And I, I wonder if one thing that I'm not doing here is looking at a number of ways in which I haven't been myself. I haven't been direct. Because right after that is this bit with Donald coming in. And I don't want to go with him, but I don't tell him so directly. I say that, ah, he had said nothing, we had said nothing about dinner. But I don't say, "I don't want to go with you." I withdraw, and am cool and distant. And, you know, in real life that wasn't the way I behaved with Donald. I told him I don't, there's, that: "I don't want to see you again." I tried to, I didn't want to be harsh, but that was what I did say. And I didn't just say, "No, I can't see you at such and such a time." And I didn't react by withdrawing. But in my dream I did. And this has been typical of the way I've behaved with, with guys I didn't care to see, for, ah, most of my life. I had a very hard time saying no. (*Silence.*) And I ended up being annoyed with Donald because he was drawing other people into the situation that concerned him, and it concerned me, and it didn't concern these others. He was trying to apply pressure on me indirectly. And that's very much the way I felt about some of the things that Irwin did at the time the marriage was ending. When, ah, I think that, ah, he tried to apply a certain amount of pressure by using others. It's almost as if my whole life was passing in review, in this dream.

Dr. C.: This phrase, "That would be almost as bad as marrying a Jew." I wonder if you're not talking about Irwin and you. (*Silence.*) Or us.

Susan: Possibly, possibly. (*Silence.*)

Dr. C.: What are you thinking?

Susan: Well, I was just thinking of little bits and pieces that have been dropped in my lap concerning Irwin, and some of his attitudes, some of his values. And I was thinking that it sounds as if we have gone in different directions during the last six years. And, ah, it sounds to me as though many things that are very important to him now weren't important to him before. And, ah, vice versa. He's a guy very much on the make, climbing professionally, socially, etc., etc. And, I don't know—

Dr. C.: Well, there's a lot in this dream evidently that isn't clear, but you do feel that the theme of it somehow involves—

Susan: Phoniness.

Dr. C.: Phoniness. The performing child, the shallow relationship, the marriage which isn't a marriage at all, but for public consumption. And then you add the thought immediately afterwards: "That would be almost as bad as marrying a Jew."

Susan: Well, I think that it also has something to do with the phoniness, some of the feeling that I used to work up, trying to feel good, love of humanity, you know, love of mankind. You forget all about man that way. (*Silence.*) You know, I think it was last week, or maybe the week before, that I was talking to you about a burden of guilt that I carry about; not understanding why I feel guilty, but feeling guilty. (*Silence.*)

Dr. C.: I wonder why this comes to mind now. (*Silence.*)

Susan: Just before, before I mentioned guilty, I thought of the dream, the anger I felt toward my mother. (*Silence.*)

Dr. C.: Anger. Any idea why?

Susan: Maybe I felt helpless. I didn't know how to relate and I felt angry. Look, she taught me how to relate in this empty way. In the dream it was the same feeling I had all my life, all my childhood with her. In some way, she still makes me feel like a child.

Dr. C.: Like a child.

Susan: Helpless. (*Pause.*) But why do I feel guilty? (*Pause.*) I guess she, it's because she does mean so well. After all, she *did* squeeze the orange juice and strain the vegetables. If I feel angry at her, I end up feeling cruel. Because she does mean so well. (*Silence.*)

Dr. C.: There was considerable anger in the dream.

Susan: I can't tell you how angry I was. I felt so angry, and helpless. (*Pause.*) I just had the thought that it might be you in the dream, and I suddenly feel a wave of anxiety, so that must be right. (*Silence.*) In the dream I talk of a relationship with a man that's, that's empty, that's not real. And later in the dream I felt this intense anger, that he was turning from me, he was leaving me, ignoring me. I felt so angry, and hurt. I guess there still is this part of me that sees my cutting down to once a week as your rejecting me. It's like standing alone and, and this is frightening to me because I still doubt if I can stand alone. There was such anger in the dream at Donald and my mother, because he turned from me, he rejected me. I felt a helpless fury, and I felt powerless to do or say anything. (*Silence.*) I think that's how part of me feels about you. And right now I feel myself getting more anxious. I feel resentful that I have only one hour a week, so I, I guess I feel deprived and angry.

Dr. C.: You feel deprived and angry. You also mentioned helplessness.

Susan: Yes, when they turned from me I felt cut off from them. I felt like a helpless child. Maybe part of me still feels that way. Maybe part of me doubts if I can make it alone.

Dr. C.: You can't make it alone—without mother, without the analysis.

Susan: I know I still am angry at her. But I don't need her as I did when I was a child. My concern now is not losing her; it's losing the analysis.

Dream 57   /   *Session 252*

Susan: I just stopped and I went blank because I started to say that, ah, you know that what I have been saying is lost and I wonder what the point of it is and that is a very difficult thing for me to say. Very difficult. (*Pause.*) I don't feel anxious now, but I noticed that I just stopped. And the reason that I stopped was because I saw where I was heading. I was heading in the direction of I don't need you any more, and I don't really believe that. I can remember when, oh, a little less than a year ago, when I felt that I didn't need to work with you any more, and I can see how wrong I was. And on the basis of some of the questions you raised then, I don't think I am ready to end. And yet everything I said since I entered tonight is an expression of I *am* ready to end. (*Silence.*)

I just thought of, of a dream that I had one night this week. I don't remember what night. It might have been last night or the night before. I have a baby in my arms. It wasn't my baby. Maybe it was related to me in some way, but the baby was an infant. It had very little hair, was very young, maybe six months old. And I said something to the baby. I think I asked the baby a question. The baby's name was Hilda, and I was quite surprised when the baby answered me in perfectly articulated speech that—"I think you will find something about it in the apartment upstairs"—and I was startled and I started to tell someone, maybe it was the baby's mother, that the baby could talk. No one had ever heard her talk before. No one knew she could. You know, I think that what I've done since I've come in here tonight is probably summed up by that fragment of the dream that I remembered. I come in and I said, I don't need you at all any more; I cut back too soon; I don't need you at all; I cut back too soon and I think, in effect, I was, I was, ah, in that dream I was the baby as well as the adult and you could substitute the word live for talk. Nobody knew the baby could talk; nobody asked her a question before. And I think that in effect what I am saying about myself is "You can"—if you give yourself a chance, give yourself the opportunity. I don't remember what I was saying just before I remembered this dream fragment. Do you? Just before . . . (*Silence.*) Was I saying I cut back too soon? (*Silence.*) You know, it seems to me that I have spent all of the time since cutting to once a week coming here and saying: It's too soon; I am not ready. I'm ready. I'm not ready. Every week it's the same. There was resentment to you; he did it.

Dr. C.: Yes. (*Laughs.*)

[*Here Susan discussed two things: her feeling that in terms of content, nothing new had been happening in the analysis for the past month, during which she had had only one session a week; and the fact that during this month she had had a feeling of greater enthusiasm about life. I restated these things for her, then brought her back to the dream.*]

Dr. C.: (*Silence.*) You come in today with a dream where there's an infant in your arms and you feel that that infant is you.

Susan: I didn't think that until I got here, incidentally. I thought about it. It never came to mind. Yes.

Dr. C.: Ah—

Susan: That she isn't really an infant because she can talk.

Dr. C.: That's right.

Susan: She can do a lot of the things she could with, that she thinks, that is, I think she can't do because I'm there in the person of an adult, too.

Dr. C.: Yes.

[*Again Susan spoke of her feeling that she was functioning better. I tried to bring her back to the dream.*]

Dr. C.: By the way, have you any idea what the question was you asked the baby?

Susan: Well, from the answer, it must have been in connection, oh, I don't really know, it may have been, you know, where something is. It may have been something along those lines. But I asked about something specific.

Dr. C.: And the baby answers: "I think you'll find it in the apartment upstairs."

Susan: Well, words, I know apartment was one, part of the answer. What do you think of when you think of the apartment upstairs? [21] (*Laughs.*)

Dr. C.: See, I don't even have to ask questions. (*Laughs.*)

Susan: You weren't really going to, were you?

Dr. C.: No.

Susan: (*Laughs.*) That's good. (*Silence.*) Really, the baby did have an amazingly small amount of hair for a six-month-old. And suddenly I remember Arlene, this girl I work with. She recently had a baby. I remember Arlene mentioned her own hair, which she said is very thin after her pregnancy. (*Silence.*)

Dr. C.: You see, in the dream you're looking for something. You asked the baby something along that line. Something specific that you don't recall, and the baby answers you: Find it.

Susan: Those words. Don't put too much emphasis on those words because—

Dr. C.: This is a reconstruction, these—

Susan: Really, it's a reconstruction that may have very little relation to the dream. I know the word apartment was in her answer and I remember it as being an extremely articulate

[21] My office was on the twelfth floor.

answer. Hardly what you would associate with a child's first words. And I also know the baby told me where to find something. To really get something. (*Silence.*)

Dr. C.: Well [*pause*], let's not force anything. Let's see what happens.

When during these last few sessions Susan discussed terminating the analysis, I thought she seemed to feel ready to go it on her own but at the same time was afraid that she had not come far enough. She had feelings of tension, vacillation, indecision.

The baby represented an immature part of herself that surprised her by being more competent than she expected, and more positively related. In saying, "I think you'll find something about it in the apartment upstairs," Susan, I felt, meant that the answers were in the analyst's office. The dream represented Susan's increased feelings of her own competence. She seemed aware that she was the adult (i.e., not helpless), and there was a feeling of hope: "She [the baby] can do a lot of things . . . I think she can't do because I'm there in the person of an adult, too." There was some ambivalence and discomfort: the baby was not her own but was related to her in some way; she commented that the baby's hair was thin.

Dream 58 / Session 256

Susan spoke about her relationship with her mother. Recently there had been much clinical material suggesting that Susan had been increasingly experiencing the following in regard to her mother: decrease in rage and in the need to punish her; devestment of intense involvement with her; increase in tolerance and compassion toward her. Susan was more and more able to see her mother and herself as two separate persons.

Susan: I had a dream last night. I don't remember much that happened, except that I did meet a man. Actually, the man in my dream was a young man, ah, I will be meeting tomorrow night. I've, I've never seen him. Ah, apparently it was, I guess it was Gale who told him that I was thirty or thirty-one. And he said something about the fact that I didn't look my age. And, gee, at this point, I don't remember whether I told him that I'm, I'm not thirty-one but thirty-six. I guess, well, I don't know whether I told him or not. I don't think I knew when I woke up. But I do remember that I had a conflict about telling him the truth. (*Silence.*) I felt I should but I don't know whether I did or not.

Dr. C.: Well, what do you make of your dream?

Susan: Well, my first impression is, ah, it's, ah, I guess this is an area in which I, I feel a little sensitive when I go out with someone who is younger than I am. And I think that this guy is younger than I am.

Dr. C.: When did you have this dream?

Susan: Last night.

Dr. C.: When are you going to meet this young man?

Susan: Tomorrow. I'm so sorry I just thought, gee, I guess when we talk about him, we do have the right to use the word young. (*Laughs.*)

In my judgment, certain subtle but cumulative changes had taken place in the quality of Susan's voice and in her way of communicating. She now spoke in a less dramatic, more even, more sincere manner, with little of the affectation and whine she showed in the earlier sessions. Susan's ability to feel and to express directly and naturally, to contradict or interrupt me, and to use humor is much improved.

I asked myself at this point whether I was the man who was too young and whom she dismissed as inappropriate, the man she felt in conflict about, on whether to give an honest picture of herself or not.

Dreams 59 and 60 / *Session 258*

Susan: I went home on Friday night and I had a dream and it was not a dream that aroused any feelings of anxiety. It was something, it was a dream about which I had no feeling. I don't remember too much about it. I remember it involved Irwin, and he was coming to see me, and I don't remember if he was coming to see me at my own home or at my parents' home. Er, as in reality, he was married, but his wife wasn't with him. And I was very surprised when he visited me. And I don't remember what we talked about, but I do remember at one point we were in bed together and, er, I reacted, I responded physically in a way that I don't remember responding to Irwin when we were married. And I began to feel that the situation is not right but he is married and, and I began to want to withdraw from the situation and I think that I had this feeling before there was actual intercourse but I am not at all sure.

And the next night I had another dream that didn't seem to be an anxiety dream at all. You were involved in this dream. At one point I remember sitting around a large, round table. There were a lot of people present. Some, there, there was a woman in the dream who was identified as your wife, but it's not someone who looked like your wife at all. It was a woman with dyed black hair, jet-black hair. And at one point I was very surprised that your wife would have dyed hair. I think that at first there might have been some feeling of discomfort in connection with being in a social situation with you. But it, it, it was very soon dissipated. I had to leave the group. I, I had to complete some preparations for a trip to Europe that I was taking. Apparently, this was a business trip. It was not just a vacation. I was going, I remember that there was something that I had to do in northern Italy. And that's about all I remember of it. I have a feeling that the two dreams are connected. You know, when I woke up on Sunday morning and thought of the woman with the black hair, one of the first people I thought of was my mother. I remember when I was a little girl, before I started to go to school, my mother was getting gray and didn't like the notion at all. And I used to have to sit and pull gray hairs out of her head. Then there were so many gray hairs that I guess it was a question of either accepting them or dyeing them or, if she continued to pull them out, walking around in a semi-bald condition. And she began to get what she called a "rinse," I don't think she ever really used the word dye, because that's not something she would do. But, in effect, she was dyeing her hair. She did it for a number of years. I remember my father and I tried to talk her out of it. Eventually, we did. But tonight when I thought of, as I was talking about this dream of Saturday, I was thinking of one of the first dreams I had mentioned to you when I started to see you. And I think that now it seems to me that I'm both people in the dream. I am myself and the wo-, the thing with the dyed hair. Only, I am getting ready to go away, and to leave behind the me with the dyed hair. (*Silence.*) I, I wonder if, if Irwin might not have represented you and I, I, it doesn't sound right to me. I think that I know the tack I'm taking is starting to be an intellectual one. I think, what I am trying to do is to piece out the same theme in both dreams and I don't, and I think, just because they followed one another they don't have to be saying the same thing.

Dr. C.: Well, let's not force anything.

Susan: Hummmmm.

Dr. C.: You prefer to start with the second dream.

Susan: Well, I had more, it seemed to have more meaning for me.

Dr. C.: Uhuh.

Susan: Incidentally, since Friday I have been thinking of David, from time to time, I have been thinking of him in a negative way consistently. Consistently hostile, and this is just something that I, that I used to experience intermittently over any period of time. But it's every time I have thought of him, I, I've thought of him in a definitely hostile way in terms of my own reactions. I, oh, I remembered incidents that occurred last year, but I've been very selective. I haven't been remembering anything positive. And I wonder if this doesn't represent a surer footing on my part. A, well [*laughs*], for these few days at any rate, a more stable image of myself, as a person. And an image that has something more of value in my own eyes than it had before. (*Silence.*)

Dr. C.: When you think of northern Italy, what comes to mind?

Susan: I always wanted to go there. I've always wanted to see Florence and the surrounding area. (*Silence.*) I've always imagined it as an area that is particularly rich in terms of kinds of lives that people lived, in terms of [*clears throat*] the way in which the arts have flowered in that area in particular. And I think that, I don't know if I'm all wet here or not, I guess my feeling was that it's not quite as poverty-stricken as some other areas of Italy. Extremely civilized. But I was going there on business; this was not a pleasure trip. Almost as though I can't quite see indulging myself to this extent. And, you know, when I straightened my glasses just now, just after I said what I did about self-indulgence, I took them off slightly. I, I couldn't remember which pair I had put on this morning. I have two pair. Sure, my eyes are bad enough so that I need a second pair in case a lens cracks in one, but I could have used an old pair of frames for my second pair of glasses. That, the second pair that I did buy was a form of indulgence, self-indulgence. But I don't think I had any real guilt feelings about it. But the importance of this being a business trip that I was taking, well, this means that I had to prove something to someone that I was not being self-indulgent.

Dr. C.: Uhummmm. You start the hour by telling us that you felt anxious as you left the office. And then you give us two dreams. One Friday night after your analytic hour here, and then one next night, and you feel the two dreams are related.

Susan: Ummmmm. Well, but, you know, they did have one thing in common. They weren't anxiety dreams. I didn't feel anxious while I was dreaming them or when I woke up the next morning and remembered them. (*Silence.*) [*After some discussion of her relationship with Irwin, then with David, and their connection with her early relationship with her father, Susan returned to the dream.*] I think that I had a brief thought about the dream I had when I was an adolescent in which I had intercourse with my father as a punishment. It was a painful experience; a tremendously anxious experience. This wasn't. This was a question of in the dream of letting myself go. I was letting myself go to such an extent that I thought I was in a situation that was inappropriate. And felt that I had to withdraw, had to use, had to use some discipline. Some self-control. And the thing that comes to mind when I say that is the situation is solved. After all, you're not a child any more. You are responsible for what you do and you do have to use some self-control. You just can't do anything you want to do. (*Silence.*)

Dr. C.: Well, I wonder if what happened here in the last hour couldn't have been a stimulus for this dream.

Susan: Oh, I think that that's, that was part of what went through my mind saying Irwin wasn't Irwin. Irwin was you. But I still have a feeling that that isn't quite right. You know, this is one hour when I feel that I have been going over material that is meaningful for me. But I have not the vaguest notion of what it means. It's, it's almost as though, well, maybe I am trying to detach myself from it, in some way. So that I don't get the full impact. And one way of, of doing this, is just not to let yourself see the meaning, the reasons. You, you, I, I, I know very well that you can't operate on a totally intellectual level, but I don't think you should leave your brains outside either. And I think that that's what I've been trying to do.

Dr. C.: Well, what do you make of this dream?

Susan: You know, well, all right. I, I, I, there was a, a, certainly a directness in the dream. There were no mechanical devices. I was perfectly well aware that this was something I wanted to do. But I think that just looking back on the dream, it was fitting that I want to withdraw from, because this was an inappropriate situation. You know that I have used sex in my time by going to bed when I, with people with whom I shouldn't have gone to bed. At times when I should not have gone to bed with them to get something from them. And I didn't want to do it this time. And I don't think it has to mean, you know, you go up to a point with people and you have to withdraw. Maybe it means that too, but there is this other fact. I mean, there's a positive side to not letting yourself go completely where it would be inappropriate.

Dr. C.: I could see that. (*Silence.*)

Susan: And now, for some reason in the last few seconds I

found myself thinking of my scared date, Todd. I am going to have dinner tomorrow with several couples and he is going to be there. This is not something that really has any relationship to me at all. And I had a fantasy in those few seconds of Todd's becoming attracted to me and making a pass and wanting to take it to bed. And I think that at, that my responding to this pass with, the phrase I was just using it was "inappropriate."

Dr. C.: Now what do you make of this fantasy? Why did you have it in relation to this dream just now?

Susan: You know that, do you think it's possible that one reason that the dream took the actual form that it did take and that I had a physical response was because, ah, I, I, I'm very frustrated physically. And I think that I, I, you know I can have these fantasies about just anyone at all right now. Anyone with whom I may come in contact in a setting like this one tomorrow night. You see, we are going to be an even number of people.

Dr. C. (*jokingly*): A large, round table?

Susan: No. (*Laughs.*) Their table is oblong.

Dr. C.: (*Laughs.*)

Susan: Sorry.

Dr. C.: Well—

Susan: Todd did go to Europe last summer, though—not on business, though.

Dr. C.: Well, what I hear you saying in this dream is that you find yourself responding and symbolically you use physical, sexual symbols. That you wonder if your response is appropriate and—

Susan: I don't wonder it was. I felt that it wasn't.

Dr. C.: O.K. And that you want to withdraw before the actual intercourse or the actual point of contact or something along this line. And I think that maybe the dream does have both sides of the coin: ability to respond in a more direct and related way, and yet also perhaps . . . (*Is interrupted.*)

Susan: A few minutes ago you asked me about why I had this fantasy about Todd just now.

Dr. C.: Yes.

Susan: (Laughs.) Actually, it would be extremely inappropriate, anything between this type of person and me.
Dr. C.: Um-hum.
Susan: It's just another bad choice. That's what it would be—

In the first dream, there was Susan's heightened experience of sexuality, and her impulsivity. I noted the thinly disguised sexual wish in relation to me, and the movement toward gratification. There were still some elements of guilt, censorship, and the realization that she should choose a more appropriate lover.

In the second dream, as I saw it, Susan was trying to diminish her emotional investment in the analysis. This was further suggested by her getting over her upset at seeing me socially. I believe she was attempting to see me more realistically.

I felt that in talking of her "consistent hostility" to David, Susan was probably referring to me. This represented her resentment toward me because of the impending termination of the analysis, and she identified me with "scared" Todd, whom she described as inappropriate though available.

Dream 61   /   *Session 259*

Susan: I, I had spent Saturday afternoon with my parents and Saturday evening with my parents. That evening Todd and Alfred and Gale came over to visit. This [her parents being present] didn't present any problem for me. [*She felt free to interact spontaneously and talk about herself in their presence.*] And at the end of the evening I got up to go, and Todd got up to go, too. He took me home. He lives in the neighborhood. And I went to sleep and I had a dream that involved a continuation of the evening. It wasn't an anxiety dream. I dreamed that Todd came back to my apartment with my parents and in the course of the conversation he referred to his twelve-year-old daughter. I was very surprised, but I made an effort to accept this without appearing startled in any way. And, ah, I had the impression in the dream that Todd had wanted to startle me, surprise me and, in some fashion. And I remember thinking that it seemed very strange that he had been able to make a marriage re-, re-, regardless of the fact that the marriage didn't last. And he, he commented on my lack of violent reaction, in an undertone. And I said something to the effect that, that this, this lack of shock is pretty amazing, wasn't it. And then I don't quite remember what happened. I don't remember what all four of us were talking about. But at, at, at some point later on, Alfred and Gale either told me about or showed me—

Dr. C.: Is this still in the dream?

Susan: Yeah. About a telegram they had gotten from Todd to the effect that Susan is not shocked at learning that I have a twelve-year-old daughter—and that was the dream. And I can't make head or tail of it. Except that while I was talking about it now, I was, as I was, as I was expressing surprise that he had been able to make a marriage, even an unsuccessful one. And I thought that I was talking about myself when I was telling you the dream. Twelve-year-old daughter. It occurs to me now that it was just about twelve years ago that Irwin and I became engaged and we decided to get married. (*Silence.*) And now I found myself, find myself thinking about money.[22] You know, I don't like being in a position that I'm in right now. But I am going to find it very, very difficult to pay you in January. And I wonder if it, if this is something that, if you would accept my trying to get up to date in February but lapsing a little in January.

[*Susan went on about her fear of asking a favor, that her fear was a way to prevent a closer relationship. She spoke about the importance of my reactions to her; about her conflict in accepting gifts. She mentioned that it was her birthday.*]

Dr. C.: Have you any idea what you're saying in the dream, what you are trying to tell yourself?

Susan: Gee, I don't, aside from what I said a little earlier in relation to twelve years and thinking of Todd as another part of me.

Dr. C.: You feel that the twelve-year-old daughter is part of you in some way.

---

[22] Susan had had unforeseen medical expenses and was having financial difficulties.

Susan: No. No. No. But I had this reaction of surprise that he had been capable of marriage, even an unsuccessful marriage. I wonder if, if that isn't part of my reaction. My reaction to me, particularly, as I was twelve years ago. But then, ah, I didn't even think of that at all until I started to tell you the dream. Up until I started to talk about it tonight, I remember at the time I thought of it, it was, I thought of it with curiosity and with surprise, you know. What could this mean? But without—this was not anything that had any great emotional involvement for me. It was just something that I could describe as interesting while I was experiencing it. But without any anxiety or panic or really negative feelings. I do, the, the only feelings involved were my surprise at the news that Todd dropped casually. And a certain amount of pride that I was able to hold back some of the surprise because I just didn't think it would be appropriate.

Dr. C.: Well, have you any ideas on that?

Susan: No. I certainly don't see what this has to do with what I had been talking about.

Dr. C.: Now, let's see. Today is your birthday.

Susan: Uhummm.

Dr. C.: When you think of twelve-year-old daughter, twelve years at any rate, you think of the time when you first became engaged to Irwin—

Susan: Well, that happened twelve years ago. (*Silence.*)

Dr. C.: And then in the dream it seems strange to you that Todd had been able to make a marriage—

Susan: Yeah.

Dr. C.: Despite the fact that the marriage did not last.

Susan: Ummmm—even an unsuccessful one. Yeah. It surprised me that he was able to go that far. I wonder if David doesn't get involved here, and possibly my feelings about that relationship. Because I think that I think that I have mentioned him in here the last couple of times. I have been thinking of him with a certain amount of hostility, resentment. And both he and Todd I think probably have some very similar problems. Except that I think that David may be a little further than Todd is.

Dr. C.: What about the idea—

Susan: I don't think that that was what I was dreaming about.

Dr. C.: The idea of your not being shocked. Your lack of shock was pretty amazing and then the idea of—

Susan: Not showing it—

Dr. C.: Not showing it. And then the telegram validating this—

Susan: Yes. Your using the word "validating" makes me think, well, it makes me think of you. After all, what of the day when I leave the analyst. And what's been going on in here. I've, I think I have been doing a certain amount of testing and tr-, tr-, trying to get validation of changes. In many ways, I was a little girl when I came, and in many ways I'm not now. But I think I'm missing the boat here too in, in, in, I, I think that all, all these things that I am thinking of may be involved in this dream. But in terms of new meaning, I'm missing the boat. (*Silence.*) And then I find myself thinking of my medical bills and thinking about money again and getting a little bit anxious. And I think that that goes back to this whole question that I raised with you a little while ago about my asking for an extension [of credit] and the fact that you haven't said a word yet. This, incidentally, is talking about an extension and wanting to get your reaction to it, is a very different kind of behavior than I have exhibited in the past. (*Laughs.*) I haven't talked about it. Just have done it and haven't talked about it. But I don't want to do that tonight, and I guess I have the feeling that this is a sign of growing up, too. I don't think it's, it's a question really of my becoming more and more comfortable with you and trusting you more and more and so on and so on. I think that I no longer duck questions that I find unpleasant in the way that I did. (*Silence.*) I think it's perfectly reasonable for me to ask for your reaction and I don't understand why you haven't given it at all until now.

Dr. C.: Well—

Susan: I don't want to nag but . . . (*Laughs.*)

Dr. C.: I'll put it this way. It does not impose any hardship on me at all to wait another month.

Susan: Yeah.

Dr. C.: And therefore I am willing to wait. If it did, then I would be able to make my needs known and tell you of that. But as it is, it does not pose a problem. Whether I get it four weeks earlier or later is unimportant. So you decide the issue for yourself.

Susan: Well, as long as you tell me that it's, it's decided.

Dr. C.: Hummm. But there's something in the dream that is evidently quite confusing to the both of us. Now I think that in some sense you may be talking about the analysis.

Susan: I just remembered something that my mother said at lunch yesterday. She was talking about how happy she is. And at one point when she was talking about why she felt good, she turned to me and she said: "I know that you are better and that's a big help to me." And when she said that, what she meant was in terms, she was talking in terms of emotional problems. And I had a slight reaction of resentment, annoyance at that point. I, I, I know that every time she has talked about the fact that she sees a change in me. She sees that I'm getting better. I reacted to it with resentment, with more in the past than I did this time. And I, I thought of this when you said I wonder if you're not talking about the analysis because my parents came back.

Dr. C.: That's right, came back with Todd. So there's the idea, Todd, parents, twelve-year-old daughter.

Susan: And you were probably there because, after all, who was in the room with me when they all came back, my mother, my father, a social psychologist [Todd]. I think that when I pick a psychologist and put him in my dream, I think, as far as I am concerned I'm putting some kind of authority figure in my dream, and I still see you as an authority figure, I think. (*Silence.*) Perhaps I was just going back to me at the age of twelve. The reference that Todd made to his daughter in the dream was in terms of a summer vacation; what she was going to do possibly at camp. The summer I was twelve was the last summer I went to children's camp as a camper. It could be in reference to a form of ending. Oh, I don't know, I guess I'm tending to push it now.

Dr. C.: Well, let's not force anything, but in the dream there is a marriage that does not last. There is a twelve-year-old child, which is the length of time since your engagement to Irwin and also the last time you went to a children's camp. And there is a lack of shock, in some way lack of surprise in the validation of this . . . (*Is interrupted loudly.*)

Susan: Well, it's the lack of exhibited surprise. It was there that, it wasn't apparent.

Dr. C.: Could you sum up what you think you're saying in this dream as you hear it?

Susan: No. I can't because I, my feeling is that I just missed the boat. That I may very well have pointed to some peripheral ideas that are involved, but that I've missed the main point.

Dr. C.: Well, should you get any further enlightenment on this dream—

Susan: You'll be the first to know.

Dr. C.: Let me know.

Susan: I don't think it's a terribly significant dream, incidentally. Probably because of the fact that there was so little emotional involvement for me. O.K.

I asked myself whether the twelve-year-old daughter was Susan's way of saying that she was startled at the fact that she was growing up. Is the age of twelve, which she associated with her last camp experience in childhood, also associated with the ending of childhood and the analytic dependence?

Termination

Susan raised the possibility of termination, with considerable anxiety, in session 262. She described her conflict: the fear that she had not gone far enough in her own growth process versus feeling that she would like to try it on her own.

Susan pointed out that she had had seven years of analysis and did not want to be in it permanently. Close friends who were psychologically sophisticated felt that she had changed significantly and was ready to continue on her own. Since she had cut down the analysis to one session a week fourteen weeks ago, she had been finding herself increasingly capable of structuring a kind of open, more direct, closer relatedness with the real world. Still, she was anxious about giving up the analysis.

Susan and I explored whether she felt she could go further in her psychoanalysis at this point. We analyzed her question about continuing and carefully evaluated what had and had not been accomplished. Susan believed she was in touch with herself, often painfully so, and was able to relate openly as never before. She carefully weighed the gains she had made, her age of thirty-six, her current dating and her feeling open to any opportunities for a relationship, her overall situation and her desire to grow on her own without analytic dependence. Her decision was to terminate and I went along with it.

Susan terminated in session 263, though she had some fear that she would regress. She felt that a leave of absence from analysis would be a good idea, however. She knew that she could return for further analytic work if she needed to. I agreed and indicated that the anxiety she expressed was natural and very much a reflection of her feelings. She suggested a break of three months, after which we would get together once. An appointment was arranged.

Susan wrote me twice during these three months. Both letters indicated that she was functioning and managing on her own, despite the anxiety aroused by her withdrawal from psychoanalysis. With her second letter, as we had agreed, she enclosed a check for the balance she owed me.

The Follow-up Session

Susan had already decided, before this session, to go it alone. She had felt upset after discontinuing the analysis, but she reported a decline in anxiety in the past three months, and an increase in energy, work output, and social activity.

Susan had been dating, and she felt that, given the opportunity, she would make a good mother and wife. She said she had not given up hope of making a satisfactory marriage despite her age, and the scarcity of available, worthwhile men. But she expressed the desire to live as complete and productive a life as she could on her own, and she knew she must face the painful possibility that she would always be alone.

Susan said, toward the end of the session: "In all honesty, I cannot exclude the possibility of wanting to come back for further analytic work. I also do not feel that I can say now that I will never come back to you. I hope I don't have to, but I don't feel that I never will. But I also am not sure that at some point I will." At the moment, however, Susan felt that living without the analysis, though more anxiety-laden, would lead to her greater growth as a person.

Index

abortion, 50–51, 115, 120, 166, 168–170, 175, 236

acceptance: desire for, 21, 28, 35, 65–66, 110, 122–124, 126, 142, 146–147, 150, 165, 167, 197–201, 211; self-, 98–99

acting out, 20 *n.*, 39; sex and, 43

active-passive conflict, 8, 23, 24, 39, 49, 51–52, 61

aggression, 18, 38, 41, 43, 47, 92, 96; oral, 46; passivity as cover for, 44

aggressive counterattack, 53

aggressiveness, embarrassment over, 92–93

aging, *see* hair

alcohol: as anesthesia, 141, 269; as escape, 141, 202

alcoholism, fear of, 141

aloneness, 73; fear of, 74, 203, 211, 218, 219, 221, 222, 282

ambivalence, 23, 74, 85; toward marriage, 77; toward sex, 24, 52–53, 60–63, 88, 167; toward therapy, 132

anesthesia, 90, 91, 267; alcohol as, 141, 269; childbirth and, 166

anger, 38, 41, 81–83, 238–240; anxiety and, 141; guilt about, 84, 85, 88, 282; inability to feel, 141

animal nature, 22, 25

animals, 5 *n.*, 22–23, 37, 39, 43, 46, 62, 78–80, 113, 144–145, 230–235, 247

anti-Negro feeling, 93–94, 280

anti-Semitism, 55, 93, 280–282

anxiety, 6, 7 *n.*, 8, 15, 16, 18, 20, 22, 25–27, 33–37; acute, 73–75, 132; anger and, 141; bypassing of, 43; denial of, 37, 46, 47, 97–102, 163, 283, 290; diffuse, 143, 155 *n.*; escape from, 11, 43, 44, 59 *n.*, 75, 91, 113; evasion of, 39; hostility and, 88; of irrationalism, 126; possessions as assuagement for, 122–123; about pregnancy, 117–118, 191–192, 194; release from, 43–44, 179; repression and, 66 *n.*; sex as assuagement for, 43, 114; sexuality and, 37, 39, 43, 44; Tillich's formulation of, 54

apathy, 141

appointments, making of, 48, 49, 165–167

approval, *see* acceptance

arbitrariness, symbols and, 16, 120 *n.*

archetypal symbols, 34, 82

art form, dreams as, 10

ascendency, feeling of, 110, 111, 126

avoidance mechanism, sex as, 40

awareness, 3; blocking off of, 31, 32, 39, 85, 179; consciousness and, 5; denial of, 6, 27, 31, 32, 86, 101, 111–112; different dimensions of, 6; generalized, 5